'The one thing that can make men march into the muzzles of the cannon which are trained at them is honour.'

FREDERICK THE GREAT

For Dvora

'A gracious woman retaineth honour.'

PROVERBS 11:16

Men, Women and War

MARTIN VAN CREVELD

CASSELL&CO

Cassell & Co
Wellington House, 125 Strand, London WC2R 0BB

A catalogue record for this book is available from the British Library

ISBN 0-304-35959-9

Printed and bound in Great Britain by
MPG Books Ltd, Bodmin, Cornwall

Contents

Preface 7

Introduction **The Great Illusion** 9

Part I **Women in the Maw of Mars** 15

1 Instigating War 16

2 Causes, Objects and Victims 27

3 Protecting Women 33

4 A World without War? 38

Part II **From the Amazons to GI Jane** 41

5 'War' in the Animal Kingdom 45

6 Warrior Goddesses 48

7 Amazons Old and New 54

8 Rulers and Commanders 67

9 Playing at War 81

10 Camp-Followers 88

11 Women in Disguise 99

12 Warrior Women of Dahomey 107

13 Revolts, Revolutions and Insurgencies 117

14 The Age of Total War 126

15 The Weakness of Women 149

16 The Glory of Men 161

Part III **1945 and After** 169

17 The Military Background 170

18 Separate and Unequal 180

19 Enter the Women 189

20 Women into Combat 201

21 The Hollow Triumph 210

22 The New World Disorder 222

Conclusions **Change and Continuity** 228

Notes to the Text 238

Index 281

Preface

This is the first of my books in which women occupy centre stage; perhaps, at number fourteen, the time has come. Until I came to write it, I never thought it important to check whether the authorities on whom I relied were male or female. In my field, military history and strategy, there were many more men than women. However, I always took it for granted that authors belonging to either sex were equally capable and equally honest.

Working my way through the literature surrounding this book, I have learned better. If the field of scholarship is at all representative, never have relations between the sexes been as poisonous as they are today. Since writers are either male or female, the very possibility of embarking on a common intellectual endeavour and reaching out for the truth is being questioned by some feminists who insist that there exist separate, if not superior, female modes of thought and knowledge. Specifically, males by virtue of their sex stand accused of being representatives of 'patriarchy' (to use one of the milder terms that feminists employ). Moreover, they are subject to the rules of casuistry; if they deny the charge, then this itself is taken as proof that it is true.

I on my part do not deny the charge. It is my view that women (like men) have their place. Whatever man's place may be, and history shows that in some respects it has changed very much, it includes the duty to protect woman, by fighting for her if necessary. Woman's place, too, has changed very much. Whatever it may be, except perhaps under the most extreme circumstances, I think it neither does nor should include war and combat. It is also my view, or perhaps I should call it hope, that in spite of the many things that seem to separate men and women these days reaching out for the truth remains possible. Or, at any rate, that some judgments are based on better evidence and are more tightly argued, and therefore closer to the truth, than others.

I realize, though, that many readers belonging to either sex may not share my beliefs. To allow them to draw their own conclusions concerning the material, much of which is either fanciful or controversial, I decided to provide this book with far more footnotes per page than any of the others. To make sure the views of men and women could be told apart, I also looked up and noted the first names of all authors referred to. Doing so was not always easy, since some authors – mostly, following a now somewhat antiquated British tradition, probably male ones – went out of their way to conceal their gender. I hope I shall be forgiven for the gaps that sometimes result.

This work could not have been completed without the interest shown by, assistance from, persons of both sexes. First and foremost I should like to thank Professor Benjamin Kedar. Professor Kedar has now been my friend for close to three decades; his encyclopaedic knowledge of history, deep understanding of its philosophy, and keen eye for its detail have been as helpful in preparing this book as in most previous ones. Next I wish to thank Ms Rivka Shaked who is responsible for women's questions in Israel's civil service; she showed more than usual generosity in discussing my views with me and in inviting me to address her subordinates. Thanks are due to Ms Katherine Aspy and her father, Professor William O'Neill, who have done what they could to encourage me in difficult times. Then there are the Alexander von Humboldt Foundation and Professor Hans-Erich Volkmann of the Militaergeschichtliche Forschungsamt, Potsdam, Germany, who helped finance my research and acted as my host during a very pleasant year in that magnificent city. Last, not least, I should like to thank my agents, Gabriele and Leslie Pantucci, for their usual patience and understanding.

Introduction **The Great Illusion**

For good or ill, ours is perhaps the most revolutionary age in history. At least since Roman ladies began to present themselves in the arena and fought as gladiators, women have often tried to enter fields previously reserved for men; however, none of these attempts was nearly as determined or nearly as widespread as the one unfolding in front of our eyes. Seeking to assist the movement and to justify it, feminist authors have produced thousands of volumes to show that women are as fit to pay any price, bear any burden, and support any hardship, as men. The same authors never get tired of claiming that any failure by women to make their presence felt in this field or that is the result not of anatomy but of ideology and culture – 'the construction of gender', as the fashionable phrase goes: by which they mean the discrimination and oppression to which women at all times and places allegedly have been and still are subject at the hands of men.

As the modern feminist movement strove to end this oppression and this discrimination, the role that women can or cannot, should or should not, play in the military and in war has assumed a special significance. As a very large number of pictures, TV shows, films, computer games and mud-wrestling contests prove, in part this is because many people find the idea of female warriors titillating: especially if, by simultaneously brandishing their weapons and showing their breasts, they can combine ferocity with sex appeal. Mainly, however, it is because violence in general, and war in particular, are often seen as the 'last bastion' of male superiority over, and control of, females.[1] Take away men's monopoly over violence, and hopefully the rest of the 'patriarchal' social order will crumble like a house of cards. Some, indeed, have gone even further than this, claiming that men are in decline and that the future belongs to women.

Whatever the reason, the military have become the favoured arena where the so-called 'battle of the sexes' is being fought and which has attracted the greatest attention on the part of the media. On both sides of the Atlantic, scarcely a week goes by without the announcement that military women are now beginning to enter some 'non-traditional' field, be it as forward artillery observers, or missile operators, or fighter pilots, or submarine commanders, or whatever. On both sides of the Atlantic, too, scarcely a week goes by without some unfortunate male officer or soldier being accused of 'sexual harassment' and being hounded out of the services. This is likely to be his fate even if the alleged incident took place many years previously; even if it was the woman who made the initial advances and seduced him; even if his record of service is otherwise excellent; and often even if he is found innocent of the charges.

Against this background, it is not the purpose of the present book to prove that the influx of women has been a disaster for the military. That mission has been successfully accomplished by others;[2] in fact, it is hardly possible to open a newspaper or switch on the TV without coming across some story of the damage that feminization is causing both in fiscal terms and from the point of view of fighting power. Nor do I intend to show that women are, on average, not nearly as fit for war as men. Considering the tremendous demands of war on the one hand and women's relative weakness and vulnerability on the other, that fact is or ought to be self-evident. It is as true today as it was when Homer's Hector advised his wife to look to her spinning while he, the man, risked his life on her behalf; at a time when people fought sword in hand as at a time when Australian infantrymen, so heavily laden they could hardly walk, landed in East Timor to restore order in that unfortunate country.

Instead of rehashing these matters, this volume argues that it is all a great illusion: that the influx of women into the military, far from representing some world-historical step in women's unstoppable march towards liberation, is both symptom and cause of the decline of the military in question. The process was triggered by the introduction of nuclear weapons over half a century ago. Since then, the armed forces of *no* developed country have fought a major war against a major opponent who was even remotely capable of putting its own national existence in danger; compared with the recent past, and with very few exceptions, all they have done was to engage in skirmishes. Even most of those were conducted in places hundreds if not thousands of miles away, against enemies who were often so small and weak they could hardly be located on a map.

Not having to fight a major war, the forces' role in national life has begun to decline until they have become almost unnecessary. The more superfluous they have become – indeed, precisely because they have been becoming superfluous – the more both society and its leaders feel able to treat them not as fighting machines but as social laboratories for some feminist brave new world. This they do by compelling the forces to pretend, against all the evidence that soldiers and doctors can muster, that women are as fit for war as men: increase the proportion of women from near zero to as many as 10–13 per cent of the troops; turn training into a mockery and humiliation for those men who are involved in it alongside women; absorb the extra costs involved in paying for everything from separate toilets to pregnancy care and from special uniforms to post-natal leave of absence; deny or cover up any damage done and loss suffered; and ignore or silence or discharge anybody who objects. Since, during the period in question, the size of the armed forces of practically all the advanced countries has declined very sharply, the more women those forces are compelled to take in the smaller the number of the remaining men and the less fit they themselves are for waging war. The vicious cycle has now been going on for about thirty years. If present trends are anything to go by, it will end only when the forces are no longer fit to fight at all.

Nor has the feminization of the military been a great success from the point of view of women themselves. The faster they run, the more they remain in place; very often it is a question not so much of women liberating themselves by overcoming the resistance of men as taking on jobs that men no longer want. Meanwhile, the extent of the change that has taken place should not be exaggerated. In all the military without exception men continue to occupy almost all top positions. In the war academies and staff colleges that this author often addresses they completely swamp the few women who are present. In these institutions, for a woman to raise her hand and actually ask a question about war or military history is almost unheard of; it is as if even the few who are present could not care less about what is going on. Meanwhile, the parts of the military where most women are concentrated, i.e. the rear services, are fast being privatized.

Not only are women no closer to controlling the instruments of violence than they were thirty years ago, but the same period has witnessed the creation of an entirely new type of armed forces variously known as private security or military contractors. Often led by retired senior officers, and drawing their manpower from former enlisted men who act as cannon-fodder, those forces are gradually taking over many of the traditional roles of the military. Needless to say, women are almost completely absent from them; to the extent that they are present, then usually it is either because they are cheaper than men or because they are needed to deal with other women.

Meanwhile, history is not standing still. Whereas it is now decades since any developed country has fought a major war, all over the five-sixths of the world (in terms of population) that are known as 'developing' wars are frequent, bloody and devastating. Over the last half-century the wars in question have changed the face of the earth. They led to the liberation of hundreds of millions of people from colonial rule and caused the number of sovereign states to treble; even as these lines are being written in the autumn of 2000, approximately thirty wars are raging in places as far apart as the Philippines and Sierra Leone, Chechnia and Colombia. In not one of these wars do women participate any more than they have always done: that is to say hardly at all. Thus it might almost be said that those armed forces that have been forced to incorporate women no longer fight; whereas those that still fight have very few, if any, women.

To penetrate behind the screen of claims and counter-claims and show the reader what really has been happening to men, women and war, this volume is constructed as follows. Part I is a brief survey of the ways in which women have always been caught up in war, whether as instigators or as causes or as objects or as victims or as the protégees of men. My argument in this part is that, acting in these capacities, women are absolutely critical to war; to the point, indeed, that the latter may almost be said to owe its existence to them. Part II provides an almost equally brief outline of the various things that women have done in war throughout the ages. Contrary to the claims of some contemporary writers, it shows that women have hardly ever partici-pated in what Clausewitz calls 'the cash payment of war' and what Tolstoy describes as 'the actual killing';[3] those few women who did participate in it very often did so at the cost of their femininity. Finally, part III deals with the period from 1945 on. It shows in detail how, in one country after another, the decline of the military led to the influx of women, while the influx of women accelerated the decline of the military.

From all this, three conclusions seem to follow. First, even if one assumes that women joining in what Lord Byron once called 'the brain-splattering, windpipe-slashing art' does in fact constitute 'progress',[4] that progress is due less to women's liberation than to the decline of major war and of the forces that are earmarked for waging it. Second, now as ever wherever there are wars men's monopoly over violence is almost as complete as it has always been. Third, today as ever it is only the smallest, most saintly and most iso-lated societies that do not require the threat of force or its use for external and internal defence. Power continues to grow out of the barrel of a gun; given this fact, any reports concerning the imminent demise of men appear to be greatly exaggerated.

Part I **Women in the Maw of Mars**

Before we examine the things that women have actually done in war, it is necessary to say something about their role in its origin and causation. Here this topic will be discussed under three headings: women as instigators of war; women as the causes, objects and victims of war; and war as an effort to protect women. The conclusion from all this is simple. In one way or another, women form a very large part of what war is all about. Take women away, and war would have been both impossible and pointless.

1 Instigating War

By some modern accounts female voters, when asked for their views, tend to be slightly less inclined towards the use of armed force and more in favour of peace than are men.[1] Whether or not this is true, the crowds that danced in America's streets during the first days of the 1991 Gulf War were made up of women as well as men. Throughout history there have been countless occasions when women actively and deliberately incited their menfolk to war. To adapt a reported saying of Karl Marx: 'it is impossible to overestimate the historical role played by women. When [war] comes they are swept along.'

As long ago as the first century AD the Roman historian Tacitus described how German (and British) women would join their menfolk in battle and encourage them by screaming and yelling. If necessary they would expose their breasts so as to demonstrate what would happen if the men were defeated and they themselves taken prisoner; 'and because of their wives the Germans are terrified of captivity'[2] (contemplating Trajan's column where bound Dacian prisoners are shown being decapitated, one suspects they had other reasons as well). Among the Thompson Indians of British Columbia, when the men went on the war-path the women performed dances at frequent intervals. These dances were believed to ensure the success of the expedition. The dancers flourished their knives, threw long sharp-pointed sticks forward, or drew sticks with hooked ends repeatedly backward and forward, symbolically killing the enemy. Likewise the women of the Yuki tribe in California spent the time when their husbands were away on campaign continuously dancing; the idea being that, so long as they kept it up, their husbands would not grow tired.[3] To remain in North America, similar ceremonies are said to have been performed among the Flathead Indians, the Arikara, Sahsta, Kiowa and Tinglit tribes, as well as some of the Sioux.[4]

Nor was the women's role necessarily limited to dances and other magic ceremonies. In many of these societies, women accompanied their men on military expeditions, acting as porters, encouraging them, and taking care of them. Next they would celebrate the warriors' return; so, to adduce just one example, among the Plains Ojibway where they painted their faces, came out to welcome the men, gave them presents, and received scalps in return. Wars often ended with a victory dance carried out by the women as well as the men.[5] Later the women would glory in wearing ornaments that indicated their husbands' success, including body parts such as severed ears.

Not the least important trophies of war were prisoners. Some societies, including the Cherokee, Iroquois, Omaha and Dakota of North America, allowed their women to torture prisoners to death, the objective being to humiliate them as well as add to their agonies.[6] Particularly when it came to female captives, the women could be worse than the men. Queen Clytemnestra put her husband's female prisoner, Cassandra, to death. The *Groenlendinga Saga* tells how, during the Viking expeditions to Vinland (North America), a woman called Freydis took up an axe and treacherously killed five native female prisoners whom no Viking man was prepared to kill.[7] Sometimes women were used to finish off any enemy left lying on the field, as happened for example after the battle of Little Bighorn (1876) when the Indian women pounded the faces of dead and wounded US soldiers into pulp.[8] In the words of Rudyard Kipling:

> If you're wounded and left out on Afghanistan's plains
> And the women come out to cut up what remains
> Just roll to your rifle and blow out your brains
> And go to your death like a soldier.

In Israel during the fighting that went on for the northern city of Safed in April 1948 at least one woman was used to cover up the atrocities that her male comrades committed against Arab prisoners.

Exhortation could also take the form of words, and Plutarch devotes an entire chapter to the sayings of Spartan women. Thus Gorgo, wife of Leonidas, being asked by an Athenian woman why it was that Spartan women were the only women who lorded it over their men, answered, 'Because we are the only women that are mothers of men.' A woman by the name of Gyrtias whose grandson Acrotatus got involved in a fight and was beaten up so badly that he was brought home for dead forbade her family to wail, saying that the boy 'has shown from what blood he was sprung'. Later the same Gyrtias, hearing that Acrotatus had fallen, said: 'It is more pleasing to hear that he died in a manner worthy of myself, his country, and his ancestors than if he had lived for all time a coward.' One woman, Damatria, killed her son who had been 'a coward and unworthy of her'; her epithet said that 'she was of Sparta too'. Another Spartan woman who killed her son for similar reasons had 'never I bore Sparta's unworthy son' inscribed on her tombstone. Yet another, hearing that her son had saved himself by escaping, asked him whether he intended to slink in where he had come from and pulled up her dress to show him. Still following Plutarch, on one occasion when Cyrus's men ran from battle they were confronted by the Persian women who lifted their skirts, called them 'base cowards' and taught them where duty lay.[9] In modern times Zulu women also stripped in order to shame their menfolk into action;[10] one might almost say the Spartan women were not the only ones who fought to the last man.

We cannot list the countless cases when women instigated warriors or rewarded them by bestowing sexual favours upon them; indeed it has been argued that the desire to gain the approval of women is one of the prime motivations that, in tribal societies (and by no means only in tribal societies) make men desirous of going to war.[11] Even if one does not accept this suggestion, the fact is that all societies at all times and places are made up of both men and women in approximately equal numbers. In all of them 'the home fires' must be kept burning; had women not supported warfare or, at the very least, acquiesced in its conduct war would have been impossible. This is not to say that, even in primitive societies,[12] some women have not been known to oppose war. It is to say that, in the vast majority of cases, they were 'swept along'.

Skipping over the biblical prophetess Debora,[13] by far the most famous battle-cry uttered by a female came from Jeanne d'Arc. Reliable information about her is hard to get: almost all we know comes from her two trials. During the first, held on behalf of the English, the judges (French ones, incidentally) were determined to condemn her as a witch. During the second, held posthumously on behalf of the king of France, they were equally determined, not to say obligated, to rehabilitate her as a divinely inspired saviour. Born in 1412 to a well-to-do peasant family at Domrémy, Lorraine, until the autumn of 1428 she led a normal life. Then she approached the castellan of neighbouring Vaucouleurs, saying she had heard heavenly voices. The voices had been carried to her by the wind and the village church bells since childhood. They told her to go and seek out the dauphin, Charles, and ask him for an army with which to deliver France from the English. At about this time, she apparently refused to marry somebody to whom she had been promised by her parents.[14]

Dressed in male clothes – later she was to explain that, 'for a virgin, male and female clothes are equally suitable; if God has commanded me to put on men's clothes, it is because I have to carry arms as men do[15] – she was given an escort and sent to court. There she was presented to Charles whom, though she did not know him, she was able to spot among the throng of attendants in spite of his attempts to disguise himself. His first step after having met her was to have the queen and other ladies examine her sex and verify her virginity; this was important, since her ability to claim supernatural power depended on her being a virgin. It having been established that she was what she claimed to be, a bishop and an archbishop took a good look at her divine mission. In the end Charles was convinced, or perhaps he merely decided that she might come in useful. He had a suit of armour made for her, complete with lance and sword.

Said to have been an excellent horsewoman, Jeanne quickly learned how to manage arms. Next she joined the army which was trying to break the English siege of Orléans. With her rode some of France's most important soldiers, including two marshals of France. The city was relieved in May 1429 after nine days of fighting. Her role in this episode was to send threatening letters to the English, which were disregarded; to take part in the councils of war where the plans were made; and also to participate in mêlées.

The result was that she was slightly wounded twice, once by stepping on a cal-trop and once by an arrow from a crossbow which hit her in the shoulder.

Following the victory at Orléans, in July 1429 Charles VII was crowned at Reims. In August and September she was with the army that tried, and failed, to take Paris, and was lightly wounded for the third time. She spent the next few months in Charles's suite. In May 1430 she participated in the attempt to relieve Compiègne which was under siege by the Burgundians. By now she had evolved from an anonymous girl into a famous personage. Wearing a conspicuous red and gold cloak she took part in a skirmish and, along with a few men of her party, was captured. Later she was sold to the English for an immense sum. It was decided to try her in front of an eccle-siastical court, the idea being to prove that her mission was inspired not by God but by the devil.

At first she was well treated, but later the conditions of her imprisonment became harsher and at one point she fell ill. Throughout her imprisonment and trial she showed both equanimity and courage. Having been caught during a daring attempt to escape – her ordeal included a 60-foot drop plus three days in hiding without food or water – she was offered parole in return for a promise not to try again, but refused. Asked whether she would prom-ise not to take up arms she refused again, thus leaving her judges no option. She was also re-examined and found to be a virgin still. She was sentenced to death 'for having fallen into various errors and crimes of heresy, idolatry, [and] invocation of demons'. A few days later she was burned at the stake, whereupon miracles began happening and she started her transformation into a saint.

Physically Jeanne d'Arc appears to have been sufficiently sturdy and tall to dress as a boy and pass as one; her health was generally excellent and she is credited with having had a powerful voice that could make itself heard over the din of battle. Though she had no official standing with the troops, she must have been a born leader: utterly convinced of her divine mission, cool, collected, well able to separate the important from the unimportant, and, for a peasant girl with no formal education beyond what was provided by the village church, remarkably eloquent. At her second trial, some witnesses praised her understanding of war, claiming she knew as much as a captain with twenty or thirty years' experience and was particularly good at siting artillery.[16] Others, who may have wanted the credit for themselves, dismissed her. Some contemporaries saw her as divinely inspired, others as demonic, others still (modern historians, mainly) as hysterical. Given her composed behaviour under interrogation, which at one point included the threat of torture, the latter position is hard to maintain.

Whatever the source of her strength, clearly the importance of Jeanne d'Arc was neither as a strategist nor as a fighter. From the moment she left home to the time she was captured her active career lasted no more than eighteen months; at her trial she herself said she had never actually killed anyone. What 'the Maiden', as she was called, did do was to excite the French people's imagination and call them to arms, a task at which she was singularly successful and for which she deservedly achieved immortal fame. Not so the legions of anonymous women who, before and after her, egged on their menfolk to war. There were such women in England in 1642 when, according to one historian, London women 'hugged' their menfolk into resistance against King Charles I.[17] There were such women during the War of the American Revolution and also during the French Revolutionary Wars. There were such women in 1806 when Queen Louisa of Prussia put on the uniform of a dragoon and played a major role in pushing her husband Frederick-William III towards war and defeat.[18] Seven years later, when Prussia rose against Napoleon, women also took an important part. They gladly gave up their gold jewellery in return for replacements made of iron: whence originated the most famous Prussian-German military decoration, the Iron Cross.

Skipping over the nineteenth century, the war hysteria that overtook much of Europe in August 1914 once again saw women playing a major part. In France cheering crowds made up largely of females accompanied the troops on their way to the railway stations, distributing food and covering them with flowers and kisses. The same was true in Germany where people spoke of 'war nymphomania' and observed 'a mighty increase in the female libido';[19] even Kaethe Kollwitz, a sculptor who was later to earn fame with her powerful anti-war works, saw her son off with flowers and a copy of *Faust*.[20] In the squares of St Petersburg ecstatic women tore off parts of their clothing and gave them to departing soldiers.[21] In England the phenomenon was known as 'khaki fever'.[22] People spoke of 'hundreds of reputable women and girls round every camp [who] seemed to have been suddenly smitten with a Bacchantic frenzy'.[23] One English woman found the war 'horribly exciting but I cannot live on it ... it is like being drunk all day';[24] another, the subsequent pacifist Vera Brittain, expressed her fear lest 'our bungling government' would remain neutral and 'desperately wished' she were a man so she could 'play that Great Game with Death'.[25] During the first days of mobilization the authorities were surprised by the powers they had unleashed; later they took advantage of the situation by calling on women to press their men to volunteer.[26] Soldiers on their part would have been less than human if they had not enjoyed their sudden popularity and tried to make the most of it. As one of them wrote: 'there were plenty of girls in fact hundreds of them it was no use making appointments with a girl as some other girl generally grabbed you before you got to the appointed place.'[27]

Nor did the war craze leave self-declared feminists untouched.[28] During the years before 1914, suffragettes had often argued that women were by nature less bellicose than men and that female suffrage would therefore make for a more peaceful world. In the event, these hopes were disappointed and no sooner had hostilities broken out than the feminist movement disintegrated just as surely as the socialist one did. In Britain the most famous feminist leader was Emmeline Pankhurst. She headed the Women's Social and Political Union and had even gone to jail for her beliefs; now she immediately declared that 'our country's war shall be our war'. Along with her daughter Sylvia she changed the name of their newspaper from the *Suffragette* to *Britannia*, dedicated it to 'king and country', and set out to convince men – not that they needed to – that only by enlisting could they look women in the eye. Most of the remaining thirty-one identifiable national women's organizations also ended by drumming up support for the war. Indeed they expelled pacifist members of their organization, thus rendering the cause of peace even weaker than it already was.

By and large, the situation in other countries was similar. In France the periodicals *La Fronde* and *La Française* dropped their feminist programmes, harnessing themselves to the war effort instead. In Germany the main feminist organization, the Bund Deutscher Frauenvereine (BDF) did the same; in both countries, as well as Italy and Britain, the day was to come when soldiers accused women of supporting the war at the expense of men's lives.[29] In the US women started joining pro-war 'preparedness movements' even before America joined the war in April 1917. The war itself gave rise to dozens of patriotic women's organizations such as the American Defense Society, the National Women's Patriotic Relief Society, the National Security League and various War Relief Commissions. Prominent among the thousands upon thousands of women who threw themselves into the war effort was Ms Anna Howard Shaw, president of NAWSA (National American Women's Suffrage Association), who left her post to lead the Women's Committee of the Council of National Defense. Another was Eleanor Roosevelt. As she later wrote, the war was 'my emancipation and my education.'[30] Along with her husband's discovered infidelity, it prodded her to leave home and assume a public role.

Against the background of nationalist hysteria, a few feminists even managed to see the war as a vindication of women. Thus, according to the Countess of Warwick, the reason why the Germans had to be defeated was because 'in their country women are kept more in the background than in the country of ... any other great Power'; by contrast, in France (which she loved) 'woman rules ... feminism is one of the strongest forces in France'. Writing in the *Suffragette*, Emmeline Pankhurst's other daughter, Christabel, explained that German cruelty in waging war was rooted in their attitude towards women. Therefore 'this great war ... is God's vengeance upon the people who held women in subjection and by doing that have destroyed the perfect, human balance.'[31] Had Britain been fighting against France instead of Germany, no doubt she would have said exactly the same with only the names reversed; as with many men it was the fight that mattered, not the name of the opponent.

Feminist or not, in all countries female poetasters joined male ones in encouraging their menfolk to enlist as did, for example, Jessie Pople in 'The

Call'. Others described the 'ecstasy' of battle against the Huns (May Sinclair in *The Tree of Heaven*); others still expressed envy of the soldiers' liberation from daily tedium (Rose Macaulay in 'Many Sisters to Many Brothers'). Quotations from these long-forgotten verses could fill volumes. By far the most famous effort was an essay entitled 'A Mother's ... Message to the ... Pacifists. A Message to the Bereaved. A Message to the Trenches'. It first saw the light of day in a British paper, the *Morning Post*, in 1916.[32] Later it was reprinted in pamphlet form and sold 75,000 in less than a week:

> [The voice of the] mothers of the British race ... demands to be heard, seeing that we play the most important part in the history of the world, for it is we who 'mother the men' who have to uphold the honour and traditions not only of our Empire but of the whole civilized world.
>
> We women ... will tolerate no such cry such as 'Peace! peace!' where there is no peace ... There is only one temperature for women of the British race, and that is white heat. With those who disgrace their sacred trust of motherhood we have nothing in common ... We women pass on the human ammunition of 'only sons' to fill up the gaps ... We gentle-nurtured, timid sex did not want the war ... But the bugle call came ... We've fetched our laddie from school, we've put his cap away ... We have risen to our responsibility ... Women are created for the purpose of giving life, and men to take it ... We shall not flinch one iota ... [Should we be bereft], we shall emerge stronger women to carry on the glorious work our men's memories have handed down to us for now and all eternity.
>
> Yours, etc., A LITTLE MOTHER.

To this day, it is not clear who wrote this wondrous war propaganda piece; for all we know, it may well have been a man!

For what it is worth, here is an explanation for the female war craze offered by the famous psychologist Helene Deutsch who herself witnessed it in her native Germany.[33] She thought it natural for men to welcome war by an orgy of sex: afraid to die, they hoped to leave something of themselves behind. As to women, their excitement originated in the fact that in tense periods humans:

> experience reality in a more primitive manner ... not only objectively but symbolically. The symbolic method of overcoming death often leads to consciously undesired but very realistic pregnancies, for girls who ... agree to [man's] unexpressed proposal and let themselves be impregnated by the 'unknown soldier'. They are seduced not as a result of their own sexual excitation but through serving the lust for life of others. This motive also plays a tremendous role in many young brides and unmarried girls who hasten to become pregnant by their husbands or lovers about to be drafted ... the danger of death that heightens the desire for a continuation of life is a much stronger, although unconscious factor.

Another eyewitness, Helene Swanwick, put it more succinctly by saying that women's eagerness to mate was 'the natural female complement to the male frenzy of killing. If millions of men were to be killed in early manhood, or even boyhood, it behooved every young woman to secure a mate and replenish the population, while it was yet time.'[34] Her statement confirms the obvious, namely that Mars and Venus have normally got along well together and that most women at most times and places have expressed their approval of warriors in the best way they could: by sleeping with them.

Nor did the First World War mark the end of the story. During the inter-war period Fascist Italy was more self-professedly 'virile' and 'anti-feminist' than any other country. From Marinetti through d'Annunzio all the way to Mussolini himself, no other group of leaders so much claimed to despise women. Still, when the invasion of Ethiopia got under way in 1935 neither the regime's male chauvinist tendencies nor its harsh exploitation of female labour could prevent hundreds of thousands of women from joining in demonstrations and donating their golden wedding rings to the war chest.[35] German women during the Nazi years also supported the party that devalued them and tried to exclude them from public life,[36] and German soldiers during the Second World War attached their decorations to female garters won in close combat, as the saying went. Finally, Israeli women following the October 1973 war were said to have welcomed their returning menfolk with the words 'mount and enter': an obscene adaptation of a traditional Jewish blessing referring to the right to read the Bible during divine service.

It is certainly true that some women (along with some men) have been opposed to war. Sometimes the anti-war movements were initiated by women. However, as they gathered momentum they were taken over by men, which presumably constitutes another proof of the latter's greater aggression. For example, in Israel in 1998–9 the most effective spokesperson advocating unilateral withdrawal from Lebanon was M.K. Yossi Beylin. He had joined the bandwagon as it was already rolling along; meanwhile the leaders of the 'Four Mothers' organization that was the first to raise the demand remained all but unknown to the public. In any case, very few of these movements appear to have been successful. The one great exception are the Sabine women of Roman legend. They owed their success precisely to the fact that they had male kin – their fathers and husbands, respectively – in each of the opposing camps; had this not been the case, then surely the entire episode would have been impossible in the first place.

Not being as fortunate – or, depending on one's point of view, unfortunate – as their Sabine/Roman sisters, most of the time in all eras and places the vast majority of women supported their menfolk. Usually their support was both enthusiastic and active. It took every form, beginning with the preparation of bandages and the knitting of socks and ending with what most people believe is 'the right true end of love':[37] namely sex either as a parting gift before battle or as a reward after it had taken place. Women who happened to live during a political crisis experienced exactly the same emotions as did men – even to the point where Rose Macaulay's sense of liberation from the daily grind echoes the feelings of the young Adolf Hitler as later expressed in *Mein Kampf*.[38] This is all the more remarkable because, in all wars, women have been among the main victims; and it is to this role that we must now turn our attention.

2 Causes, Objects and Victims

Under the prevailing bio-sociological wisdom,[39] the one great goal of every piece of DNA in the universe is to reproduce itself. Thus the male's best strategy to achieve this aim is to impregnate as many females as possible (the female's best strategy is said to be to find the best possible male and stick with him; which, as we shall presently see, contains an implicit threat to males who for one reason or another are not 'the best' or have ceased being so). This leads us to some other roles that women have played in war, namely as its causes, its objects and its victims.

Much has been written about women as a cause of tribal warfare, and the available evidence is conveniently summed up by a Dutch anthropologist, Jan van der Dennen.[40] Apparently many tribal wars were triggered by quarrels over women, such as the payment of bridewealth, or divorce, or rape, or the elopement of a woman with a man belonging to another tribe (what one side called elopement the other might call rape, so that the last-named two occasions were often the same). This was the situation among many Indian tribes living along the Californian coast. It also prevailed among the Yanomamo of the Amazon Forest,[41] the Mundugumor of New Guinea,[42] and many other peoples including the biblical Israelites who once went to war against the tribe of Benjamin after some of the latter's members had abused a woman of another tribe.[43] The Maori of New Zealand used to say that 'land and women were the causes of war'. From which we may learn that among all those people women were but one cause among many and on a level with disputes over homicide, injury, insults, trespassing, theft of livestock, and the like.

To say that quarrels over women sometimes gave rise to war is one thing; that men went to war in order to obtain women, another. For example, the *Iliad* mentions many occasions when cities were razed, their menfolk killed, and the women captured;[44] however, among the Greeks as among many other peoples they were often valued less for their reproductive facilities than for their labour, which put a premium on skills such as spinning and weaving. In California, the Pomo and the Nisenan regularly incorporated captive women into their own tribes by way of marriage. Early Viking warfare also provided frequent opportunities to procure women by force, a practice known as *herfang*.[45] We are told that, when King Helgi of Norway harried Sweden, 'he got plenteous plunder, and laid hands on Yrsa the queen, and had her away with him'.[46]

On the other hand, many tribes put no particular value on women, either killing them along with their male relatives or setting them free. Thus the Yurok sometimes carried off women as captives but normally returned them to their relatives after a settlement. The Mattole, Nongatl, Sinkyone, Lassik and Wailaki took no prisoners and sometimes killed women as well as children. The Quenchan and Mojave sometimes took female captives but considered it dangerous to have intercourse with them. Among the Asmat head-hunters of New Guinea, a warrior interested in saving a woman or child as a captive (something rarely done) experienced considerable difficulty in preventing his over-excited comrades from dispatching his chosen prisoners.[47]

Thus, on the whole, the evidence that tribal societies go to war in order to capture women and use them for recreation or reproduction is ambivalent. Nor did the tactics they used make it easy for them to do so. One of the most prevalent was the pre-dawn attack on isolated settlements, in which case the entire population was normally killed irrespective of sex. Nor could raiding parties take prisoners, given that they would obstruct mobility; thus females belonging to a hostile tribe who had the bad luck to run into such parties were likely to be raped and then killed, but not captured. Finally, in the form of war known as the pitched battle – a sort of ceremonial encounter familiar to many tribes around the world – women were considered exempt. They might, indeed, act as spectators, encouraging the warriors and egging them on.

In all this, much depended on the political structure of war-making society. For males in a comparatively egalitarian tribe to resort to war in order to procure additional women for themselves can make good sense, and in fact there are tribes where captive women made up a considerable percentage of the population.[48] For a king or emperor to engage in hostile acts with the same objective probably did not make sense, since such august personages already had access to all the females they could possibly want from among their own people or peoples. The more complex and hierarchical any given political entity, the less the evidence that those who governed it went to war in order to obtain women as opposed to slaves of both sexes; the more so because female captives were often considered less valuable than male ones.[49] In fact I can think of no political organization more sophisticated than a chiefdom using war as a method for procuring women *qua* women. For example, when Virgilius makes his hero Aeneas wage war against King Turnus in order to secure the Latin Princess Lavinia for himself it was high politics, not sexual gratification, that he had in mind.[50] The same was true of the Persian Emperor Darius, who, as he laid siege to the Milesians in 490 BC, threatened that if they did not submit they themselves would be killed, their sons castrated, and their daughters carried off to Bactria.[51]

From the women's own point of view, whether they served as the object of war or were merely made to suffer as a result ('collateral damage', is the modern term for this) made little difference. Either way they would be victimized by stronger, more aggressive and better organized males against whom they were unable to defend themselves. As described by authors from Euripides in *The Trojan Women* to Susan Brownmuller in *Against Our Will*,[52] the sufferings that war has always inflicted and still inflicts on women are notorious and do not require elaboration. If anything, given the post-1945 shift from inter-state to intra-state war and so-called 'ethnic cleansing', compared to the period between 1700 and the beginning of the Second World War those sufferings have increased; in Bosnia-Herzegovina in 1992–5 rape is said to have been systematically used by the Serbs in order to humiliate and punish their Muslim enemies,[53] and the same occurred in East Timor. Still, the fact remains that, as is already the case in chimpanzee 'warfare', females have generally received better treatment and fared better than males. For tribal societies, the best available figures are as follows:[54]

society	male deaths as per cent of total	female deaths as per cent of total	all deaths	female/male deaths ratio
Jivaro	59.0	27.0	32.7	1:2.8
Yanomamo-Shamatari	37.4	4.4	20.9	1:8.5
Mae Enga	34.8	2.3	18.6	1:15.1
Dugm Dani	28.5	2.4	15.5	1:11.9
Yanomamo-Nanowei	23.7	6.9	15.3	1:3.4
Huli	19.6	6.1	13.2	1:3.2
Gebusi	8.3	8.2	8.3	1:1.02

The mean for all seven societies is 1:6.1, so that for every woman who died as a result of war just over six men met the same fate. Moreover, there is no correlation between a tribe's overall ferocity – as expressed by the third column – and the ratio in question. In other words, warlike societies do not lose proportionally more women than do peaceful ones. Instead the one society in which as many women are killed as men (the Gebusi) is far and away the most peaceful of all, as it would have to be in order to avoid extermination.

What applies to tribal warfare is no less true of its 'civilized' counterpart. As Julius Caesar reports,[55] for examples women, though no doubt often raped and mistreated, were seldom killed out of hand; and indeed all over the ancient Mediterranean it was standard practice to kill the men of cities taken by storm while selling the women and children. The reliefs that were commissioned by the Assyrian King Sancherib to commemorate his capture of Lachish in Judaea in 705 BC, and which have been found in the ruins of his palace at Ninveh, illustrate the point as well as anything can. The city having fallen, the women, along with their children, are shown being led away with the rest of the booty, apparently unharmed. The men, however, were impaled.

One of the first codes for protecting women from the evils of war is represented by Deuteronomy 21:10–15. Going on 'optional war' (in other words, a war that was not explicitly ordered by the Lord) the Israelites were enjoined to kill all male captives. However, the law required that they refrain from 'tormenting' female ones. Instead, the women taken in war were to be allowed adequate time to grieve for their dead relatives before being married to their captors in due form; only then could sex follow. Since then there have been countless attempts to protect women from the worst that war can do, most of them inspired either by religion or by some kind of chivalrous code. A typical example is Honoré Bonet's *The Tree of Battles* (*c.* 1400).[56] It bristles with injunctions concerning the need to spare women who, along with ecclesiastics and domestic animals, were classified as 'innocent' and thus deserving of Christian mercy; as late as the sixteenth century German articles of war still contained strong exhortations that young mothers, pregnant women and '*Maedchen*' (which might be translated either as 'virgins' or as 'young girls') were not to be harmed.[57]

The modern world has approached these problems in a somewhat different way. From the second half of the seventeenth century Western warfare has been waged not by individuals or by peoples but by states.[58] A state by definition had the right to wage war; accordingly, the problem was not so much to separate the 'innocent' from the 'guilty' but to establish exactly who had the right to fight in the name of the state and who did not. Once that problem was solved by the introduction of uniforms, jurists such as Emmerich Vattel[59] drew a line between combatants and non-combatants. The former had the right to kill and could expect to be killed in return; the latter, as far as 'military necessity' permitted and so long as they did not resist, were supposedly immune. Thus the separation by age and sex was replaced by one between soldiers and civilians. In theory at least, women were left better protected than ever before.

That the injunctions against killing women (as well as, at various times and places, taking them prisoner and subjecting them to some kind of sexual mistreatment) have often been violated goes without saying. In the ancient world, Alexander and Scipio Africanus were specifically commended for *not* abusing the fair captives delivered to them.[60] The former's behaviour in this respect led to some discussion concerning the possibility that he might have been a homosexual; the latter had his attitude commemorated in a special painting produced by the sixteenth-century painter Domenico Beccafumi.[61] Also during the sixteenth century Pierre de Bayard, 'the cavalier without reproach and without fear', owed part of his reputation to his unusual chastity.[62] By contrast, to mention but a few occasions, mass rape accompanied the sack of Rome in 1527 and the destruction of Magdeburg in 1631, both by imperial troops who had broken loose and acted without their commanders' permission. Mass rape took place at the hands of the Japanese Army at Nanking in 1938, and mass rape was practised by the Red Army as they invaded Germany in 1945.[63] Indeed it was with these events in mind that the obligation to treat female prisoners 'with all the regard due to their sex', was written into the Second Geneva Convention of 1949.[64]

In peace and in war, whether carried out on an individual basis or in an organized way as a matter of policy, the maltreatment of women – including, above all, rape – is a hideous and, unfortunately, all too prevalent crime. Still, on the whole there is reason to think that women have come out of war much better than men. Even the medieval Celts, notorious for their refusal to grant quarter, preferred to capture 'soft, youthful, bright, matchless girls' and 'blooming, silk-clad, young women' rather than kill them out of hand;[65] the Belgian Fascist leader Leon Degrelle describes how, amidst the immense carnage that took place on the Russian Front in 1942, both sides permitted Ukrainian women to continue working the fields between the lines.[66] Women taken prisoner could expect to be treated less harshly than men. Thus Allied troops captured by the Japanese during the Second World War died like flies; by contrast, though the US Army nurses captured at Bataan were also ravaged by hunger and disease every single one of them survived.[67] Here is the Reverend A.E. Winnington, Bishop of London, as he was exhorting his countrymen to wage war against Germany in 1914:[68] 'Kill Germans – to kill them, not for the sake of killing, but to save the world, to kill the good as well as the bad, to kill the young men as well as the old, to kill those who have shewn kindness to our wounded as well as those fiends who crucified the Canadian sergeant [referring to a widely circulated propaganda myth] ...'

Note that, even in this outpouring of outraged rhetoric, Britons are not called upon to kill German women.

3 Protecting Women

If women have not been victimized by war as often or as much as men, on the other hand victimizing women always has been and still is one of the principal objectives for which war is waged. The point is well made in a story told of Genghis Khan, the Mongol chieftain who at the peak of his power ruled over one-quarter of the entire earth and, needless to say, had his pick among the fair sex. Seeing that he was more able to do what he pleased than perhaps any other man before or since, his advisers once asked him what was the most marvellous thing in life. Ghengis's answer, 'to watch one's enemies bathing in tears even as one embraces their women', speaks for itself.

In part, rape is motivated by the need for physical relief: all soldiers know the effect that a period spent in the field, without women, can have. However, to quote Aristophanes' *Lysistrate*,[69] a man's pleasure depends on a woman's goodwill. To force a woman against her will is not fun. Certainly not if the act has to be repeated; in which case, instead of demonstrating the power he has over her, it merely emphasizes the perpetrator's degradation. Hence there is good reason to suspect that, in war at any rate, the real motive behind rape is often not so much sexual as symbolic. More than any other act it proves that the enemy has indeed been 'thrown to the ground' (as Clausewitz puts it) and his will 'broken'.[70] In other words, that the objective of war has been achieved and that he is no longer able to protect his nearest and, presumably, dearest.

To make things worse for the defeated, the women themselves are not passive. If they do not feel protected, they may go over to the other side: flirt with him, live with him (formally or informally), have sex with him, and bear children for him. Voluntarily if they live under occupation, or involuntarily if they are prisoners, those who can may strike a deal with the victor. Presumably not all the women who were ever captured by tribal warriors and incorporated into their societies' stayed against their will; in the *Iliad* the woman Briseis, a helpless captive whose male relatives had been killed, lamented Patroclus who had shown sympathy with her and even promised her that she would become Achilles' wife.[71] Simone de Beauvoir recorded how, in 1940, no sooner had Paris been occupied than the Boche were approached by French women, professional and amateur alike.[72] Over the next few years Dutch, Belgian, French, Danish and Norwegian women gave birth to 200,000 children of German soldiers (the real figure may have been higher, since presumably not all the women hastened to report to Himmler's *Lebensborn* organization, which compiled the statistics). Of those, probably only a small minority – perhaps 10 per cent – resulted from rape.[73]

When the Allies liberated Europe a few years later the roles were reversed. In the Netherlands this led to the so-called 'dancing tents' inhabited by Canadian soldiers and their local paramours. In Germany the outcome was various obscene variations on the famous popular song, 'Lili Marlene'.[74] As had also happened in the countries occupied by Germany, Japan and their allies, very often it was a question of the women asking for, and obtaining, scarce goods such as food, liquor and tobacco in return for sexual favours; however, behind the persuasion and the various forms of mercenary sex ranging from concubinage to straightforward prostitution the threat of force is always present. By demonstrating the domination of enemy women and the ultimate humiliation of enemy men, rape is what war is all about. Even if those among the victors who are guilty of it are apprehended and punished, and even if it never takes place.[75]

Conversely, protecting women against rape has always been one of the most important reasons why men fought. In the *Iliad* the Trojan Hector prefers 'going to hell and be covered by soil and ashes' rather than witness his wife, Andromache, 'being led away, crying, by one of the copper-armoured Achaeans'.[76] Some of the reliefs of the Athenian Parthenon show Lapiths defending their women against Centaur attack. About five hundred years after those reliefs were made Elazar Ben Yair, commander of the Zealots at Masada, was trying to persuade his men to commit mass suicide in the face of inevitable defeat. His first attempt failed. Speaking for the second time, among other things he described their wives' and daughters' 'shame' if they should fall into the hands of the Romans while their own hands were tied. This time his words had the intended effect. Yet presumably shame was no worse than being thrown to the lions, which is how many Jewish men captured during the war ended their lives.[77]

Passing to modern times, the annals of the American West are full of accounts of lascivious redskins lusting for white ladies' flesh; some, written by women who claimed to have been victims, became best-sellers.[78] The Confederates during the Civil War invented the myth of Yankee desire for the 'Southern Belle'. Throughout the First World War, troops of all nations saw an urgent need to protect their womenfolk against rape.[79] At various times during the Arab-Israeli conflict, Israeli determination to fight was fuelled by what they saw as the threat that sex-starved hordes of Arab savages presented to their women. Thus, for example, in 1948 when a few women in Gush Etsion, to the south of Jerusalem, were actually raped by Trans-Jordanian troops; and again during the first desperate days of the October 1973 war when husbands departing for the front advised their womenfolk to try and take refuge in hospitals if, as seemed possible, everything were lost. Whatever the time and the setting, there is always a ferocious enemy positively slavering after one's own women, who, depending on the prevailing fashion, are portrayed as exceptionally thin, exceptionally thick, exceptionally modest, exceptionally forthcoming, at any rate exceptionally beautiful and exceptionally desirable. Always they must be saved from that horrible fate, even at the cost of one's own life and even if, as may happen once in a while, they do not want to be saved.

At times, the threat of mass rape and the enslavement of the entire female population was real enough; by showing conquered countries in the form of captive women, Roman art in particular often made the connection between defeat and rape quite explicit.[80] Often the fear of rape was spontaneous, but as often it was deliberately manufactured and systematically used in order to incite men to war. For example, in 1914 French and British propaganda presented German troops as pausing between one crucified Canadian sergeant and the next in order to rape Belgian nuns and French women;[81]

there were also stories of German troops cutting off ladies' breasts.[82] During the Second World War all belligerents produced posters that spelled out the fate that women could anticipate at the enemy's hands, often leaving little to the imagination.[83] The ploy worked; for example, late in the Second World War news of atrocities committed by the Red Army against German women proved to be 'extremely effective' in maintaining the Wehrmacht's will to fight.[84] During the 1991 Gulf Crisis the Kuwaiti government in exile hired an American public relations firm to make its case. Among other rumours spread as part of the campaign to discredit Saddam Hussein were lurid stories concerning the rape of Kuwaiti women by Iraqi troops.

Sometimes entire countries were cast in the form of ravishing women about to be ravished. Like Athene, her prototype, Britain's Britannia was much too imperious to play the role; it is impossible to imagine either lady being approached by any man. However, during the first World War France ('Marianne'), Italy and Austria–Hungary were often portrayed in this way. In 1917–18, American propaganda posters portrayed the US in the form of so-called 'Gibson Girls' (after their creator, Charles Dana Gibson) with apple-red cheeks and rounded breasts; others showed a poor Belgian maiden about to be dished by a German soldier who looked like King Kong, wore a spiked helmet, had saliva dripping out of his maw, and carried a truncheon marked '*Kultur*' against a background of ruins.[85] Some of these posters may appear crude, but their very crudeness suggests that the fears to which they appealed were real and that the artists knew what they were doing. As propaganda pieces they have never been surpassed. Similar imagery was used during the Second World War, for example by the Dutch government in exile. In 1943–4 German posters in the occupied countries often presented Europe itself as a women being crucified by capitalists, communists and Jews.[86]

In some cases the women gave to rise to protective feelings even though they were enemies and even after they were dead. The following account of the death of the Amazon queen, Penthesilea, was written by the Greek poet Quintus Smyrnaeus during the second half of the fourth century AD:[87]

Though she lay fallen in dirt and gore, beneath her lovely eyebrows shone her beautiful face, even in death. The Argives, crowding about, were amazed when they saw her; she seemed like the blessed immortals. She lay on the ground in her armour like tireless Artemis, daughter of Zeus, sleeping when weary from chasing swift lions in the lofty mountains. Aphrodite, beautiful garlanded wife of mighty Ares, made Penthesilea radiant even in death to cause the son of blameless Peleus [i.e. Achilles, her killer] to grieve. Many men prayed that when they came home they would sleep in the bed of a wife like her. Achilles suffered greatly in his heart, that he slew her and did not bring her to Phthia as his shining wife, since in height and beauty she was blameless like the immortals.

To sum up, in myth – and, often enough, in fact as well – protecting women (and, of course, children) is one of the prime objectives for which wars are fought and for which men are expected to lay down their lives. As the numerous stories about females inciting their menfolk to war prove, the initiative may come from the women themselves; if necessary they will even lift their skirts for the purpose. Often the fears for women's safety are deliberately spread by the powers that be, which of course does not necessarily mean they are either unreal or unfounded on fact. It follows that women who consort with the enemy (and even those who are simply unfaithful to their soldier husbands)[88] must be punished, for by doing so they undermine the purpose of the entire war. This is what happened in France in 1944–5, when thousands of them, accused of 'horizontal co-operation' and 'unpatriotic love', were paraded half naked and had their hair shaved off in public;[89] in Norway during the same period they were abused and even imprisoned.[90] If the propaganda is to succeed it must emphasize women's relative physical weakness and inability to fight. Conversely, if they *could* fight then much of the war's purpose would be lost. This, then, is another reason why women have hardly ever fought and, even more rarely, killed.

4 A World without War?

By some feminist accounts, in a world without men there would be no war. Whether or not there is any truth in this, so long as humanity is made up of men *and* women the latter's role will remain important, even vital; in the words of Horace, 'long before Helene the female sex (*cunnus*) was the cause of terrible war.'[91] Women have always acted as instigators, causes, objects, victims and protégées. Very often the same women have played different roles at different times. Occasionally they even played different ones at the same time, for example by instigating men while they were being victimized and clamouring for protection even as they felt themselves threatened as objects.

It is often said that behind every successful man there is an ambitious woman; as the Spartan women's sayings prove, this is even more true in the case of war than in any other field. Had it not been for women who, in reality as well as imagination, demand protection from their menfolk, cheer them as they march away, pray for them while they fight, wait for their return, embrace the victors, console the losers, dress the wounded, mourn the dead, and act (in one way or another) as spoils, war would have been both pointless and impossible; in these ways as well as many others, it would scarcely be too much to say that women are what war is all about. In the words of Virginia Woolf: 'women have served all these centuries as magnifying mirrors possessing the magic and delicious power of reflecting the figure of men at twice its real size.' Without that power, 'probably the earth would still be swamp and jungle. The glories of all our wars would be unknown … mirrors are essential to all violent and heroic action.'[92]

Conversely, the only way to make men cease fighting is to cause women to cease to admire warriors. Here is one ancient Greek woman explaining how she would go about it:[93]

Lysistrate: First we will stop the disorderly crew,
               soldiers in arms promenading and marketing.

Stratyllis: Yea, by divine Aphrodite, 'tis true.

Lysistrate: Now in the market you see them like Corybants,
               jangling about with their armour of mail.
               Fiercely they stalk in the midst of the crockery,
               sternly parade by the cabbage and kail.

Magistrate: Right, for a soldier should always be soldierly!

Lysistrate: Troth, 'tis a mighty ridiculous jest,
               Watching them haggle for shrimps in the market-place,
               grimly accoutred with shield and with crest.

Stratyllis: Lately I witnessed a captain of cavalry,
               proudly the while on his charger he sat,
               witnessed him, soldierly, buying an omelette,
               stowing it all in his cavalry hat.
               Comes, like a Terus, a Thracian irregular
               shaking his dart and his target to boot;
               Off runs a shop-girl, appalled at the sight of him
               down he sits soldierly, gobbles her fruit.

If war is a man's glory, then assuredly the best antidote to it ought to be a woman's ridicule.

Part II **From the Amazons to GI Jane**

Whereas, in our own day, women's participation in war has become the subject of a fierce debate, previous periods up until the late 1960s usually took it for granted that men and women possessed different qualities, and that the qualities they did or did not possess made women inherently unsuited for war.[1] If anything, it was the expressed wish of some women to participate in the slaughter that was considered abnormal and in need of an explanation.

For example, during the 1940s and 1950s – in fact, until the influence of psychoanalysis began to wane in the late 1970s – the world's most important authority on the psychology of women was Helene Deutsch. Deutsch was a student of Freud who had come to the US during the 1930s in order to escape the Nazis. Writing during the early years of the Second World War even as women's auxiliary corps were being formed in the US and elsewhere, she devoted much of her work to the question of why some women should want to emulate men. To her, woman's essential quality was her 'passivity'. Passivity was something all women were born with and, if they were to stay mentally healthy, had to learn to accept. If they failed to do so, the outcome was a 'masculinity complex' and 'bizarre' attempts by women to become men.[2]

For Deutsch, any woman who wished to participate in combat was clearly abnormal and had to be psychoanalyzed. To the extent that they addressed the question at all, other female authors agreed. Thus, the fourteenth-century writer Christine de Pizan set out to refute the slanders aimed at the members of her sex. Though convinced that women were by no means without either strength or courage, she took it for granted that men alone had the 'hardy bodies' that enabled them to fight.[3] Writing during the first heady months of the First World War, the British suffragette Helene Swanwick argued that most women did not share men's 'exhilaration' in war (in fact, as we saw, quite a few did). Therefore, unlike British men who at that very time were joining the armed services by the hundreds of thousands, there was no question of them taking up arms. Instead she explained the numerous negative effects war had on women, the most important of which were 'millions of young bodies made barren by the premature death of those who should have been their mates'.[4]

Thanks to her *Vindication of the Rights of Women* (1792),[5] Mary Wollstonecraft has a claim to be considered the mother of all feminists.[6] An Englishwoman born and bred, Wollstonecraft was a disciple of Rousseau and, like him, wanted a society based on freedom and equality. Accordingly, she applauded the French Revolution which had just granted citizenship to men. Now Rousseau in *Emile* (1762) had a lot to say about the education of women whom he regarded as being governed by emotion rather than by reason. Hence he opposed their enfranchisement and suggested that, in the utopian community of soldier-farmers which constituted his political ideal, they should remain under the tutelage of their fathers and husbands. While agreeing with Rousseau as to women's nature, Wollstonecraft argued that it was the result not of biology but of the lack of education. She demanded that women be given equal rights in the new polity, but only after they showed themselves worthy of the honour by abandoning their addiction to 'wild nights' of pleasure and developing man-like civic virtue.[7]

As it happened, the very year her book was published saw the enactment by the French National Assembly of universal conscription which 'permanently requisitioned' all male citizens for military service. One would have thought that a better opportunity for women to develop civic virtue could scarcely be imagined; the more so because Wollstonecraft spent part of the year in France – where she masqueraded as the wife of an American officer – and was thus able to observe events at first hand. Yet she did not follow her own logic. Possibly because she considered the idea too absurd, she did not demand that women fight like men. Instead she suggested that men behave like women; even in defensive war, they should turn their muskets into prunes. Coming at a time France was about to be invaded by a coalition comprising all Europe's remaining principal powers with the aim of putting an end to the very revolution that Wollstonecraft so admired, this advice was not very practicable.

Since few if any women either wanted to fight or thought they could,[8] perhaps men may be excused if they did not expound on the subject either. For example, James Stuart Mill was as ardent a feminist as has ever lived. In his *Subjection of Women* – written in 1861 but only published eight years later – he denounced the legal handicaps that surrounded the lives of women in his time and demanded 'perfect equality' for them. Yet it never occurred to him to suggest that, as part of women's liberation, they should also join the British armed forces. Nor is this omission surprising, given that, at the time, those forces themselves were regarded very much as a refuge for unsuccessful men who were unable or unwilling to make a decent living.

Turning our gaze to military theorists, the Byzantine Flavius Renatus Vegetius (*c.* AD 380) wrote that 'fishermen, fowlers, confectioners, weavers, and all those who appear to have been engaged in occupations appropriate to women should not, in my opinion, be allowed near the barracks'.[9] Eight hundred years before him the Chinese *Art of War* narrates how Sun Tzu formed the Duke of Wu's concubines into an army – after having resorted to drastic means (execution) to stop them laughing at him.[10] These two apart, no other theorist of war with whom I am familiar so much as considers the possibility of including women in the military or excluding them; indeed during most of history 'effeminate' and 'warlike' were considered to be opposites.[11]

Departing from tradition, this part of the study will present a brief outline of the things that women *have* done in war at various times and places. As we shall see, sometimes their role was real, but quite often it was either mythological or legendary. Sometimes women took centre stage, but most of the time their role was marginal. Often women who wanted to participate in combat had to disguise themselves or else surrender their femininity in some other way; in other cases what mattered was not so much their military feats as the titillating effect they had on men. Very occasionally women were formally incorporated into whatever armed forces were in existence, but most of the time they remained on the sidelines. The vast majority of women did not participate in war proper but were active in a variety of supporting tasks as camp-followers, nurses, and so on. Finally, a survey of all the roles that women have played in war shows that there has been remarkably little change over time and that what change did take place was often illusory. In this, perhaps, is an indication that the psychology of both men and women is not nearly as flexible as some historians would have us believe.[12]

5 'War' in the Animal Kingdom

War might be defined as the use of organized violence waged in order to achieve collective goals. Therefore the combats that frequently take place between individual members of the same animal species – let alone between members of different species, such as hunting and its reverse, defence against predators – need not concern us here. From fish through birds to mammalians, often the objective of such combats is the defence or extension of territory.[13] In other cases it is a question of exercising dominance, or else of males competing for females as among rats, red deer, mountain sheep, baboons, seals and numerous other species.[14] The fact that males often fight each other for access to females does not necessarily mean that the latter are always passive: in many species they exercise choice in selecting their mates.[15] However, there are very few species, and no mammalian ones, in whom the roles are reversed and whose females fight each other in order to obtain the favour of males.[16]

Combats between individuals apart, the closest thing that the animal world has to war is that waged between ants.[17] Ants live in highly organized colonies with a clear division of labour among the members. Those members are known to fight the members of other colonies in an organized way, conquer them and exterminate them. When they win a campaign some species of ants will even take prisoners and carry off booty, thus further increasing the similarity with humans. The trouble, though, is that ants are about as far removed from us on the evolutionary scale as it is possible to go. Nobody knows what an ant feels and thinks, if it does so at all in our sense of those terms. Furthermore, colonies of ants consist entirely of females, albeit such as are (with the sole exception of the queen) sexually neutral, do not seek to copulate with males during the course of their lives, and do not have offspring. For these reasons their relevance to the subject at hand is virtually zero and they will not be discussed further.

Aside from ants, the members of some mammalian species appear to engage in collective 'military' action against each other. Among those species, the majority are primates.[18] Some, including baboons, vervet monkeys, redtail monkeys, grey langurs and rhesus macaques have been observed forming in long parallel lines numbering as many as one hundred individuals. They confront each other and threaten each other by screaming, grimacing, thumping their chests, and exposing their teeth. At some point one group will break and flee, pursued by the other; actual violence, let alone injury and death, seldom results.[19] The members of other primate species, including chimpanzees as our closest living relatives, participate in a different form of collective action. These animals will form groups numbering around ten individuals and aggressively patrol their territories' 'borders'. If and when they encounter the members of another group, fights and injuries, including lethal ones, may – but need not – ensue; over time, this may lead to the extermination of one of the groups and the take-over of its territory.[20]

Assuming such activities deserve the appellation 'war', female participation in them is said to depend on the extent to which the males and females of the species are, or are not, philopatric (i.e. mate within the group). Where females are the philopatric sex males mate outside the group. Hence the bonds between individual males are weak and female participation in 'combat' is high. This, for example, is the case among lemurs, macaques and vervets, all of which also have this in common: that the differences in body size between the sexes are minimal. Conversely, in species where males are the philopatric sex the bonds between individual males are strong and female participation in conflict is low. As it happens, among chimpanzees it is the male sex that is philopatric. All the male members of a group are related; this enables them to create strong bonds, including the kind of bonds needed to wage 'war'.[21]

Partly because they are considerably smaller and weaker than the males, partly because they are infrequently free from pregnancy and nursing,[22] adult female chimpanzees who are involved in fights are limited to a 'supporting role';[23] one is almost tempted to say that they act as camp-followers. Here and there young female chimpanzees, usually while in oestrus, will accompany the males on patrol. However, they do not initiate hostilities. If they participate at all, they will take as their opponents the females who accompany the males of the opposing group.[24] Being considerably larger and heavier, male chimpanzees on their part seldom launch serious attacks on females belonging either to their own group (which, by our definition, would not count as war) or to another one (which would).[25] Should a group of male chimpanzees be successful in its fight against a neighbouring one, then the females belonging to the losers will probably end up being assimilated by the victors.[26]

Given the immense gap that separates even a chimpanzee from a human being, too much should not be made of these considerations. Neither chimpanzees nor any other living primate are included among our direct ancestors. Therefore there is no way of knowing whether warfare as it was practised, if it was practised, by hominids living hundreds of thousands of years ago resembled the observed fights of chimpanzees or baboons.[27] Still, the fact that female primates will participate in fights only if the males of the species do not mate within the group – and consequently do not form strong bonds among themselves – is significant. Some human societies are matrilocal, which means that the groom goes to live with the family of the bride, whereas the great majority are patrilocal. However, and if only because of the need to make a living, in no known society have males systematically left their own societies to marry complete strangers belonging to other groups.

6 Warrior Goddesses

Given that very few women have ever fought in reality, the prominent role that female warriors have played in religion and myth requires an explanation. This is all the more true because, in the vast majority of cases, the imagination that created them seems to have been male.

From India to Scandinavia and from Sumer to Peru, the most important deities which various religions credited with the creation of the world were usually male. Whether his name was Ra or Osiris or El or Zeus or Odin, it was 'the Father of the Gods' who occupied the centre of the pantheon. The wives of such male gods, such as Isis or Asherah or Hera or Freya, were seldom warrior queens in their own right. If anything they tended to be gracious and wise (though sometimes jealous of their husbands' philandering), bearing children to them, and helping them rule the world. For example, Asherah was known as 'The Lady'.[28] 'White-armed' Hera as she prepared to sleep with Zeus was described as having 'attractive flesh'.[29] Her Scandinavian counterpart Freya stood for desirable femininity in the eyes of gods and men alike.[30]

Not too far away from the royal couple, though, there often stood a female deity who had selected war as her special domain. Terrifying to look at, she personified destruction much in the way that early cannon often bore such names as 'Mad Margaret' and hurricanes used to be called after women. Here is a hymn written in honour of one of the earliest of them, the Sumerian Inanna:[31]

> That you totally destroy rebellious lands – be it known!
> That you roar at the land – be it known!
> That you kill – be it known!
> That like a dog you eat the corpses – be it known!
> That your glance is terrible – be it known!
> That you lift this terrible glance – be it known!

> That you glance flashes – be it known!
> at those who do not obey – be it known!
> That you attain victories – be it known!

She was the very spirit of battle, which throughout Sumerian history is often referred to as 'Inanna's dance'. Iconographic evidence shows her armed with the bow, which from Anatolia to China was the classic weapon of war and also served as the standard symbol of manliness: 'speak the truth and shoot the bow' was Zarathustra's advice to those who would be men. More information about Inanna comes from a lament dating to the first millennium BC. In battle she holds the spindle and the whorl, making skulls roll. As she whirls around in her 'manliness', her ferocity and rage so trouble heaven that another goddess has to be created especially in order to keep her under control.[32]

A marginal figure standing between gods and humans, Inanna did not have a husband. That was precisely the quality that enabled her to take the king of Sumer (whose daughter, Enheduanna, composed the hymn just quoted) as her lover so that he might 'plow her vulva' for her. Still they did not have children; instead, by copulating with her, the king made sure that the land should be fertile.[33] Most other warrior goddesses also tended to be unmarried and childless. So, for example, Anath, sister of the Canaanite god Baal, described as the 'virgin' who delighted in slaughter:[34]

> Anath … violently slays the sons of two cities;
> she hews the people of the sea-shore;
> she destroys the people of the rising sun;
> under her, heads [fly] like vultures;
> over her, hands [fly] like locusts …
> she attaches heads to her back;
> she attaches hands unto her girdle;
> she wades knee-deep in blood …
> Anat exults, her liver is filled with laughter,
> her heart with rejoicing.

Innana and Anath were not alone. Equally ferocious was the Indian goddess Kali, a hideous, black-faced hag who had a protruding tongue and was smeared with blood. Possessed of four arms with four hands, she held a sword, a shield, the severed head of a giant, and a noose. She wore a tiger skin and a necklace made of skulls. In battle she was quite capable of devouring entire armies, infantry, cavalry, elephants, chariots and all.[35]

Although she was sometimes identified with Anath,[36] compared with her fellow divine she-dragons the best known of all warrior goddesses, the Greek Athene, makes an almost sympathetic impression. Described as 'robust' (*palas*), she is the goddess not just of war but of handicraft and wisdom. By Hellenistic times the latter qualities had won the upper hand; there exists a famous representation of her leaning on a spear, lost in thought. Still her civilized appearance should not deceive. To the poet Hesiod, who flourished around 700 BC, she was 'a fearsome queen who brings/the noise of war and tireless, leads the host/she who loves shouts and battling and fights'.[37] During the Trojan War she lived up to her reputation, roaming the battlefield, inciting to slaughter, bullying, bellowing, and fending off weapons with her bare hands.

In her role as 'first in battle' (*promachos*) Athene stood erect, carrying spear, helmet and shield. That shield, the *aegis*, was even equipped with a special refinement in the form of the head of another goddess, Medusa. Having been severed by the male hero Perseus, the head was presented to Athene as a gift. It turned those who looked at it into stone, thus making Athene into the equal of any male warrior except Zeus himself.[38] Yet for all the ruckus she raised, as far as I am aware she never actually killed anybody, preferring to leave that task to others. For example, at one point during the Trojan War she leaped into the chariot of a hero by the name of Diomedes. Getting rid of his driver (Greek chariots carried two men), she personally took hold of the reins and egged her human companion forward. Diomedes, in turn, challenged the war god Ares, wounded him in the groin, and sent him packing to Mount Olympus where, even as he was being cured of his wound, he complained to Zeus about his 'terrible' opponent.[39] As befits the original meaning of *sophia*, Athene could also be tricky; fair play was definitely not among her attributes, and she herself said as much.[40] When her favourite hero Achilles engaged the Trojan Hector in a duel she posed as the latter's brother. Then, after Achilles had cast his spear and missed, she retrieved it and returned it to him, thereby deciding the fight and dooming Hector to die.[41]

These qualities apart, the decisive fact about Athene – as about most other warrior goddesses – was that she was childless, unmarried, and a virgin (*parthenos*). For seeing her naked, the seer Tiresias was struck with blindness. Her own womb remained untouched by any man; she herself sprang straight out of her father Zeus' head without any female intervention, thus validating his patriarchal regime.[42] Later, in her role as 'guardian of young men', she aided and assisted a whole series of heroes including, besides the above-mentioned two, Odysseus, Perseus, Bellerophone, Jason, Theseus and Heracles. Several of these gentlemen had deserted or killed their wives. Others were guilty of rape or had fought against the Amazons, defeated them, killed them, and stripped them of their armour. As we shall see, Athene is typical both of mythological warrior women and of real-life warrior queens in that (except for her role as the patroness of weaving and spinning) she had no sympathy for the members of her sex who were weaker than herself. She herself proudly proclaimed:[43]

> I honour the male, in all things but marriage.
> Yes, with all my heart I am my father's child.

Whereupon, acting as a judge in the trial of Orestes, she acquitted him of his murder of his mother Clytemnestra.

The other Greek martial goddess was Artemis (the Roman Diana). Unlike Athene, she did not carry armour but wore a light hunting tunic in which, surrounded by her maidens, she roamed the countryside. Unlike Athene she was armed with the bow, which the Greeks – in contrast to the peoples of Asia – considered the weapon of the weak and the cowardly.[44] Physically she was no match for her half sister (she was the daughter of Zeus by Leto, a minor deity). Indeed she was said to be more fit 'to pursue roes in the mountains' than to fight in earnest with her 'light arrows'. When confronted head-on she was apt to break into tears, drop her bow, and escape 'like a dove'.[45]

Like Athene, Artemis was a fanatical virgin who hated 'the flying arrows of Cupid'.[46] Like Athene, her attitude to men was ambiguous. She took savage revenge against the only man who ever saw her naked, transforming him into a stag and having him torn to pieces by her hounds; on the other hand she was regarded by gladiators as their patroness.[47] Though surrounded by maidens like herself, like Athene she had little sympathy for other members of her sex. On the eve of the Trojan War it was she who demanded, and obtained, the sacrifice of Agamemnon's daughter Iphigenia in order to assuage her offended pride. On another occasion she used her arrows to kill all six daughters of a woman (Niobe) who had given offence by boasting of her own fertility; on yet another, she killed a queen who had been captured by Achilles and set free by him.[48] Finally, also like Athene, Artemis did have a role to play in the life of women, bearing special responsibility for menstruation, defloration and childbirth. One modern scholar explains that, like men, she made women bleed. Which is why, also like men, she herself did not bleed.[49]

Though probably the most famous, these five were by no means the only divine or semi-divine females whose special domain was war. The ancient Celts had Andraste, Baudihille ('ruler of battle'), Bede and Bebhionn.[50] The Gaels had Bodb, and the Scots had Cailleach – and so to the end of the alphabet where we encounter the Slavic version of an armed virgin warrior, Zarya, who plays a role akin to that of Athene by 'bearing her father's sword'.[51] Some of these goddesses are shown as beautiful maidens, others as terrifying monsters. Often bearing appropriate names such as 'Frenzy' (the Irish Nemen) or 'The Terrifying' (the Egyptian Net), the role of the monsters was to wreak vast destruction while literally wading in blood. Some of the maidens specialized in serving male warriors, gathering their souls after battle and presenting them to the father of the gods: that was the task of the Valkyries, and, perhaps, Freya before she lost her virginity.[52]

Monster or maiden, each goddess in her own way seems to have suffered from problems of sexual identity. Some were expressly 'masculine', their fathers' favourites. Others did not bleed, and others still were androgynous (the Russian Vasillisa Vasily). At least one – the Egyptian Sekhmet, who was among the less gentle characters – resembled Athene in that she had sprung out of her father Ra's body without any female intervention and served as his 'eye'. In view of their qualities it is hardly surprising that none of them seems to have acted as the vast majority of real women did, loving a male, marrying a male (though not necessarily in that order) and bearing the children of a male. At most, some of them demanded to be serviced by a male before helping him in battle and became terribly angry if he dared to refuse.[53]

Certain female scholars have claimed that warrior goddesses reflected some long-lost historical reality when women ruled and, consequently, fought;[54] others, on the contrary, that they were originally nice, loving goddesses who did their best to *avert* war and who owed their subsequent nasty characteristics to some trick of 'patriarchal' imagination.[55] The first argument makes as much sense as to say that, since the Athenians for example had a story about a king (Erechtheus) who was half man half snake, serpents with human upper bodies must once have roamed the earth. The second may apply to a few goddesses – deities, like the people who create them, sometimes change – but totally misrepresents many others who were horrible from beginning to end.[56]

Some of the myths – particularly those involving Valkyries and the like – were probably designed to instigate warriors to fight by promising them female delights in the afterworld. Others present women as fearsome furies whom neither man nor god could (or would, unless on pain of death) touch, as in ancient Chinese thought where war was associated with the female element or *wu*.[57] Nor is the idea of woman as destruction incarnate dead even today. In 1894 the French Impressionist painter Henri Rousseau depicted *La guerre* as a witch riding her horse over the prostrate bodies of male and female dead.[58] Early in the First World War, the British periodical *Punch* published a cartoon in which a sword-wielding hag called the Spirit of Carnage was said to be 'the Kaiser's only friend'.[59] Other myths still create an inverted world, which in turn is supposed to help explain and justify the real one.[60] Whatever their purpose, the myths concerning martial goddesses do not prove that real-life women have ever participated in war and combat. If anything, the contrary.

7 Amazons Old and New

The legend of the Amazons is an ancient one. It is also extraordinarily persistent; in the words of one modern American feminist: 'Amazon society was probably better for the development of women's bodies and emotions than any male-dominated society has ever been.'[61]

The fact that the Amazons were pure invention was clear to the ancients themselves. None of them had ever seen a member of the Amazon tribe, and one author dating to the fourth century BC even declared that, since the Amazons were reported to engage in fighting, they had to be men.[62] Originally they were thought to be located beyond the Black Sea. Over time, however, the Greeks' geographical horizons expanded; failing to find the Amazons in the designated places, they kept moving the women's habitat further and further into the 'frontiers of the universe'.[63] Much like modern tribal societies who are being pushed into less and less hospitable parts of the world, the legend presents them as a defeated race.[64] From Heracles and Theseus down, many Greek male heroes made their names by fighting and killing Amazons among others; conversely most of the Amazons' own names are known only because their owners were killed by this hero or that. Pictures of Amazons in combat almost always show them as being seized by the hair or by the helmet, or else collapsing at the knees while spears are being driven into their throats.[65] Whatever the reason for the myth's popularity, it cannot have depended on the victories that the Amazons won or the conquests they made.

The earliest mention of the *amazones* is in the *Iliad*. From the first, their exact gender turns out to be problematic. They are there described as *antianeirai*, 'equivalent to men';[66] in all of Greek literature, the Amazons are the only noun to which this epithet is applied. The form *amazones* itself is masculine. It is prefixed by the definite article in its (plural) masculine form, *hoi*, and corresponds with the normal way in which Greek designates peoples made up of both men and women. The same form may also be used to describe armies; in which case of course it refers exclusively to men. Thus the term *amazones* differs from those used to denote other groups of mytho-logical women, such as the *Nymphai*, which are clearly feminine. Judging solely by Homer, and ignoring the tradition that grew up after him, had it not been for the epithet *antianeirai* there would have been no way of knowing they were female.

Nor is Homer the only source to emphasize that Amazons, though not men, are somehow equivalent to them. Pindar calls them *androleteirai*, 'destroyers of men'; Aischylos in *Eumenides* says that they were 'man-hating' (*stuganoor*). Aischylos also says that they were 'martial' (*thourios*), an epithet often applied to the war god Ares who was their father. As if to empha-size their problematic gender, Aischylos always uses the masculine terminations for the epithets with which he describes the Amazons. And no wonder: while not married to men (*anandroi*), they behave like men and fight in the open like men. In this they differ from others of their sex, particularly that cowardly Clytemnestra, who murdered her husband in his bath.

For the Amazons to be 'equivalent to men' was extremely important. In Arctinus's poem *Aethiopis* the villain Theristes is killed by the hero, Achilles, for suggesting that he (i.e. Achilles) was sexually attracted to the Amazon Queen Penthesilea whom Achilles had just killed; the point being that, had the accusation been true and had Penthesileia been primarily a woman, then of course her death would have been transformed from a glorious feat of arms into mere murder. The same reasoning may explain why, in all repre-sentations until the middle of the sixth century BC, no Amazon, alive or dead, is ever shown naked as many male warriors are. Instead they are always dressed and armed as hoplites. They wield spears, carry shields, and wear body armour that effectively hides their breasts; had it not been for their given names, as well as the white colour of their faces and bodies and sometimes a characteristic piece of attire such as the skin of an animal, it would have been impossible to know they are actually female. In this way their 'equivalence to men' served a double purpose. On the one hand it permitted them to participate in war and to fight. On the other it enabled those who fought against them and, often enough, killed them to take pride in their actions.

At some point during the fifth century BC, Greek ideas of the Amazons began to change.[67] The first evidence for the change is iconographic: instead of being presented as hoplites as previously, more and more often the Amazons started being depicted as women. To achieve this, much of the armour that they used to wear on their bodies had to be discarded, its place being taken by loosely fitting clothes which often left one or even two breasts exposed. With their identity as women now fully revealed the Amazons continued to fight, that is go from one defeat to another. More often than not they are shown desperately seeking shelter behind their shields as their male enemies prepare to run them through with the spear, as, for example, on a vase now in the Mansell collection.[68] Alternatively they are being pulled off their horses, as on a frieze from the temple of Apollo at Bassae;[69] or being seized by the hair while trying to escape, as on Phidias's shield of Athene Parthenos that has survived only as a marble copy.[70]

Later still, Amazons began to be shown in all kinds of lively scenes. They don armour, leave for the fray, return from battle with their dead, lead, ride or dismount from horses, equip chariots or ride in them, or simply wash themselves as their weapons lean nearby. The more varied the activities in which they are shown, the less often they fight. They start wearing Scythian and Persian dress and carrying characteristic Asian weapons including, besides the bow, a light battleaxe.[71] Since the Persians were repeatedly defeated by the Greeks their weapons, including specifically the small shields that they carried, counted as second class[72] and their dress as effeminate; on the other hand that dress, being made of fabric or leather, permitted the Amazons' anatomy to be displayed as never before. Briefly, in dress as well as the activities in which they engaged, the Amazons were being turned from 'the equivalents of men' into women. As they became women, gradually they ceased to fight.

From painting, the 'debellicization' of the Amazons spread to literature. In the words of Lysias, an Attic orator who flourished during the fourth century BC, originally 'they were accounted as men for their high courage rather than as women for their sex'. Later, having met with 'valiant men' (i.e. the Athenians, who defeated them) 'their spirit now was like to their sex … They stood alone in failing to learn from their mistakes, and so … perished on the spot.'[73] Once the Amazons had ceased to fight it became necessary to find some other characteristics by which they might be defined. Attempts were accordingly made to explain the origin of the word by deriving it either from *a-mazos* (without breasts) or from *a-mazas* (those who did not eat bread). The first, and most famous, interpretation gave rise to an entire mythology: the Amazons, or their offspring (by the Scyths, who had resorted to sex in order to 'tame' them)[74] the Sauromatae, used a special bronze instrument to excise the right breast of young girls and divert the body's energy into the shoulder and the arm, needed for drawing the bow.[75] The second led to the idea that they were half-wild creatures of the steppe who fed on snakes and lizards (*sauroi*). Later still yet another interpretation put the emphasis on the prefix *ama*. Accordingly, *amazones* was derived from either *amazoosai*, 'living together', or *amazoonais*, 'with girdles'.[76]

Since the word *amazones* is probably non Greek by origin, none of these interpretations makes sense. What they do show is that ideas concerning them were changing. Originally they were warrior women, 'equivalent to men'. Later they came to be seen in a somewhat less heroic light and the emphasis changed to the exorbitant price they had to pay for their martial qualities: either mutilation or a nomadic, uncivilized life that did not include any of the amenities which the Greeks held dear.[77] Attention shifted to the way in which, as women living on their own, they reproduced;[78] hence the story – recorded by Strabo, who himself doubted their existence – that they met with the men of a neighbouring tribe for two months a year. During that period they had sexual intercourse 'in the open and at random'. Once the children were born they handed the boys to their fathers (another version says the boys were mutilated and raised as slaves)[79] while keeping the daughters and teaching them to ride and fight in the approved Amazonian manner.[80] By this time the 'golden-shielded, silver-axed host' of women was becoming decidedly 'friendly to men'.[81] They welcomed their advances and even initiated trysts, as when the Amazon Queen Thalestris proposed to mate with Alexander the Great to produce the best possible heir.[82]

Briefly, as warriors the Amazons were unremarkable, merely one out of hundreds or thousands of tribes whose customs are recorded by ancient authors and one who, on the whole, went from one defeat to the next. As *female* warriors, though, they left a lasting impression. Late in the third century, the Roman Emperor Aurelian decorated his triumph with a troupe of captive Gothic women who were labelled 'Amazons'.[83] Subsequent Western literature is full of references to them, and to this day their name is synonymous with women warriors, real or imaginary.[84] During the Middle Ages their story was retold by Boccaccio.[85] He was followed by Christine de Pizan whose *Book of the City of Ladies* contains many references to them, though she, like her master, fails to distinguish between mythical Amazon queens and real-life female rulers such as Zenobia of Palmyra.[86] In keeping with medieval ideals, all of Christine's women are chaste, beautiful, wise and good. This also applies to the Amazons, causing their martial accomplishments to be overshadowed by the other qualities she attributes to them.

By the time of the Renaissance a vast number of stories concerning warrior women, some old, some new, were in circulation. Many went back to the story of Camilla as narrated by Virgilius in the *Aeneid* around the time of Christ.[87] Born to King Metabus of the Volscians, who had been exiled by his own people, Camilla was raised in the woods. She was dedicated to Artemis and fed on a diet of mare's milk in an apparent attempt to prevent her from turning into a real woman and receiving her period – from which it follows without saying that she was and remained a virgin. 'At the head of her maidens' and 'with one breast exposed' she fought against the Trojan refugee, Aeneas, and his conquering band of heroes. She died when her breast was pierced by a 'cowardly' arrow fired by a man.

Camilla's sad fate did not prevent the heroines of the Italian Renaissance poets Ariosto (1474–1533) and Torquato Tasso (1544–95) from following in her footsteps. The former in *Orlando Furioso* created Marfisa who was fed on lioness's milk. The latter in *Gerusalemme liberata* conjured up Clotilde who was fed on tigress's milk (in both cases the choice of animals seems to have been dictated by the metre). Both ladies were raised as

Saracen princesses. The former fought against the Christians until she discovered her true birth and changed sides. The latter clung to her Muslim faith and, as her reward, ended up by being killed by the Christian hero Tancred. Accompanied by entire races of fighting maidens they represented a man-woman type which was very popular at the time, alternately fascinating and repelling people.[88]

The Elizabethan vogue for Amazons – some bad, others good, but all of them virgins until either death or marriage terminated their careers – may have had something to do with the fact that, around the middle of the century, the possibility that such a race might actually exist presented itself.[89] The story begins with one Francesco Orellana (1511–?), a distant relative of Francisco Pizarro and a *conquistador* in his own right. In 1541, with fifty companions, he set out from Quito to the east, crossing the Andes, reaching the Amazon (which they called first the Orellana, then the Maranon), and following it to its mouth. An account of the expedition was written by one of his men, Friar Gaspar de Carvajal. An abbreviated version is given by another Spaniard, the historian Oviedo, who claims to have talked to Orellana himself.

According to Carvajal, as Orellana led his expedition through the Amazonian forest he was told by a captured Indian of 'certain women' who had come to help the Indians fight the conquistadors. Ruled by a queen, they led an independent life but

> consorted with Indian men at times; when that desire came over
> them, they assembled a great horde of warriors and went off to
> make war on a very great overlord whose residence is not far from
> the land of these women, and by force they brought them to their
> own country and kept them with them for the time that suited
> their caprice, and after they found themselves pregnant they sent
> them back to their country without doing them any harm; and
> afterwards, when the time came for them to have children, if they
> gave birth to male children, they killed them and sent them to
> their fathers, and, if female children, they raised them with great
> solemnity and instructed them in the art of war.

They rode camels (!) and lorded it over numerous surrounding Indian tribes.

Oviedo's account largely agrees with that of Carvajal. Orellana, he says, had told him that 'among ourselves we gave them the name of Amazons, though improperly: for 'Amazon' in the Greek language means 'having no breasts', in order that they might have nothing to hinder them in shooting with the bow ... But these women that we are dealing with here, although they do use the bow, do not cut off their breasts nor do they burn them off, albeit in others matters, such as in taking men unto themselves for a certain period of time for the propagation of their kind and in other respects, it does seem as if they imitate those whom the ancient called Amazons.'

How much truth the stories contained is impossible to say. In spite of a 1971 claim by a German anthropologist,[90] a kingdom made up of warrior women never existed; at most a few Indian women may have fought with their menfolk, pouring arrows at the Spaniards as they floated down the river. Writing early in the seventeenth century, Garcilaso Inca de la Vega believed that Orellana's tales had something to do with the fact that, technically speaking, he was a deserter. His unauthorized expedition having failed to locate gold, he needed some great feat to justify himself to Emperor Charles V; what better discovery than a kingdom of Amazons?

The fact that Orellana's story was never substantiated did not prevent other tales of warrior women from retaining their appeal. In Britain and the Netherlands their exploits were celebrated in stories, dramas and popular ballads, most of them published in cheap editions and intended for low-class audiences.[91] They had titles such as *Mary Ambree, The Valiant Virgin,* and *The Famous Woman Drummer*. Usually they tell how the daughter of a well-to-do family falls in love with a low-class man. Refused permission to marry him, she leaves home to follow him into the army or navy and joins in his many adventures. Their mutual loyalty undergoes severe tests – hers consciously and deliberately, his in all ignorance as, remembering his darling, he refuses the advances of other comely maidens. Finally her true identity is revealed among many tears. Thereupon the pair obtain their discharge and travel back to the girl's father; having obtained his pardon, they get married and live happily ever after.

Some of the ballads make fun of the disguised heroine, such as Jane in
The Female Smuggler:

> In sailor's clothing Jane did go
> Dressed like a smuggler from top to toe
> With a brace of pistols all by her side
> Like a warlike hero, like a warlike hero
> In all his martial pride.

Most of the time, though, the women are presented as both feminine and
heroic or, in the words of a modern author, 'Venus playing Mars'.[92] They
engage in the same strenuous activities as the men by whom they are surrounded, living aboard ship, pulling ropes, climbing masts, withstanding
difficult weather, and fighting; as in ancient Greece, they sometimes have
the quality of 'manliness' attributed to them. Yet their hands are always soft,
their fingers 'milk white', their breasts 'snow white'; a miraculous combi-
nation which, if nothing else, suggests that the songs were not meant to be
taken too seriously.

As had happened to the Greek Amazons, as time went on the typical heroine tended to change. Earlier ballads concentrate on their martial prowess
and often present us with fighting viragos who performed heroic deeds.
Later ones put greater emphasis on their role as suffering helpmates, in other
words as women. Some of the ballads are ribald as wounded men, all unknow-
ing, have their injuries dressed by their paramours who take the opportunity to engage in a little sexual exploration. After 1850 the genre all but
disappeared. Some authors have blamed their demise on the decline of transvestism.[93] Equally likely, though, the growing professionalism of armed forces
and the institution of regular pre-enlistment medical checks by qualified
physicians (who were male) was putting an end to disguised women, both
fictional and real.

Nor was classical Christian civilization the only one to delight in tales of
warrior women. Celtic legends also abound with legendary female fighters,
and pictures of the ladies in question are carried on Celtic coins. The most
famous one was Medb who, resorting to treachery, tried (and failed) to

overcome the hero Cuchulainn;[94] other women allegedly ran 'martial-art academies' in which men were taught to fight as well as being offered 'the friendship of the thighs'.[95] In China, the tale that attained the greatest fame was Luo Maodeng's *Sanbao's Expedition to the Western Ocean* (1597). The novel's male hero, Sanbao, travels to the country of Jinlin. There the natural order is inverted as *yin*, the female principle, rules over *yang*, the male one. A wicked warrior queen called Huang Jinding rules an all-female country and commands lascivious warrior women. Known as Shizhiyu, they are awful creatures who symbolize both female might and sexuality: fearsome and tempting at the same time. Like the Greek legends, the work is meant to emphasize how monstrous woman-rule is. At the same time the hero, by fighting women, being captured by them, and being rescued by one (Hang Fenxian) is taught a lesson in humility.[96]

The best-known Japanese female warrior was a lady by the name of Tomoe, a medieval heroine whose name, meaning 'comma-shaped swirl pattern', is still used for women today. Modern scholars believe that a lady by that name did exist;[97] however, her story as we know it is probably romance. Along with her two brothers she fought for her lord (who may also have been her lover), 'The Rising Sun General' Kiso Yoshinaka during the civil wars of the late twelfth century. She was said to have been 'of very light complexion and her hair was long. Her face was quite lovely. She was an archer of rare strength and skill, a mighty warrior who could stand alone against a thousand and who with bow and arrow or the sword was a match for any god or demon.' In battle this prowess stood her in good stead, partly because her opponents were afraid of her and partly because they were reluctant to fight her; as one of them put it: 'it is galling to be forced back by a woman, but if I attack her, and then make a slip, I will be dishonoured forever.' As it happened, Yoshinaka lost the war. About to die he sent Tomoe away, saying that 'I am ashamed that people will tell of me how at last I had a woman precede me in battle. I release you from your duty. Go now, quickly, leave.' Deeply distressed, Tomoe obeyed. Later she became a nun.

Though anything but exhaustive, the above list is enough to show that women warriors have always made good subjects for fiction. Nor, of course, are they dead today. For example, in the 1930s the English writer Robert E. Howard wrote two pseudo-historical tales, *Sword Woman* and *Blades for France*, set in the Middle Ages. In them he created Agnes de Chastillon, also known as Dark Agnes, a heroic French she-warrior. Proudly taking her 'place among men', like so many other viragos she had little sympathy for her weaker sisters; these she called 'cows, slaves, whimpering cringing serfs, crouching to blows, avenging themselves by taking their own lives'. At roughly the same time American comic strip writers created Sheena, Queen of the Jungle as a female counterpart to Tarzan. Her books lasted into the 1950s when the character was adapted for television and played by a 'strapping beauty', Iris McCullough.[98]

Sheena's success gave birth to quite some copycats. By the late 1940s comic books sported several jungle Amazons. They were clad in skins of leopard, tiger, panther, or zebra, carried knives somewhere near their crotches, and swung through trees to save wildlife or, from time to time, their friendly but only moderately competent boyfriends such as Sheena's 'milquetoast' Bob. Their names were Princess Pantha, Zegra, Judy of the Jungle, Rula, Tiger Girl and Camilla, Queen of the Jungle. As late as the 1970s there was Rima the Jungle Girl. Perhaps because there are so few jungles still left in this world, the genre has been worked for all it was worth and has been obsolescent for some time; whether Tarzan's revival at the hand of Disney will cause it to resurface remains to be seen. Tales of half-naked women warriors armed with edged weapons remain popular, however, as is shown by the fearsome creatures often displayed on the cover of publications such as *Dungeons and Dragons*.[99]

In 1968 the fad for female fighters spread into intergalactic space. The heroine of *Barbarella* was played by Jane Fonda before she became a feminist. She wielded a ray gun and, like so many of her kind, exposed very long legs and rather more of her breasts than is customary while fighting legions of wicked enemies. *Barbarella* was followed by *Charlie's Angels*, a group of three policewomen who, as they shot their way through 'sophomoric' plots, always owed more to the way they looked in their bikinis than to their intelligence.[100]

Charlie's Angels in their turn had to give way to *Wonderwoman*, a sort of female counterpart of Superman who delighted viewers with her capers.

The fashionable heroine of the mid nineties was *Xena the Warrior Queen*. Like Athene, Xena had blue eyes and an imperious glare. Also like Athene (and Wonderwoman) she was handsome in a grenadier sort of way; still the film's makers, perhaps in order to keep her moderately attractive, did not give her the kind of muscle sported by Rambo. She was unattached to any man, even to the point where she did not have a father and where an elderly male who tried to present himself as such was revealed as an impostor; men who tried to court her were treated with a bored look if they were lucky and by a resounding blow if they were not. Like her male enemies, Xena fought with every kind of edged weapon. Unlike her male enemies, she could fend off such weapons with her bare hands. Her speciality was a magic disc which she alone possessed and which, once hurled on its way, came back to her of its own accord like an Australian boomerang. Her subjects consisted of a troupe of other females, all of them much smaller and weaker than herself and most of them perfect ninnies. Always about to be raped by evil men, they had to be rescued by their queen.

Next, 1996 saw the screening of *GI Jane* with Demi Moore cast in the title role. Unlike so many others, *GI Jane* claimed to be more than entertainment for slightly retarded teenagers; whether it succeeded is another question. Prodded by a female under-secretary of defense, a female navy officer circumvents US law which bars women from slots involving ground combat behind enemy lines. She joins in SEAL (Sea-Air-Land, an elite commando unit) training. She fails to gain the approval of her instructors and fellow trainees, all of whom are male; by alternately patronizing her and humiliating her, they turn her life into a misery. Towards the end of the course students are engaged in SERE (Search, Evasion, Rescue, Evacuation) training, one of whose aims is to teach them how to deal with torture. A hefty male instructor tells a weeping, spluttering GI Jane (she has just been roughed up and held under water) that all she has to do to be let off the hook is to strike a bell; to which she responds with the memorable phrase, 'suck my dick'. Having thus pretended to be a man she is finally accepted as one, more or less. From this point on the film loses any interest as it degenerates into the usual good heroic Americans fighting wicked cowardly Arabs stuff.

What one is to make of these and countless other tales is hard to say. Some, particularly the most recent ones, seem to say that the best a woman can do for herself is to join with men, undergo every sort of hardship along with them, and, by way of a crowning achievement, grow a penis. Others are meant to entertain by combining combat with cleavage, no matter how idiotic the plot. For example, *Barbed Wire* (1998) was specifically designed to permit Pamela Anderson to display her considerable treasures. The *GI Joe* series is aimed at young boys under the age of consent, yet here too female characters such as Lady J and Scarlet wear specially designed, sexy uniforms.[101] As we saw, an element of titillation was by no means lacking either from the stories produced during the eighteenth century, the Renaissance, or classical antiquity.[102] Then as now, providing women with armour so as to turn them into credible fighters while at the same time exposing just enough of their bodies to make them sexually alluring presented a challenge to those who painted them, sculpted them, or stage-managed them. The most recent manifestations of the phenomenon may be found in computer games. For example, a game called 'Sin' has a long-legged, big-busted heroine who goes by the name of Alexis and who wears a sort of plastic bikini and high boots. Dressed in this improbable costume, she plans to flood the streets of 'Freeport' with DNA-altering drugs, in which endeavour she is opposed by the head of the largest local security firm, Colonel John R. Blade.[103]

Today, as ever, many of the stories carry a lesson for both men and women, their purpose being to reaffirm the existing, male-dominated world by describing its 'monstrous' opposite.[104] To achieve this last-named end, there is often a distinction between two kinds of warrior women. Good women, including also the heroines of the various ballads, fight with or for their menfolk. One, Tomoe, becomes a nun after her lord and master has fallen when she did not stand with him to the last. Others end their fighting careers by explaining, amidst a flood of tears, that they were only forced to kill by circumstances and are not *really* tough;[105] which confession having been made, they are presumably fit to get married and raise a family. Evil women are represented by Shakespeare's 'Amazonian trull[s]' who have 'tiger[s]' heart[s] wrapped in a woman's hide'.[106] They act on their own behalf, subdue men (by sex as much as by fighting), try to create an upside-down world, and end up dying for their sins. These categories may have something to do with the fact that, though many women have sought to put their wartime experiences into writing, from the Amazons on the overwhelming majority of fictional heroines were produced by men with the intent of offering amusement to other men. Perhaps understandably, original military fiction written by women for women is rare. In one of the few specimens I could find, the heroine is distinguished above all by the fact that she has six husbands whom she would like to turn into drumskins; even so, her main instrument is magic, not violence.[107]

Returning to the Greek Amazons as the prototype of them all, there is no reason to believe that they ever existed any more than Barbarella or Wonderwoman did; had they lived in any of the various habitats attributed to them, then they ought to have been known to other peoples besides the Greeks.[108] The closest available historical evidence connected with them is made up of a few 'genuine' Sauromatian graves. Those were dug up in southern Russia and found to contain female skeletons as well as arrowheads, daggers, and, in one case, scale armour as well as equipment proper to female burials.[109] The Sauromatians, it will be recalled, were supposed to be the offspring of the Amazons after the latter had been 'tamed' by the Scyths; the Scyths themselves, according to Herodotus, were the offspring of Heracles and a 'viper woman' who was human from the buttocks upwards but snake below. Just as the fact that some Israeli women died while wearing uniform and received military burials does not mean that Israel is a matriarchy, so the discovery of these graves does not prove that a tribe of independent, male-less, male-baby-killing race of warrior women ever existed. What it *may* prove is that, among the Sauromatians as elsewhere, women sometimes acted as rulers and commanders; it is to the subject of such women that we must next turn our attention.

8 Rulers and Commanders

To fight is one thing, to command is another. As has already been noted, during much of history commanders were expected to fight in person and very often did precisely that. Still, even in hoplite warfare waged by democratic city-states, there were some exceptions;[110] during the Middle Ages, though commanders were constrained by the knightly ethos, some of them preferred to control their forces from the rear as England's Edward III for instance did at Crécy in 1346. In this way, it is precisely the fact that commanders did not *necessarily* fight which sometimes enabled women to act as commanders.

The ways whereby one became a commander depended on the type of military organization.[111] Often it was a question of learning how to command by being commanded by others, as Plutarch puts it.[112] One joined the army, gained experience, rose through the ranks, and obtained a senior position either by being elected (as in Greece or Rome) or by receiving an appointment at the hands of one's superiors. Since women, even the very few who did fight, were never accepted as regular members of any military establishment this path was closed to them. It was, however, possible for women to become commanders if they lived in societies where government was hereditary and if they happened to be close relatives of kings, feudal lords, or tribal chieftains; in short, of non-elective rulers who also acted as commanders-in-chief. Sometimes rulers died without a male heir. In other cases the widows, daughters, or (rarely) sisters of deceased rulers pushed aside such male heirs as did exist by means of intrigue or civil war. If so, they succeeded both to command and to government. To avoid being burdened with children, many of these women refused to have sex; one of them, the eleventh-century Countess Matilda of Tuscany, apparently managed to remain a virgin in spite of having been married not once but twice.[113] Others must have left what children they did have to the care of female servants.

In discussing female commanders, perhaps the best starting point is an anonymous Greek tract entitled *Women Intelligent and Courageous in Warfare.*[114] The author of the treatise and date of its composition are unknown. However, some of the women it lists can be dated to the fourth century BC; hence it must have been written after 300 BC and possibly as late as 100 AD. The six pages of which it consists sum up the deeds of fourteen outstanding women, some Greek and others barbarian, each of whom performed some notable feat, principally in war. Some, such as Semiramis or Artemisia, were well known to the ancient world, whereas others are fairly obscure figures. Though not all can be identified from other sources, most are apparently historical. At any rate none is either a goddess or obviously mythological.

The essay's title notwithstanding, only seven of the ladies in question actually fought or commanded in war; one more, Queen Nicotris, is said to have fortified the city of Babylon. Of the remaining six, some have interesting stories. Take, for example, the Egyptian Queen Nicotris (not to be confused with her namesake, who is Babylonian). She cannot be identified by other sources; her place in the *Women Intelligent and Courageous* is due to the fact that she avenged the murder of her brother, inviting the assassins to a treacherous feast and letting the river in on them. Another queen, Theiso (Dido of *Aeneid* fame) committed suicide after being deserted by her lover Aeneas. That deed was undoubtedly a brave one and must have been the reason for including her in the list. However, it scarcely qualifies her as a warrior queen.

Of the seven women listed who did participate in war in one capacity or another, two did so along with, or at the orders of, their husbands. This applies to Semiramis whose portrait as presented in this and other sources is based on Smmuramat, a ninth-century BC Assyrian queen, as well as Zerinea, a queen of Parthia. The last-named was wife of King Mermerus and helped him fight the Persian King Stryangaeus. Having suffered a wound, she fled but was captured by Stryangaeus who, recognizing her as a woman, presented her with her life.[115] Not long afterwards Stryangaeus himself was captured by Mermerus who wanted to execute him. But Zerinea did not agree and, failing to persuade her husband, conspired against him and had him killed. Thereupon she became Stryangaeus's wife and ally and, presumably, lived happily ever after.

This leaves us with five warrior queens who commanded and fought on their own. The first, Atossa, of unknown nationality, is said to have 'inherited the kingdom' from her father Ariaspes. 'Hiding her feminine mentality, she was the first to wear a tiara, the first to wear trousers, and to invent the use of eunuchs and to make her replies in writing. She ruled many tribes and was most warlike and brave in every deed.' Neither this source or any other gives any details. She cannot be identified: she is, however, clearly associated with the Amazons. In many ways she is only half woman, disguising herself by wearing trousers, surrounding herself with eunuchs with high voices to make her own appearance less conspicuous, and giving her replies in writing. She is thus a model of a false ruler who disguises everything about herself, even her sex.

Next in line comes Rhodogyne, said to have been queen of the Persians (although she cannot be identified) and a true warrior queen. Courageous and, with her half-combed hair, 'terrifying' to her enemies, she was able to quell a tribal revolt. Other sources present her as a man-hater,[116] a quality, as we shall see, by no means rare among her kind. Finally there were Tomyris, Artemisia and Onomaris. Of these three, the first was queen of the Massegetae (living in what is now western Iran) and is credited by Herodotus[117] with having defeated the great Persian Emperor Cyrus. The second joined Xerxes in his expedition against Greece as already mentioned, commanding a naval squadron and earning his praise for herself,[118] whereas the third is said to have been 'one of the distinguished Galatians' who defeated neighbouring tribes in battle.

Of the five women who acted as warrior queens, only Artemisia was clearly a historical figure. The rest may, or may not, have existed. Like Christine de Pizan, whoever wrote the essay about them may well have been a woman: a favourite guess is Pamphile of Epidaurus, a bluestocking who lived during the first century AD and who is known to have produced thirty-three historical works.[119] Man or woman, he or she undertook the task precisely because of its esoteric nature. All fourteen characters were understood as paradoxical creatures: women who, in spite of being women, yet displayed 'manliness' (*andreia*) and were even 'very manly' (*andreiotate*). Two of them, Atossa and Semiramis, dressed to hide their femininity. The last-named one is described by other sources as 'a liminal figure of indeterminate gender, partially male and partially female'.[120]

Women Intelligent and Courageous in War is the first work of its kind to have come down to us. Though it does not bear a mythological character, it fails to distinguish between legendary women, real women, women who accompanied their husbands, women who fought, women who commanded, women who intrigued and gained or maintained political power with or without bloodshed, and women who displayed all sorts of courage, including the kind of courage that is necessary for committing suicide; in this respect it has set a bad example which has lasted to the present day.[121] Here we are concerned with female rulers who, in their capacity as independent rulers, exercised command in the same way as men in their position would. Out of the fourteen listed in the essay under consideration only seven, and possibly only five, fit that description. Out of the seven, only two are definitely historical.

This is not to say that there were no real-life female commanders. In the millennium and a half between *c.* 1000 BC and AD 500 there were many cases when women inherited power or seized it. It is hardly surprising that some of them also conducted wars. Limiting ourselves to those who are clearly historical, even a short list must include the Illyrian chieftain(ness) Teuta who, in 230 BC, foolishly took on the Roman Republic and was easily defeated.[122] Next in line came several Hellenistic queens, particularly Egyptian ones. Though none was a titular ruler in her own right,[123] several did govern in the name of, or along with, their incompetent menfolk. Some accompanied armies on campaign and took part in top-level decision-making, though they did not actually command. One, the famous Cleopatra VII, led the resistance to the Roman occupation of Egypt in 48 BC until her troops grew sick of their 'girl commander'.[124] Thereupon she changed tactics and, instead of trying to fight Caesar, made love first to him and then to his successor, Mark Antony. Later she married the latter, sat in his council of war, contributed to his treasury, and went down with him.[125]

Probably the most famous ancient female commander was the British Queen Boudicca.[126] Just why she rose in revolt is not known; whatever the reasons, they included her own humiliation (she was flogged) and the rape by the Romans of her two daughters. In AD 60 she captured three undefended towns, Camulodunum, Londinium and Verulamium. Next, far from showing any special sympathy for the members of her own sex, she ordered or at least permitted her Iceni warriors to commit a series of incredible atrocities against them; in Londinium, we are told by the ancient historian Dio Casius, 'the noblest and most distinguished women' were hung up and had their breasts cut off and sewn to their mouths so that they appeared to be eating them.[127] Boudicca's triumph did not last long, however, since the Roman garrison, though greatly outnumbered, rallied and defeated her with the loss of 80,000 lives.

As the queen herself told her men before the decisive battle, 'we British are used to women commanders in war'.[128] Though their names are unknown, the Celts must have had others like her, as is proved by the fact that, in AD 590, an Irish cleric by the name of Colmcille banned women from serving in war and in council.[129] In between these two dates, far away at the other extremity of the Roman Empire, there lived Queen Zenobia of Palmyra. She mounted the throne after having her husband, Odaenathus, and his eldest son, the heir-apparent, assassinated. Like Boudicca she resented her status as a client of Rome and around AD 270 she launched a revolt. For a year or two she and her male general, Zabdas, campaigned all over the Middle East before suffering the usual fate of those who opposed Rome. Taken captive she begged for her life as 'a mere woman', in which she must have been assisted by her beautiful voice and 'incredible sex appeal'.[130] Her efforts were successful. Realizing that to punish a female too harshly is bad publicity, Emperor Aurelian blamed the revolt on her chief adviser, the philosopher Casius Longinus, and had him executed. Zenobia herself marched in her conqueror's triumph and was pardoned. She ended her days as a great lady in a villa put at her disposal by the victor.[131]

As noted, whether or not there would be women commanders around depended primarily on the political structure of the society in question and, specifically, on whether government was hereditary. Imperial China, India and the Maya all had them,[132] but they were most often found in the kind of tribal society to which Boudicca too belonged. To adduce but one additional example of the same kind, the Viking *Erik's Saga,* a fourteenth-century composition, tells of one Aud the Deep-Minded. She is supposed to have lived in the eleventh century and was the wife of a 'warrior king called Olaf the White'. After his death she continued the family business of raiding and harrying, allying herself with another chief by the name of Thorstein whom, however, she did not marry. By the time he too was killed she had acquired enough confidence to strike out on her own. With twenty of her husband's men she sailed to Iceland and conquered one of its districts for herself. Though the record does not say that she fought in person, given the small size of her party she may well have.[133]

In feudal societies, too, political power was hereditary. Hence the Middle Ages were a great time for female rulers who, if they got the chance, might try to liberate themselves from the tutelage exercised by their male relatives and act as independent rulers.[134] The list of ladies who did exactly that is almost endless: here all we can do is give a few names by way of illustrating the point. In the years immediately after 910 Aethelflaed, daughter of Alfred the Great and widow of Aelthelred of Mercia, successfully helped her brother Edward campaign against the Danes before losing out to him in the ensuing struggle for power. In the 1020s Guidinild of Catalonia led a campaign to recapture her family holding of Cervera.[135] In the 1070s Mabille of Belleme, wife of Roger II of Mont Gomeri, formed her own army and led it in sieges and skirmishes. This particular lady made herself widely hated by her cruelty and avarice, and ended up being murdered by one of her own vassals.

Many medieval rulers spent months if not years away from their own countries. Hence it often fell to their female relatives to step into their shoes and defend their castles. For example, the exploits of Matilda of Tuscany, widely known as 'the Pope's handmaiden', began in 1061 when she helped

Alexander II fight schismatics in Lombardy; one year before her death, in 1115, the seventy-year old was still threatening to lead an army against Mantua. In 1129 Sophia, sister of Henry the Proud of Bavaria, held one of his castles against an attack by imperial troops. In the same year Agnes of Saarbruecken performed a similar task for her husband, Duke Frederick II of Swabia. In 1136 Queen Matilda of England opened her military career by taking the field and accepting the surrender of Derby, whereas eighty years later one Nichola de la Hay defended Lincoln in the name of King Henry III of England.

The tradition of warrior queens, or princesses, standing in for their male relatives was carried on throughout the late Middle Ages and the Renaissance. A famous instance involved Caterina Sforza. An illegitimate grand daughter of Duke Francesco Sforza of Milan, in 1500 she unsuccessfully defended the fortress of Forli against Cesare Borgia and was raped by him.[136] As late as the middle of the seventeenth century both sides in the English Civil War sometimes boasted heroic women who defended their absent husbands' estates.[137] By then, however, five centuries during which England had been free from foreign invasion and almost a century and a half of domestic peace had turned it into an essentially unfortified country. Thus most of these sieges involved country houses. They were conducted on a very small scale and, a few shots having been fired, were over in a matter of days if not hours.

Though Machiavelli commented that real men did not require fortresses to protect them,[138] there can be no doubt that conducting the defence of a besieged castle, let alone commanding a field army, took skill, leadership and courage. Certainly it deserves to be considered as 'active' participation in war.[139] On the other hand, how many of the women who withstood sieges or led armies also fought weapon in hand – as, facing similar circumstances, their male relatives were expected to do – is not clear. Of Alexander the Great's older sister, Cynane, it was told that she accompanied her father Philip II into battle and on one occasion killed 'an Illyrian queen'.[140] The remaining Hellenistic queens left the business to professional generals. At the decisive battle Boudicca presented herself to her troops wearing armour and riding a chariot just as a male commander would have done. Though she may have provided them with directives, there is no record of her leading a charge or fighting hand to hand. Following her defeat she fled from the field, which is just what many a male commander would have done in her place. She probably ended by killing herself.[141]

Then there were the exploits of 'The Lady with the Golden Spurs', Eleanor of Aquitaine. In 1146 she helped her husband, Louis VII of France, stir up enthusiasm for the (disastrous) Second Crusade. Next she braved custom, took the cross, and accompanied him to the Middle East. A thirteenth-century Greek historian, Nicetas, presents her as a new Penthesilea: she and her maidens are said to have dressed as Amazons, ridden on horseback, and wielded lances and war axes. How Nicetas, an author noted for his florid, rhetorical style, got his information is impossible to say. At the time he wrote, Eleanor, who on top of her various extramarital affairs had married two kings and had given birth to two more, was already growing into a legend. Nicetas's purpose may have been to inflate the power of the Franks by saying that 'even women travelled in their ranks'. Whatever the truth of this matter, even if his description of her dress is accurate there is no evidence that she commanded, let alone fought.[142]

The French writer Jean Froissart (1333?–1400) also liked to describe extraordinary feats of arms. Most of his information probably came from English and French noblemen with whom he maintained good contacts even as they were fighting the Hundred Years' War against one another; on occasion he must have been an eyewitness. His *Chronicles* tell how, during the War of the Bretonnic Succession, Jeanne de Monfort, 'armed all over', 'mounted on a fine horse', 'held a sharp cutting sword upright and fought well with great courage'.[143] When Charles VI of France invaded Flanders in 1382 the Flemish banner was carried by a woman who was killed when her people were defeated. During the war between Frisia and Hainault in 1396 there appeared a Frisian woman dressed in blue. She fought 'like a madwoman' and died pierced with arrows after 'defying the enemy in her own way'.[144] What that 'way' was we do not know; judging from several similar instances, one of them recounted by Machiavelli (who was an eyewitness) of the above-mentioned Ms Sforza,[145] she probably put her genitals on display. Be this as it may, clearly she did not act as a commander.

In the West, the most famous female ruler-commander was Queen Elizabeth of England (1533–1603). Daughter to King Henry VIII, she was as well educated as any Renaissance ruler and followed her father in her predilection for the chase. Coming to power in 1558, she abhorred war, partly because the expense that it involved threatened to make her dependent on the goodwill of parliament, and partly, as one modern female historian has noted, because it might cause control to pass 'from the woman on the throne to the man on the spot'.[146] To assuage her subjects' worry concerning her anomalous position as a female ruler and commander-in-chief (and also in reference to her perennial refusal to marry and produce an heir), she presented herself as both man and woman, queen and king, mother and first-born son; briefly, as an androgynous creature capable of filling both the male and female roles at the cost of being neither. Born a princess, after her coronation she was properly a 'queen'; the longer her reign lasted, however, and especially at critical moments, the more she favoured the form 'prince'. Over time, 'princess' became a term she reserved to other female monarchs – with the curious result that we find 'Prince' Elizabeth deciding the fate of 'Princess' Mary of Scots. In sermons and public entertainments she might be addressed as Belphoebe or Astraea or Gloriana. As often, she was portrayed in male form as St George, David, Moses, Solomon and Alexander.[147]

During the first thirty years of her reign Elizabeth intrigued against King Philip II of Spain, sent out military expeditions against him both on land and by sea, and shared in any profits there were to be had. Finally Philip, provoked beyond endurance (previously he had tried to marry her, thus making her take the place of her sister Mary), launched the Great Armada against her in 1588. There is a famous description of her as she visited Tilbury in August of that year to review her troops: appearing without her usual retinue of ladies, she was 'habited like an Amazonian Queen, Buskind and plumed, having a golden Truncheon, Gantlet, and Gorget; Armes sufficient to expresse her high and magnanimous spirit'. She harangued the troops, assuring them that, though she well knew she had 'the frail body of a woman', she had 'the spirit of a king'.[148] As it happened, and though the English did not yet know it, by the time she delivered this stirring speech the main danger posed by the Armada had already passed.

Other warrior queens, such as the twelfth-century Tamara of Georgia and Isabella of Castile, also had themselves called 'kings'.[149] This shows how hard it was for women to be accepted as soldiers and commanders; then as now, this was normally something they could do only at the cost of denying their sex. As it happened, and at any rate in the West, the problem was about to be solved. Medieval and early modern rulers down to the first half of the sixteenth century led itinerant lives, headed their armies on campaign, commanded them, and, as noted, often fought in person. The consolidation of states and the rise of impersonal bureaucracies changed this situation. Government was becoming too important and too complicated to be left alone while the ruler took the field. Conversely, war was becoming too complicated (and too dangerous) to entrust to royal persons who might or might not have the necessary qualifications. A monarch who was taken prisoner – as happened to France's Francis I at Pavia in 1525 – might literally require a king's ransom; nor was it unknown for kings to die on the field, as happened to Sweden's Gustavus Adolphus as late as 1632. As a result, starting with Elizabeth's enemy Philip II, one ruler after another dropped out even though they retained their titles as commanders-in-chief.[150]

By the eighteenth century only a few kings, such as Sweden's Charles XII and Prussia's Frederick II, still exercised personal command. Most considered themselves civilians and preferred to remain in their palaces. From there, they worked by way of the minister of war and the commander-in-chief; if they took the field, as the king of Prussia for example did in 1793, normally they only played a symbolic role and made themselves a nuisance to their own subordinates. In short, there had come into being a *de facto* separation between rulers and commanders. Like their male opposite numbers, females on the throne – including Anne of Austria (who acted as regent for France's Louis XIV, 1643–61), Sweden's Christina (reigned 1644–54), England's Anne (1702–14), Russia's Catherine I (1725–7), Anna (1730–40), Elizabeth (1741–61) and Catherine II (1762–96), and Austria's Maria Theresa

(1740–80) – were no longer expected to be paragons of military virtue. They did not supervise operations at anything below what today would be termed the grand strategic level, let alone lead their forces into battle.

Owing to the laws of succession, female rulers remained a small minority. Of Maria Theresa Frederick II said that she 'wept but took' (meaning that she, like him, participated in the dastardly act that was the partition of Poland). Tsarinas Elizabeth and Catherine the Great launched numerous wars against both Turkey and Persia and the latter brought Russian rule to the shores of the Black Sea for the first time. Contrary to the claims of some feminist authors who believe a world ruled by women would be a peaceful one,[151] these queens proved themselves neither more nor less aggressive, neither more nor less capable of supervising the higher levels of war, than their male colleagues. Still, one wonders what would have happened if Prussia's 'soldier king' Frederick-William I (1713–40) had produced no male heir and Frederick the Great had been born female. In that case, however great her genius, she would never have gained military experience and never commanded her troops in the field. The history of Prussia, Germany and the whole of Europe might have been different.

Even in the nineteenth century some rulers continued to command in person. The most famous one was Napoleon; since he had started his career as an officer in the French Army and worked his way up the chain of command, there was no way his place could have been taken by a woman. Napoleon's nephew Louis Napoleon also commanded in person. 'Louis, do your duty,' was the parting shot of his empress, Eugénie, as she saw him off to the field. At Solferino in 1859 he won a great victory. At Sedan in 1870 he was incapacitated by kidney stones and suffered an even greater defeat. Although he (like his Prussian opposite number, King Wilhelm) was physically present at the battle in question, he (also like his Prussian opposite number) delegated command to a professional military man. Except for somebody with the name Bonaparte, by that time personal command had long become an anachronism.

In most modern countries women received the vote in the wake of the First World War. Once they had been enfranchised, it was only a question of time before some would be elected to office and find themselves in charge of matters related to war and defence.[152] Still, even in the US, women in the Department of Defense only constitute a tiny minority;[153] to the extent that senior decision-makers continue to be surrounded almost exclusively by male advisers, there has been little change from previous periods. For example, the War of the Spanish Succession was the largest in history until then and the first in a series of 'global' conflicts that culminated in 1914–1945. The person in charge of the English war effort was Queen Anne; it is said that her 'intellectual limitations' forced her to depend heavily on her secretary of war, Sydney Godolphin.[154] Maria Theresa during the War of the Austrian Succession (1740–48) and the Seven Years War (1756–63) relied on her male commanders-in-chief, the most important of whom was Field Marshal Daun. Catherine the Great had Suvorov.

Like Maria Theresa in the eighteenth century, Israel's Golda Meir, India's Indira Gandhi and Britain's Margaret Thatcher all found themselves in charge of their countries' affairs at wartime. As such, they were responsible for making critically important military-political decisions under enormous stress. On the other hand, none of them had any military knowledge or experience to speak of. This even applied to Ms Meir as prime minister of the only country in history that has conscripted women. Too old to have served in PALMACH, the Jewish community's pre-independence striking force, her way to the top led through the Labour Party apparatus. On the morning of 6 October 1973 she was called upon to decide whether to mobilize either two or four reserve divisions; whereupon, as she subsequently admitted, it turned out that she did not know exactly what a division was.[155] Throughout the war she was surrounded exclusively by male advisers such as the minister of defence, the chief of staff, the chief of intelligence, and so on. As far as military operations were concerned, if her advice was asked at all – even over crucial issues such as the decision to cross the Suez Canal – it was pure formality.[156] The same applies to Ms Gandhi and Ms Thatcher. All three ladies governed with a firm hand but, wisely, left the conduct of operations to the (male) professionals. These and other female rulers prove, if proof were needed, that the capacity to exercise government – has nothing to do with sex.

However, except in so far as rulers also commanded, government is not our concern in this volume.

To sum up, it is clear that many – maybe most – societies whose political structure did not rule out such a possibility have always had occasional female rulers. Some of those also commanded in war, either independently or, perhaps more often, while standing in for their male relatives. While some of these women were legendary, others were real. Unlike men, they were normally unable to attain command by training for, and gaining experience in, war. Usually they limited themselves to the council-room on the one hand and the parade-ground on the other; perhaps their absence from 'the sweaty battlefield'[157] explains why none developed into a really great commander. To quote one well-known female historian of the Hellenistic age: 'no woman … rivaled the splendid recklessness of a Philip or an Alexander, the spirit ... [which overran] the countries like a forest-fire or a hail-storm, sacrificing any part of his body, his eye, his hand, his leg, for the sake of ambition and glory.'[158]

In the West the period after 1600 saw the establishment of regular armed forces. As social position came to be separated from military rank women could no longer stand in for their male relatives, causing female commanders to disappear. Some women continued to exercise government, even in wartime. On the whole they probably did so as well as men; however, the growing separation between government and command prevented them from taking the field. Finally, during the twentieth century the advent of democracy and the enfranchisement of women enabled a few women to act as prime ministers in peace and wartime alike. As was only to be expected, when asked to direct their countries' affairs some did very well, others less so.

However good or bad the performance of queens and female prime ministers whose fate it was to preside over wars, perhaps it is worth noting that none was a declared feminist or came to power on a feminist programme. Thus, the very first historical warrior queen, Artemisia of Caria, told her superiors in the Persian Army that, at sea, 'the Greeks were as superior to the Persians as men are to women'.[159] Queen Elizabeth liked to poke fun at members of her own sex, claiming that it was much easier to teach a woman to speak six languages (as she herself did) than to make her hold her tongue.[160] Another, Christina of Sweden, was famous all over Europe because of her 'butch' lesbian tendencies and masculine affectations; she ended up by resigning the crown, arguing that to govern was too heavy a burden for a woman (the real reason may have been her reluctance to marry and produce an heir).[161] A fourth, Catherine the Great, always regretted she had not been born a man. If her memoirs may be believed, already during her youth she rejected everything girlish; later, in her own words, she developed 'a mind infinitely more masculine than feminine'.[162]

In the twentieth century, Ms Meir ruled a country whose women wanted nothing better than to retreat inside the home.[163] In an interview with the Italian journalist Oriana Fallaci she once called feminists 'crazy' and 'nuts';[164] her own political career ended before feminism became an effective force. Ms Gandhi explicitly said that, as prime minister, she did not regard herself as a woman,[165] whereas Ms Thatcher was at pains to point out that she owed the feminists nothing.[166] As one feminist critic pointed out at the time, throughout the Falkland Crisis she ignored women and emphasized the value of 'masculinity' instead.[167] Like the warrior queens of *Women Intelligent and Courageous in War*, all of these are best understood as honorary males. Deriving their status from the fact that they had competed with men and beat them at their own game, they identified with them. None was especially sympathetic to the members of her own sex. If anything, their prowess caused them to despise other women even more than men did.

9 Playing at War

As Clausewitz pointed out in the first book of *On War*,[168] there exist strong affinities between war and a game; indeed it could be argued that, from football all the way to chess, many and perhaps most human games are either a substitute for war or an enactment of it. Already the Roman vestal virgins were given reserved seats in the circus. Some gladiators received the same kind of female attention as do today's pop stars; at least one was known as 'the boss and healer of girls in the night'.[169] Similarly, medieval ladies crowded the tribunes during tournaments. They adjudicated on what was acceptable and what was not and, at the end of the day, awarded knights with the symbols of victory. In subsequent centuries women were both the most frequent cause of duels and among the most enthusiastic admirers of those who participated in them; in Wilhelmine Germany young people belonging to the appropriate classes sometimes had their faces slashed especially in order to render themselves more attractive to women.[170] As the cheerleaders who are a vital part of any modern American team sport event prove, without the active and willing support of women male competition would have been almost inconceivable. To put it in a different way, war-games are at least as dependent on women as is their real-life equivalent.

Though the vast majority of those who participated in combat sports have always been male, some females have also taken part. While surviving Athenian vases show hundreds of male athletes, we do not have any with female athletes.[171] The single exception is the sportswoman Atalante. Best known for her prowess as a runner, she is sometimes shown engaged in a wrestling match with the male hero Peleus; contrary to the beliefs of some modern authors, though, she was a mythological character rather than a real one. In one example she is leaning on a pickaxe, the instrument used by wrestlers to break up the earth in the competition area. She is dressed in skull cap, bra and shorts, which was probably based on something worn in real life.[172] As far as ancient Greece is concerned, this is all the evidence concerning female participation in combat sports that we possess.

In Rome the situation was rather different.[173] Beginning already during the late Republic, some women entered the gladiatorial arena. They continued to do so during the empire until Emperor Septimus Severus prohibited their participation early in the third century AD. Since there is no record of female slaves being ordered to fight as male ones were it has been argued that many of these women were the daughters of gladiators;[174] however, and in spite of several laws that attempted to exclude them, they also included a sprinkling of upper-class females. Thus Tacitus disapprovingly notes that, under Nero, 'many upper-class women and senators denigrated themselves in the arena'.[175] Also referring to Nero's time, Petronius's *Satyricon* contains some idle chat about a forthcoming show which was to include a *mulier essedaria*. Now *essedarius* is the standard term for a gladiator who fought from a chariot. Since only one *essedaria* is mentioned, possibly she was to fight against a man; another possibility is that she did not fight but acted as a driver in what were normally two-men vehicles.

In one of the compositions he wrote in honour of the Emperor Domitian, the court poet Publius Papinius Statius (*c*. 45–96) praised the gladiatorial games of AD 88. The programme was unusual in that it included Moors, women and pygmies; possibly the idea was to pit the last-named against the second. What a female gladiator may have looked like is described by his rough contemporary, the poet Juvenal:[176]

> And what about female athletes, with their purple
> Track-suits, and wrestling in the mud? Not to mention our lady fencers –
> We've all seen *them*, stabbing in the step with a foil,
> Shield well advanced, going through the proper motions;
> Just the right training needed to blow a matronly horn
> At the Floral Festival[177] – unless they have higher ambitions,
> And the goal of all their practice is the real arena.
> But then, what modesty can be looked for in some

Helmeted hoyden, a renegade from her sex,

Who thrives on masculine violence – yet would not prefer

To *be* a man, since the pleasure is so much less?

What a fine sight for some husband – *it might be you* – his wife's

Equipment put up at auction, baldric, armlet, plumes

And one odd shinguard! Or if the other style

Of fighting takes her fancy, imagine your delight when

The dear girl sells off her greaves! (And yet these same women

Have such delicate skins that even silk chafes them;

They sweat in the finest chiffon.) Hark how she snorts

At each practice thrust, bowed down by the weight of her helmet;

See the big coarse puttees wrapped around her ample hams –

Then wait for the laugh, when she lays her weapons aside

And squats on the potty!

Some women also hunted in the arena. In AD 80 the Emperor Titus inaugurated the Coliseum by holding extensive games. According to Dio Cassius, the self-appointed recorder of the emperor's 'noteworthy' deeds, 9,000 animals were killed 'and women – not those of any prominence, however – took part in dispatching them'.[178]

Outside the circus, hunting was often considered as preparation for war.[179] A few mythological figures apart, we have no record of real-life ancient females participating in it. Medieval and Renaissance women certainly did so, however, riding astride instead of sideways as was the normal practice. Women skilled at hunting included Queen Tamara of Georgia (1184–1212), and Isabella Clara Eugenia who, along with her husband Archduke Albert, governed the Spanish Netherlands early in the seventeenth century and was known as a crack archer. Then there was England's Queen Anne of whom Jonathan Swift said she was 'furious like Jebu, mighty as Nimrod'. On state visits she liked to surround herself with a guard of women archers attired as Amazons.

As mentioned above, throughout the Middle Ages and as late as the beginning of the seventeenth century women often went to watch male knights fighting each other in tournaments and handed out the prizes. Initially these competitions were held in the open field and did not differ much from real war,[180] but later they tended to become formalized. Teams of warriors were replaced by individual contestants and a wall was built to separate them from each other; although, as the accidental death in a tournament of the French King Henry II in 1559 demonstrated, they never became quite safe. From about 1350 on they became more and more elaborate. Entire scenarios were written about, and stage-sets constructed for, weeping damsels in distress. They, or their effigies, were held captive by wicked dragons, had to be rescued by bold knights, and, of course, ended up by giving themselves to those knights by way of the latter's reward; on other occasions the loser undertook to wear shackles which could only be unlocked by the mysterious lady who possessed the key.[181] In at least one tournament, known to have been held at Acre in 1286, the participating knights dressed up as ladies and nuns.[182] Similarly in a tournament held by Queen Elizabeth of England, a group of male warriors entered the lists disguised as 'Amazons'.[183]

For real-life women to participate in tournaments was rare, but not unknown. Here and there women apparently were permitted to 'defend' mock towers. Thus, at Treviso in 1214 when a troop of ladies defended a Castle of Love against two rival bands of gentlemen who used cakes and fruits and flowers to bombard the ladies and each other; the dangers of such a game became evident when the rivalry got serious and the authorities had to separate the quarrelling males. On at least one occasion at Ferrara in 1438 the programme of a tournament included a foot race for female participants. As the reference to cakes and fruits shows, these occasions were supposed to provide comic relief from the otherwise serious proceedings. There is no record of women fighting against each other, or against men, with the weapons normally used in tournaments – which themselves were increasingly different from those used in war.

Depending on the time and place, women also participated in other combat sports. One of them was sumo wrestling, a popular spectacle in

Tokugawa, Japan, in which women were sometimes pitted either against each other or against blind men.[184] In eighteenth-century England there were female pugilists: thus the *London Journal* of June 1722 gives an account of 'boxing in public at the Bear-garden ... when two of the feminine gender appeared for the first time on the theatre of War at Hockley in the Hole, and maintained the battle with great valour for a long time, to the no small satisfaction of the spectators.'[185] Other women, mostly belonging to the lower classes, wielded swords and held duels against each other for a living. Towards the end of the century spreading middle-class respectability began to look at such displays as indecorous. Among the first to condemn them was Mary Wollstonecraft.[186]

What one is to make of these and other exhibitions of female pugnacity is hard to say. In some cases the sports in which the women participated were well-known ones, cherished both for their own sake and as preparation for warfare. Still, even here women tended to be restricted to less strenuous activities such as shooting the bow or flying the falcon; often their participation was itself the best proof that the activities in question were no longer dangerous. Most contests involving women derived whatever appeal they possessed less from the ladies' martial prowess than from other factors. This is most obvious in the kind of night-club contest where nude or semi-nude women wrestle each other in a bath of mud in front of an audience made up largely of leering males; some escort agencies will even provide female wrestlers for a fee. When women were made to confront men directly the latter were usually handicapped. During the early Middle Ages, a man who confronted a woman in juridical combat would be buried up to his waist in a pit. In a boxing match held in the US in October 1999 a male teenage boxer was beaten by a female three years older and much bigger than himself.[187] In no case I could find were women made to engage men on equal terms. In view of the physical disparity between the sexes, to do so would be pointless.

In recent years the media often report the growing participation of women in this combat sport or that. Thus in Finland hunting has become largely a women's sport and there are now 10,000 registered female hunters.[188] In the US women have taken up riding in rodeos. Now it is a little-known fact that the spectacular leaps of bulls and broncos are the result less of the animals' reluctance to be ridden than of their groins being bound so as to put pressure on their testicles; it is almost as if the female participation in this cruel sport were intended to produce a literal enactment of the proverbial castrating woman. In England in 1997 two sixteen-year old girls wearing helmets, mouthpieces and breast-covers boxed against each other in front of a paying public.[189] A year later a similar event was scheduled to take place in New South Wales but had to be moved to Tasmania where there were no laws to prohibit it.[190] Some upper-class Israeli women also turned to boxing as a sport. Fearing for their looks, though, they preferred hitting to being hit, either limiting themselves to the punching bag or taking on male sparring partners who were forbidden to punch back.[191]

As if to prove that boxing is an occupation like any other, the reaction of male athletes to the influx of women into their sport has been to invent even more violent contests, variously known as 'cage boxing' or 'ultimate combat'. As the name implies, the bouts are held in tall wire cages from which there is no escape and in which the men are shut up as if they were members of some species of dangerous animal. Any part of the body may be used to hit any other, which leads to much use of the feet, knees, elbows and head. In contrast to ordinary boxing no gloves are worn. Nor is there any question of putting on earcaps and the like; the (intentional) result is that the number of bloody injuries suffered is much larger. Though a referee is present, there are no rounds that allow the participants to staunch their wounds or catch their breath. Thus a man who is down will continue to be hit until he asks for quarter.

If history is any guide, women's main role in combat sports will continue to be that of spectators (women usually form a minority on the tribunes, but a vocal one and one whose members often engage in blatant sexual displays). Another role is to award prizes. Sometimes they themselves have served as prizes, as during the games which Achilles held in honour of his dead friend Patroclus;[192] according to Arrian, Indian fathers at the time of Alexander bestowed their daughters on the victors in boxing and wrestling matches.[193] If history is any guide, too, female participants in these sports are doomed to remain a tiny minority whose members are valued, if that is the word, not so much for their own prowess as for the titillating effect that their capers have on many men. Finally, if history is any guide, combat sports involving women do not prove that women, as part of their 'progress' in every field, are on their way to join in war or capable of doing so. What they do prove, I leave it to the reader to decide.

10 Camp-Followers

Since the time when some tribal women first began to accompany their menfolk on campaign, armies have always been trailed by female (and male, but that is another story) camp-followers who supported the troops and provided them with various kinds of services. Here we shall limit ourselves to those women who took the field, which means that peacetime military families, whether official or not, are largely excluded.

The information we have on camp-followers in the ancient world is rather limited,[194] and what we do know is sometimes coloured by prejudice. The wives and concubines of Persian kings and nobles often accompanied their husbands into the field,[195] and from time to time we hear of their being taken prisoner. After the battle of Palataea, says Herodotus, the victorious Greeks divided the Persian 'women, horses and camels' among themselves. A Greek woman by the name of Aspasia who was mistress to Cyrus the Younger and accompanied him during his revolt against Artaxes II was captured during the battle of Cunaxa;[196] a similar fate overtook the wife and daughters of Darius following the battle of Issus. By contrast, Greek armies were supposed to be without female camp-followers – the rationale being that war was above all a question of coping with hardship and that the presence of women would soften the men.[197] In this way literature created a contrast between the manly Greeks who renounced women on campaign and the effeminate Persians who could not do without them, with the aim of explaining the defeat of the latter at the hand of the former.

In fact, Greek armies also had their female camp-followers, especially on prolonged campaigns. It is true that Achilles, according to Euripides, was surprised to see King Agamemnon's wife, Clytemnestra, 'a respectable woman among shield-bearing men';[198] it is also true that Clytmnestra did not accompany the army in its voyage across the sea. Still, the Homeric poems

themselves make it abundantly clear that numerous female slaves were present during the ten-year siege of Troy who were captured on the way and
who served their masters as well as sleeping with them.[199] Much later,
a woman by the name of Antigone who was captured at Issus became mistress
to the Macedonian commander Philotas and followed him on his
campaigns;[200] another Macedonian camp-follower, Ptolemy's mistress Thais,
supposedly initiated the burning of the Persian royal palace at Persepolis
during a drunken orgy. It stands to reason, though it cannot be proved, that
many of the 10,000 Persian women whom Alexander married to his
soldiers[201] had originally been camp-followers.

By the second century BC, the boot was on the other foot. Instead of
defeating Barbarians who could be presented as effeminate, Hellenistic
armies themselves were being regularly defeated by the Romans who, as
victors, went on to write history. As a result, it was now the middle-aged
king of Syria, Antiochus III, who was accused of wasting his time with a
young woman and, consequently, losing the campaign that ended with the
battle of Thermopylae in 191–190 BC.[202] The next time female camp-
followers are mentioned is in 134 BC. Taking up his new command in
Numidia, (present-day Algeria) Scipio Aemilianus found the army in disorder. To restore discipline, he had 'whores, seers and prophets' expelled from
camp,[203] the implication being that such persons tended to assemble around
any army, particularly during pauses in operations.

Early Roman emperors, concerned lest the army lose its mobility, forbade
soldiers up to and including the rank of centurion to marry and even made
them break up existing marriages. Augustus, who when it came to others
had a conservative streak, also tried to prevent senior commanders from taking their wives into the field,[204] but his efforts were not always crowned with
success. This became evident when, during the reign of Tiberius, a high-
ranking lady called Munatia Plancina not only visited her husband Gnaeus
Calpurnius Piso but, 'violating the customs of her sex', participated in military exercises.[205] This and similar outrages caused the Senate to consider
the advantages and disadvantages of having women follow their menfolk.
After listening to the usual arguments concerning their 'softening' effects, it

concluded that their presence was permissible so long as they retained their modesty and did not so far run out of hand as to entice the men to abandon duty.[206]

Whatever the requirements of policy, clearly it was unable to prevent soldiers from forming unofficial unions with women. As time went on emperors had no choice but to recognize them to some extent, as Claudius for example did when he exempted serving soldiers from the laws that Augustus, attempting to raise the birth rate, had enacted to penalize bachelors. Much later, the soldiers' marriages were gradually legalized by means of edicts issued by Septimus Severus (AD 197) and Caracalla (AD 212).[207] Probably the change both reflected and was responsible for the declining mobility of Roman field armies, most of whose troops could increasingly expect to spend their entire careers in town-like garrison camps along the border.

The progressive immobilization of the Roman Army by the marital attachments that its soldiers formed must have contributed to its division into *limitanei* (border guards) and *comitatenses* (mobile striking force) that took place during the fourth century AD. Fortunately for the Roman Army, it was not the only one to suffer from the problem: Lactantius, the third-century AD father of the Church from whom much of our knowledge of the period derives, notes that the Romans' Barbarian opponents were likewise handicapped by their female camp-followers.[208] If anything this understates the difficulty. It was typical of Celts, Germans and other tribal peoples that they did not distinguish between adult men and warriors so that the German '*Volk*' could apply to either or both. Hence their campaigns were hardly military expeditions as we understand them. Instead entire peoples left their habitats and moved to foreign countries, men, women, children, livestock, wagons and all, of which the warriors only formed the cutting edge.

Nor, as might be expected, was the tradition of female camp-followers broken during the Middle Ages. They were known as 'bad women' and attempts were often made to get rid of them or limit their numbers; never, as the frequent repetition of the decrees suggests, with lasting success.[209] Just as there were always some women who were determined to follow the armies, so few armies could do entirely without women. In particular,

Arabic accounts of the Crusades often dwelt upon the scarlet women who accompanied the Latin warriors; then as later, Muslims were partly repelled, partly enthused, by the greater freedom that Western women enjoyed. Here is one, Imad a Din (1303–73), writing after the Crusades were over:[210]

> There arrived by ship [at Acre] three hundred lovely Frankish women, full of youth and beauty, assembled from beyond the sea and offering themselves for sin. They were expatriates come to help expatriates, ready to cheer the fallen and sustained in turn to give support and assistance, and they glowed with ardor for carnal intercourse. They were all licentious harlots, proud and scornful, who took and gave, foul-fleshed and sinful singers and coquettes, appearing proudly in public, ardent and inflamed, tinted and painted, desirable and appetizing, exquisite and graceful, who ripped open and patched up, lacerated and mended, erred and ogled, urged and seduced, consoled and solicited, seductive and languid, desired and desiring, amused and amusing, versatile and cunning, like tipsy adolescents, making love and selling themselves for gold, bold, and ardent, loving and passionate, pink-faced and unblushing, black-eyed and bullying, callipygian and graceful, with nasal voices and fleshy thighs, blue-eyed and great-eyed, broken down little fools … They said that they set out with the intention of consecrating their charms, that they did not intend to refuse themselves to bachelors, and they maintained that they could make themselves acceptable to God by no better sacrifice than this. So they set themselves up each in a pavilion or tent erected for their use, together with other lovely young girls of their age, and opened the gates of pleasure. They dedicated as a holy offering what they kept between their thighs; they were openly licentious and devoted themselves to relaxation; they removed every obstacle to making of themselves free offerings. They plied a brisk trade in dissoluteness … made themselves targets for men's darts … made javelins rise towards shields … and raced under whoever bestrode them at the spur's blow …

Another Muslim writer claimed that Christian soldiers would not fight unless they had first been satisfied by women.[211]

More detailed, if less romantic, information about female camp-followers is available for German armies from the sixteenth century on.[212] Contemporaries expected each regiment to be followed by 'at least' 4,000 women and children.[213] Some of the women were married to soldiers, others formed unofficial liaisons with them, and others were unattached. Some acted as entrenchment workers, some marched with the baggage train and provided every kind of logistical support, whereas others attended to the men's sexual needs. Probably there existed no strict dividing line between the various categories. This is evident from the fact that *any* woman associated with the army used to be called by such names as 'whore' or 'doxy', though it has been suggested that these terms were slightly less derogatory at that time than they are today. The women were not soldiers and were not sworn in. Still many commanders, recognizing that they were needed or simply to keep them in some kind of order, made arrangements to look after them, appointing an official who was responsible for them (the *Hurenwebel*), and providing them with quarters, transport, rations, and so on.

In Germany and elsewhere, the second half of the seventeenth century saw a switch from mercenary forces (troops mustered at the beginning of each war who would be disbanded at its end) to standing armies. Attempts were made to regulate female camp-followers and limit their numbers by allowing some soldiers in each company to marry – one out of three in Prussia, one out of twenty in Bavaria, Wuertemburg and Austria.[214] During peacetime 'authorized' wives lived with their husbands in a corner of the barracks. In wartime they followed their husbands on campaign and provided the entire company with services such as nursing and mending and laundering uniforms. In return they received provisions as well as a small wage, the expense of which was borne by a special fund. Should a soldier be killed, his widow often married his comrade so that the company would retain her services, and she herself, her living. That apart, periodic attempts were made to rid the army of other female followers but not, as one might guess, with great success, if only because the authorities themselves were not above using 'horny tarts' to 'debauch' men and entice them to enlist.

The eighteenth-century British Army operated a somewhat similar system.[215] Taking the field, it was accompanied by swarms of women, some of them married to soldiers and enjoying semi-official status, others not. Frequently they were put under the command of one of their number who was responsible for keeping them together. Some observers thought the women were 'of great assistance to the regiment, for they brought and prepared the food for the Company, brought in fuel for the fire, washed the linen, and generally tended the men. Especially they were useful in camp, for then they were permitted to go miles ... in search of victuals and of other necessaries.'[216] Others, including the Duke of Marlborough, regarded them as pests and tried to get rid of them. In 1758 a compromise was struck and ten women per company were authorized. This number did not include the commanders' wives or mistresses who, like Martha Washington during the War of the American Revolution, often joined their husbands on campaign and provided them with comfort. They distinguished themselves from the rest by riding in coaches;[217] one eighteenth-century handbook for ADCs even has a chapter on the way the commander's wife or mistress should be treated. Nevertheless, the army still did its best to prevent soldiers from getting married.

In theory camp-followers of the British Army came under the Articles of War and the Mutiny Acts. But men were reluctant to inflict serious punishment on the women who accompanied them and looked after them; such was the resulting disorder that even forming an idea of their number was difficult. Whereas eighteenth-century armies thought nothing of executing a man or flogging him half to death,[218] normally the worst that could happen to a woman was to be drummed out of the regiment. One punishment devised especially for females was the whirligig. It consisted of a sort of cage mounted on a pivot and rapidly rotated until the inmate became violently sick and, much to the spectators' amusement, emptied her body through every aperture; elsewhere women offenders might have their hair shaved or be paraded in the buff.[219] On one occasion the Duke of Wellington was criticized for having female camp-followers flogged. He vented his frustration by writing that, though there was no order for punishing women, neither could they be made exempt. It was 'well known that, in all armies, the women are at least as bad, if not worse, than the men as Plunderers; and the exemption of the ladies from punishment would have encouraged Plunder.'[220] Contemporaries agreed with him, claiming that the ladies' penchant for plunder sometimes caused them to be mistaken for raiding parties.[221]

Like his fellow commanders in other countries, George Washington lamented the 'pernicious consequences' of female camp-followers' presence, although he realized that they performed some useful services as cooks, laundresses, menders of clothes, nurses (of whom there were never enough)[222] and prostitutes (of whom there were always too many). Above all, also like his fellow commanders, he knew that the best he could do was not to get rid of them but to reduce them to some kind of order by issuing those who were 'authorized' with rations (which would prevent plunder) and appointing somebody to oversee them. He ended by decreeing that there should be no more than one woman per fifteen men but, as usual, found that the order could not be enforced.[223]

Finally, when the French National Assembly declared general conscription it also authorized a number of *viviandières, cantinières*, and *blanchisseuses* who were to follow the forces and serve their needs. However, the Revolutionary and Napoleonic armies differed from the professional ones of the eighteenth century in that they were based on conscripts aged eighteen to twenty-six. Married men were exempt; hence it stands to reason that more of the female camp-followers were unattached as opposed to being soldiers' wives. As in other armies, the swarm of official – they were issued a special badge and were entitled to receive rations – and unofficial low-class women offering their services was supplemented by officers' wives. Napoleon himself never took either Josephine or Marie Louise on campaign. Instead he preferred to sleep with local women who were procured for him as the occasion demanded by his Master of the Palace, General Duroc;[224] unless they caught his fancy, in which case the outcome might be a short affair, he would pay them generously and send them on their way. Many of his senior commanders were more faithful or less lascivious, however, and had their womenfolk accompany them in the field. As the common wisdom of the time had it, the higher-ranking a wife's husband the greater the nuisance she made of herself.[225]

On campaign, female camp-followers shared the hardships including heat, cold, hunger, thirst, long marches, heavy burdens and uncomfortable quarters; one early nineteenth-century English print shows a woman attached to Wellington's army carrying her soldier across a stream. Some fell ill, others died, particularly during retreats when confusion often reigned and the logistic arrangements were apt to break down. Still, compared to their male comrades they did enjoy some privileges. With or without authorization women often rode the wagons provided for the unit's baggage. Their normal place was in the rear in order to keep out of harm's way and, almost as important, not to impede mobility. Thus, when the Duke of Cumberland was about to fight the battle of Culloden in 1746 he ordered that the women 'remain with the horses, between the general officers' luggage and the wheel-baggage of the rest of the army'; any woman found forward of the wagons was whipped by the drummers at sunset.[226] Straying from the main body of troops, some women were killed in skirmishes and ambushes. A few may have participated in combat when the occasion presented itself, although the 'Molly Pitcher' stories that came out of the War of the American Revolution are notoriously unreliable and cannot be tied to any real woman.[227] Some, as we shall presently see, disguised themselves as men. Often both sides co-operated in offering their respective women a modicum of safety. They treated them as non-combatants, allowed them to pass between the lines in their search for victuals, and returned them unharmed when they were captured.[228]

Navies too had their camp-followers, and most early modern warships probably went to sea with at least a few of them on board.[229] As on land, some of the women received permission to sail whereas others did not. The former included the wives of officers, petty officers (who had this particular privilege attached to their rank) and some seamen; the latter, prostitutes and other low-class women who made their way aboard with the connivance of male crew-members. As on land, women at sea were sometimes able to earn some money by performing various services for the sailors. During battle they would act as nurses, whereas others could be found racing up and down ladders carrying bags of gunpowder from the storage rooms to the gun-decks. Sometimes women gave birth at sea, particularly – it was claimed – during battle when the stress, noise and vibration brought on pangs. If the ship in which they sailed was sunk and they were lucky enough not to go down with it they might be fished out of the sea afterwards. Seamen who were captured under similar circumstances were apt to be jammed into the hull of some out-of-comission ship or else confined in the cellars of a castle. The women, however, could expect to be put ashore at the nearest port, as happened to some French ones captured by the English during the battle of the Nile.

Most of the information concerning women at sea comes from the British navy. During the nineteenth century that navy enforced the orders against the presence of women aboard, and, to supply the services that they provided, replaced them with Chinamen. On land, too, the role of female – and male – camp-followers declined after 1815. In part this was because of the growing militarization of rear services. Step by step, the bureaucracy expanded; by the First World War, visitors to the British Army on the Western Front were surprised to discover that virtually every service that government offered to civilians at home was also provided to soldiers by uniformed personnel.[230] This cut into the role of female cooks, food-providers, seamstresses, laundresses and the like, until after the middle of the century there were only a few left.

Equally important was the introduction of the railways as the standard means for mobilization, deployment and strategic movement. Though the railways were civilian-owned, during wartime they operated under military control. That control was necessarily centralized at the top and very carefully planned; in both 1866–71 and 1914 the railway department of every self-respecting army calculated the traffic down to the number of axles passing over any given bridge during any given hour. Thus units being transported from one base to another, or on their way to the front, lost their autonomy. No longer could they use their own transport to give the ladies a lift – indeed the wagons themselves might be entrained. The outcome was that camp-followers, including women, tended to disappear. As to soldiers' wives, they might, if they were lucky, be given a free ticket home when their husbands left base and went on campaign.[231]

The American Civil War still saw some female camp-followers. A few even came under fire, as did a certain Dr Mary Walker (who was decorated for bravery) and a certain Mary Bickerdyke.[232] A much larger number of women, mostly of the middle classes, helped the war effort by collecting supplies, manufacturing bandages, setting up kitchens to feed passing units, establishing homes for orphans, and the like.[233] Nursing remained a favourite occupation for women and many of them found it an outlet for their energies. Whether from a humanitarian or from a military point of view, the efforts and achievements of the gathering of 'American Florence Nightingales' (as one contemporary account put it)[234] deserve recognition. Not, however, because they were in any danger; no more than their heroine, who never came anywhere *near* a battlefield but spent the Crimean War at Scutari, near the Hellespont.

By the beginning of the twentieth century camp-followers in the traditional sense had all but disappeared. Conversely, to the extent that they had not disappeared their presence with the army was understood as a typical sign of military backwardness.[235] Both because of the rise of the railways and because governments had started paying money to soldiers' families, wives normally no longer tried to follow their husbands on campaign. Most of the functions of serving-women were taken over by uniformed members of the forces themselves, with the result that those forces became more exclusively male than at any other period before or since. Of course, soldiers so fortunate as to spend any length of time at one location still formed links with the local female population. The latter would often provide them with the same services as before in laundries, restaurants, bars and of course brothels. Unlike their predecessors, however, they did so as civilians and were not considered semi-official members of the forces.

More than ever, the vast majority of women remained at home, now officially designated as 'the zone of the interior'. Many replaced their menfolk in the fields. Others undertook paid work in factories and offices, but that subject is outside our purview. Some upper-class women who either did not have to work or did not want to continued to occupy themselves by organizing collections and volunteering for hospital and other charitable work – carding and feeling nationally into the bargain, as one of them, dating to an earlier age, put it.[236] The *viviandières*, the *cantinières*, the *blanchisseuses* and their less respectable sisters disappeared, so that the only women still attached to the British Army were its corps of nurses. On the other hand, the relationship between women, men and war was about to enter a new era with the outbreak of the First and Second World Wars and the establishment of the various women's corps.

11 Women in Disguise

The vast majority of female camp-followers always wore women's clothes and operated in the open. Not so a relative handful who, in spite of the most severe legal sanctions (which, however, were rarely enforced), passed themselves off as men, donned uniform, and joined the ranks as ordinary soldiers. Although there have always been some disguised women, in the main the practice originated around the middle of the seventeenth century and thus coincides with the establishment of the first standing armies. It lasted throughout the eighteenth century and into the nineteenth.

Individual cases apart, the only modern statistical study of the women in question deals with 119 who are known to have enlisted in the Dutch armed forces between 1550 and 1840.[237] Of the 93 whose military 'careers' are known, 61 had served – at least for part of their time in disguise – as sailors and only 32 as soldiers. Their over-representation in the navy may have been due to the fact that life aboard ship afforded hardly any privacy; in other words, proportionally more female sailors than female soldiers were discovered. Practically all came from the lower classes, in which respect there was no difference between them and contemporary male soldiers. Many had been born abroad, mainly in present-day Germany, England, Scotland, or Scandinavia. Presumably what attracted them to the Netherlands was that country's wealth.

At the time they made the decision most of the women were between sixteen and twenty-five years old. Their motives, as spelt out by them at their trials in order to arouse sympathy, varied. Some wanted to escape an unhappy home, whether that of their fathers or the one provided for them by their husbands or husbands-to-be. Others followed their menfolk owing to emotional attachment or economic necessity; in the absence of a family to fall back on, the wife of an eighteenth-century soldier who was away on campaign might well be faced with starvation, particularly if she had children. Others still may have been driven by a desire for adventure. Probably the motives of women in countries other than the Netherlands were not dissimilar. Especially in the US, where the tradition of disguised warrior women was carried on well into the nineteenth century and thus into the age of nationalism, patriotism may also have played a part.

The first step towards enlistment was to migrate to another town where they were unknown. Next, to quote a woman who called herself Christian Welch and who joined the English Army in 1693: 'I cut off my hair, and dressed me in a suit of my husband's, having had the precaution to quilt the waistcoat to preserve my breasts from hurt, which were not large enough to betray my sex, and putting on my wig and hat … I went to the Sign of the Golden Last, where Ensign Herbert Lawrence was beating up for recruits … I was called a clever, brisk young fellow, given a guinea enlisting money, and a crown to drink the King's health and ordered to be enrolled forthwith.'[238] Some may have got an artificial penis: 'she pissed through a horn pipe just as a young man might,' as one popular ditty had it. Some must have suffered from problems of sexual identity, as in the case of one Maria van Antwerp who married not one but two women in succession, took them to bed, and was then found not to have what it takes. A few were probably hermaphrodites or pseudo-hermaphrodites, others 'large and coarse in body'; at which point reality and fiction as presented in the English ballads in particular part company.

The length of time the women spent in the forces before being discovered varied very much. Some served for only days or weeks, others for as long as ten years and more. What personal records we possess tend to show that the women did not either create or face any special problems. Their superiors were usually satisfied with them. Thus a certain Maria Schellink was awarded the *légion d'honneur* by Napoleon.[239] Another, the Italian noblewoman Francesca Scanagatta, served in the Austrian Army from 1794 to 1801. She was discharged as a lieutenant, got married, but continued to refer to herself in third person male singular; much later, she had a march written in her honour by Franz Lehar.[240] Often discovery was due to treatment received while the women were ill or wounded. They might also be subjected to punishment, particularly flogging which demanded that they strip to the waist; or give themselves away while drunk; or run into somebody they knew. Some women were only discovered after they were killed in action and their clothing was being stripped off them.

Dead or alive, the unveiling of a women in disguise always created a small sensation. Most were discharged, some only to re-enlist. If they had also committed some other offence they would be tried. On the other hand, rulers sufficiently astute to appreciate the propaganda value of a woman fighting for them might provide her with a pension – even if she had committed an offence, such as desertion, which would have cost a male soldier his life.[241] At least one, the above-mentioned Christian Welch, switched from a male role into a female one, working as a sutler and becoming known as 'Mother Ross' after her husband whom she had followed into the army, a certain Captain Ross, died. A few lived to a ripe old age: one, Phoebe Hessel, was born in Stepney near London in 1713 and died in 1821 at Brighton after having married no fewer than five times. At least one, the Englishwoman Hanna Snell, made her living by giving exhibitions of the drill she had learned while in the service to gaping crowds before dying in Bedlam; some, such as the American cross-dresser Debora Sampson, wrote their memoirs.[242] The strangest fate of all befell a Dutch transvestite nicknamed Aal the Dragoon. She was stabbed to death during a game of cards by a fellow soldier. After which, probably because she had committed some offence and was delivered to the medical authorities, she and her horse were stuffed and put on display.

As long as they stayed in the service women had to avoid drawing attention to themselves. Sometimes this forced them to extreme measures: for example, when Hanna Snell was sentenced to the lash 'the Method she used to prevent the Discovery of her Sex was this, according to her own Declaration: her Breasts, which were then not so big by much as they are at present, her Arms being extended and fixed to the City Gates, her Breasts were drawn up, and consequently did not appear so large; and besides this, her Breast was to the Wall, and could not be discovered by any of her

Comrades.'[243] That apart, contemporaries were more interested in titillation than in the women's military feats, with the result that information about their activities is hard to get. Usually all we know is that they served aboard this or that ship, participated in this or that campaign, and were present at this or that battle. Some must have fought and were wounded. At least one, the Englishwoman Mary Anne Talbot who enlisted with her lover's connivance, became a drummer. This job was often reserved for boys and could be very dangerous. However, it meant she did not enjoy full combatant status.

Probably the woman cross-dresser about whom we have the most information was a Russian lady, Nadezha Durova. Most of it comes from her own memoirs, written when she was much older, but some bits and pieces are from contemporary records.[244] The daughter of a noble family in the provinces, by her own account she was born in 1790 although other sources prove her to have been seven years older. The difference is explained by her forgetting to mention that, at one point, she was married to a man by the name of Chernov by whom she had a son. The marriage must have been extremely unhappy or else she would scarcely have run away (in 1806, when the child was three years old), disguised herself, and enlisted in the tsar's army.

Perhaps Durova's silence concerning these events derived from her fear lest, had she recounted them in her memoirs, she would almost certainly have been accused of being a bad wife and mother. Be this as it may, she claims that her parents had wanted her to be a boy. The mother hated her and made her life a misery, whereas the father is presented as kind and affectionate. Still, it was mainly his attitude which made her 'search actively for means to realize my previous intention: to become a warrior and a son to my father and to part company forever from the sex whose sad lot and eternal dependence had begun to terrify me'. To her men were tricksters who seduced women and then deserted them. Others married for money and, having done so, kept their wives in servitude while they themselves led a dissolute life.

Assuming the name of Alexander Vasilevich Sokolov, she joined a regiment of Polish horse and served under a Captain Kazimirski. Though the training was hard, she enjoyed the military life, particularly for the independence that it offered: 'You, young woman of my own age, only you can comprehend my rapture, only you can value my happiness! You, who must account for every step, who cannot go fifteen feet without supervision and protection … only you can comprehend the joyous sensations that fill[ed] my heart.' She spent the next seven years campaigning and was present at the battles of Friedland (1807) and Borodino (1812). Both were among the more bloody battles of the Napoleonic period, counting their casualties in the tens of thousands. At the former, she writes, 'instead of splendid feats I committed scatterbrained pranks'.[245] At the latter she suffered contusion from a passing cannon-ball.

Originating from the lower classes, most of the female transvestites were completely anonymous both during their service and after it. Not so Durova who, early during her service, made the mistake of sending a letter to her father in order to assure him that her elopement had brought her to no harm. He in turn addressed the minister of war, asking that she be found, and found she was. In 1807 she was summoned to St Petersburg and interviewed by Tsar Alexander I. He began by asking her whether it was true she was a woman. Being told she was, he said he had received reports of her bravery and proposed to send her home with honour. However, she begged him not to do so, saying she wanted 'to be a warrior, to wear a uniform and bear arms'.

Having made her point, Durova was given a commission and sent back to her regiment. Rumours about her existence were, however, already beginning to circulate among the troops. Fortunately for her, the authorities appreciated her propaganda value and treated her as a pet of sorts. Time after time she ran out of money, having been swindled by Jewish sutlers as she claimed; on each occasion all she had to do was to write to the minister of war who promptly refilled her pockets. In 1812 she was introduced to the commander-in-chief, General Mikhail Kutusov, who told her that he knew who she was and that he was delighted to meet her. Later she participated in the campaigns of 1813–14 but, judging from her own story, saw little action.

Once the Napoleonic Wars had ended, Durova says, she left her beloved army at her old father's request in order to look after him; much later she also got married. If her own account is to be believed she was a woman who, albeit possibly with good reason, hated her sex and was 'not fond of gatherings where there were many women'. Though always in the thick of things, somehow she contrived never to kill anybody. In battle she was completely fearless, but otherwise a rather timid soul, easily frightened by lonely places, shadows and unexpected noises. As an officer she was hopeless. Time upon time she lost her unit and it became necessary to send out search parties. Consequently some of her fellow officers, none of whom knew her true identity though they may have suspected it, told her to her face that she was not fit to command.

During the nineteenth century most of the disguised female warriors about whom we have information came from the United States where a republican regime, as opposed to the reactionary monarchical ones that existed almost everywhere else, encouraged virtuous women or at any rate stories about them.[246] Thus the war of 1812 is said to have witnessed a 'Louisa Baker' (real name Lucy Brewer) of Massachusetts who served in disguise aboard the USS *Constitution* and later published her memoirs.[247] A woman named Elizabeth C. Smith of Missouri served for eight months during the Mexican War and, upon being discovered and discharged, successfully appealed for a pension from Congress.[248] The Civil War is said to have witnessed some 400 fighting women on both sides – compared with 2.7 million men who enlisted or re-enlisted.[249] One woman, Jennie Hodges of Illinois, differed from most in that, after being discovered and discharged, she continued life as a man. Her true identity was only revealed in 1911 when she was injured in an automobile accident.

Even in 1914–18 some disguised women were to be found, particularly during the early years when the war was still regarded as a great adventure. The British, French, Italians, Germans and Austrians all had them. So did the Russians, who, true to tradition, differed from the rest in that they allowed women who had been discovered to remain in the military and even decorated them. By this time psychiatry had established itself as the science in charge of the human soul, and psychiatrists were frequently called upon to deal with the women and explain the phenomenon. They had scant sympathy for the women in question, claiming that for females to involve themselves in the 'most manly profession' of all was indicative of mental illness. For example, Sanitaetsrat Magnus Hirschfeld, later the author of a book on the 'sexual history' of the war, was called upon to examine a Berlin woman who pestered the military to be admitted and would not take no for an answer. On the basis of this experience, as well as his colleagues' reports, he concluded that they were frequently 'homosexual' and that the presence of 'sadistic inclinations' could often be suspected.[250]

What one is to make of these other female soldiers in disguise is hard to say. Some were imaginary, but others were undoubtedly real. Sometimes the two categories were confused. Thus a picture alleged to be of Hanna Snell, musket and all, was used to illustrate a book by one Mary Rowlandson who claimed to have been captured by American redskins,[251] even though Ms Rowlandson's only weapon, by her own account, had been a Bible. Nor was this the only case when fact and fiction became mixed up. For example, we are told that the War of the American Revolution and the American Civil War each produced a heroine called Nancy Hart. The Revolutionary Hart allegedly lived in Georgia and, wielding a rifle, held a party of Loyalists who had invaded her cabin captive until help came. Her Civil War-vintage namesake is sometimes described as a 'noted Confederate Spy'. Supposedly she was captured by the Federals, in which case one wonders why she wasn't executed; others claim that she was not a spy but a daring cavalry leader who took the town of Summersville, West Virginia, by storm. The Civil War also saw a group of women in La Grange, Georgia, who formed a militia and called themselves the Nancy Harts. Whether their Revolutionary prototype, or any of the others, ever existed is hard to say.[252]

Among the real-life women, most probably had good reasons – either personal or patriotic – for doing what they did. However, some clearly suffered from problems of sexual identity: dressing like men, living like men, and even going so far as to marry and bed other women. Most served without giving rise to any special complaint until discovered and/or discharged.

On the other hand, it stands to reason that many of those who did give trouble were discovered early on and got rid of. In at least some instances they were put under special protection and permitted to stay, as happened to a drummer-woman known as 'chaste Suzanne' who served with Napoleon in Egypt.[253] Some must have been as courageous as any man, and a few are known to have been wounded. However, it so happens that some about whom we are best informed claimed never to have killed – including, besides Durova, 'chaste Suzanne'.

As we saw, another woman who was reluctant to kill was Jeanne d'Arc. In some cases this reticence may have been imaginary, part of an age-old literary convention; the idea of killer-women is simply not compatible with their image in the eyes of men. On the other hand, in at least some cases it may have been real. Partly because of their comparatively small numbers, partly because the desire to avoid discovery presumably prevented them from attracting attention and rising in rank even if they were otherwise capable of doing so, militarily the women were totally without significance. At most their presence, whether known or rumoured or merely suspected, may have encouraged some men to fight harder. Thus, ironically, whatever impact they had was due more to their identity as women than to their efforts to act as men.

12 Warrior Women of Dahomey

With the exception of cross-dressers, so far in this study virtually all women of whom it has been said that they entered combat turned out to be mythological whereas those who were not mythological were found not to have entered combat. There does, however, exist one fairly well-authenticated account of women warriors, and that one refers to the so-called Amazons of Dahomey.

This story opens towards the end of the sixteenth century, a period when Europeans travelling to other continents competed with each other as to who could bring back the strangest and most fanciful tales. Some who had been to what is now Brazil reported the existence there of a race of arrow-shooting, camel-riding, Amazons;[254] not to be outdone, travellers to West Africa provided their audiences with similar tales.[255] For example, Theodor Bry in *Vera Descriptio Regni Africani* (Frankfurt-am-Main, 1598) wrote of a king whose palace guard consisted of women. He even attached a picture, which showed them holding their own against devilish male cannibals with turned-back eyelids.

In the event, the tales of the Brazilian Amazons were recognized as fabrications even at the time. Not so those concerning the West African ones, which turned out to have some foundation in fact. More information about them comes from the records of several Englishmen who visited the region between about 1730 and 1790. Most were merchants; however, some also carried military rank as their careers took them in and out of the West India Company which maintained its own armed forces. Their principal business was dealing in slaves, whom they bought from local chieftains and transported to the Caribbean as well as the English colonies in North America. In return they brought industrial products, including, as the most important product of all, firearms which were then put to use in order to capture even more slaves.[256] Their accounts, most of which run to several dozen pages, were often published in the form of pamphlets. Collected and republished, these pamphlets are now available in convenient form.[257]

Dahomey at the time[258] was a semi-absolute kingdom, said to be comparable in its level of development to England during the early fourteenth century and slowly moving towards greater centralization. At the apex stood a king whose position was sacred and, in theory, hereditary. In practice, though, endless civil wars and attempts at usurpation meant that dynasties seldom lasted more than two or three generations; the name Dahomey (Dan-Homey, 'in the belly of Dan') itself is said to have been derived from that of a pretender to the throne over whose dead body the capital was built. The king was the owner of all the land, part of which he worked by means of his own tenants but most of which was leased to members of the nobility, known collectively as 'Fon'. Intermarrying with the royal family and with each other, the nobility provided the palace officials and provincial governors.[259] Apart from them there was a small class of artisans and merchants who manufactured items for court use, traded with other tribes, and found occasional employment as spies. However, the bulk of the population consisted of peasants. They worked the nobles' land and paid their taxes in kind.

What excited the foreigners' curiosity was the fact that the kings of Dahomey sometimes had women guarding their thrones and that they liked to display themselves surrounded by hundreds of serving-women. One knelt in front of the king while holding up a golden cup so that he might spit into it; others bore arms.[260] Of those who bore arms, a few – described as 'fat and over-grown women' – were used to execute other women, a task they carried out under King Adahoonzou's personal direction but in such an incompetent manner that the victims' sufferings were protracted.[261] The Dahomean nobles imitated their king as best they could, setting up their own harems. Between them they withdrew so many women from circulation that low-class people were unable to marry and had to resort to 'moderately priced' prostitutes.[262]

One of the visiting foreigners has left a description of a procession held in a king's honour.[263] First came a guard of 120 men carrying blunderbusses. Then came fifteen of the king's daughters, attended by fifty female slaves, followed by 730 of his wives, carrying provisions. They were followed by a 'guard of ninety women under arms, with drums beating'. Led by King Bossa Ahadee's four favourite wives, 'very fine women' six troops of seventy women each provided entertainment during brunch; these were followed by 'seven troops of fifty women' who, like their predecessors, 'amused his majesty with their songs and droll dances'. Four of them had tails fitted to their rumps, which they whirled around most graciously. All this, exclusive of fifty to sixty women employed about the king's person as messengers. A picture provided by another visitor[264] shows the king walking up front, wearing a Napoleon-style triangular hat and carrying a naked sword; protection from the sun is provided by a parasol carried in the hands of a male servant. He is followed by a troop of women armed with blunderbusses, who in turn are surrounded by men playing horns and drums. The entire picture is deliberately designed to create as outlandish an impression as possible.

To arm women and put them on parade is one thing, to use them in real-life war another. In the normal course of things the Dahomean Army consisted of men.[265] However, some time in 1781 the neighbouring king of Eyeo (Oyo) demanded that King Adahoonzou pay him tribute in the form of women.[266] Being reluctant to part with his own wives, Adahoonzou sent out officials to take other women away from his subjects, but these officials met with resistance and were unable to get their way. Thereupon an outraged Adahoonzou put himself at the head of a hunting party made up of 800 armed women and took the field. Confronted by this 'uncommon army', the people fled. Adahoonzou ended up by obtaining the women he needed. Meanwhile, though, his male army had defeated Eyeo, making it unnecessary to deliver them.

Apparently the reason why, on this occasion, Adahoonzou departed from the normal practice and used women was because his army was occupied elsewhere; possibly, too, his objective was to humiliate his recalcitrant subjects. Be this as it may, the next time we hear about the Dahomean women soldiers is during the ceremonies that marked the king's funeral in April 1789. Though the details are somewhat obscure, we are told that *'five hundred and ninety-five women* [emphasis in the original] were murdered by their companions on this occasion and sent, according to the notion that prevails in this unhappy country, to attend Adahoonzou in the other world.'

After an interval of thirty years, we find ourselves in the reign of King Ghezo (1818–58). Ghezo was a usurper and never quite secure on his throne. He is said to have told a visiting Englishman, Captain William Winniet, Royal Navy, that he felt he could trust women better than men; possibly this was because, unlike men, they could be kept living permanently in the royal palace and were completely dependent on him.[267] Several different accounts tell of the women's identity and the way they were recruited. Some say that there took place an annual levy when the king, or his officials, had the people present their daughters as a form of tribute, selecting such as were fleshy for the royal bed and such as looked strong for his guard. Others have it that they were selected by lot or else that they were captives from other tribes;[268] it is not impossible that all three explanations are correct. One writer, the British traveller Richard Burton, claimed that the women were 'Xantippes who make men's hours bitter'. They were given to the king by their husbands and 'very properly put into the army'.[269]

The women so lucky or, depending on one's point of view, unlucky to be chosen entered his court which, at peak, may have contained some 8,000 people most of whom were women. They were reviewed by the king who pointed out those whom he wanted to marry. The rest, instead of learning 'games of love', would be 'trained in the use of arms'[270] as well as, presumably, other tasks needed to maintain the court. Forming the lowest rank among the palace women, they were known as 'the king's wives'. If they did well they might be promoted into the ranks of 'wives of the Leopard'; these were the women who lived with the king, slept with him, and bore him children. To complete the hierarchy of women there was a small group known as 'those who have borne Leopards'. They included the dowager queen as well as other women appointed to represent the deceased mothers of all previously deceased kings.

Like any Dahomean woman about to be married, 'the king's wives' were circumcised.[271] They went through a swearing-in ceremony which took place in the royal mausoleum. Their arms were cut, some blood was let out and mixed with powder and alcohol, and the mixture drunk after taking an oath of loyalty and of chastity. Having been turned into the king's soldiers, they spent their lives in seclusion in one of the king's palaces, dividing their time between exercises and work, and rarely meeting with men. In theory they were supposed to remain celibate on pain of death, but this law seems to have been enforced more strictly by some kings than by others.[272] One story has it that, to satisfy their sexual appetites, they enjoyed the services of a special corps of female prostitutes.[273] Certainly they could not marry – since this would have meant leaving the palace – without the king's consent. However, he gave it reluctantly and only if and when they were no longer fit to serve.[274]

Except for the swearing-in ceremony and their subsequent use as bodyguards, so far the accounts of the king's female retainers differ little from similar ones pertaining to many other times and places; moreover, some neighbouring chieftains also used women as bodyguards.[275] As far as may be determined, the women first went to war in 1839. Over the next twelve years they took part in various campaigns against neighbouring tribes, giving a good account of themselves. In 1851 they underwent a major test in the war against the Egba people. Aiming to take prisoners who could be sacrificed to his ancestors,[276] Ghezo laid siege to the Egba capital of Abeokuta. Apparently the Egba warriors did not expect to fight women. When they learned that the Amazons were indeed present – they may have formed about one-quarter of Ghezo's army of 16,000 – and preparing to castrate a prisoner, understandably they redoubled their efforts.[277] The assault ended up by being repulsed with heavy loss as the Dahomeans suffered 3,000 dead of whom perhaps 2,000 were women.[278]

Nevertheless the experiment must have been regarded as a success, for Ghezo's successors Glele and Behanzin decided to increase the number of warrior women. Precisely how this was done is not clear. Apparently the kings of Dahomey, like so many other tribal chieftains, surrounded themselves by permanent bodyguards made up of retainers who, in this case, included more females than usual. During wartime they also had the right to call the remaining male members of the population into service. It is possible, though by no means certain, that King Glele expanded this system to include women. More likely it included some women – the reason being that, given women's life cycle as described above, he could hardly have called them all.

If this is the correct interpretation, it would explain the distinction between a reserve corps and an active corps that is mentioned by several observers. Their description almost certainly reflects contemporary European debates as to the respective advantages of professional soldiers and reservists. The latter were said to be a useless lot: armed with sabres and cutlasses, negligent of their exercises, distinguished only by their 'horrible cries reminiscent of the hideous scenes of the ancient Bacchantes' and interested in nothing but drink. Not so the active 'Amazons'. Numbering 3,000, they had been brought up as soldiers from a tender age, 'supporting hunger and thirst with admirable courage, and their spirit, submitting to a machine-like discipline [one might think it was the Prussian Guard the writer had in mind], only knows one thing: absolute obedience to the king. Ardent, intrepid, without their aid the monarchy of Dahomey would long ago have lost the rank it occupies among the states of the West African Coast.' On a certain unspecified occasion King Ghezo was abandoned by his male soldiers and 'only the Amazons stood between him and capture'.[279] Though they failed to mention the distinction between active and reserve troops, most other sources agreed the women were effective.[280]

The Dahomean order of battle was complex, and different sources describe it in different ways. Apparently the army was divided into a right and left wing, both male. In the centre were the women, which, supposing they were originally a bodyguard, makes good sense. Like the army as a whole they were divided into a right and a left wing which, again supposing they were originally a bodyguard and formed a force within a force, also makes good sense. Still, the real cutting edge of the entire army is said to have been an 'elite male unit' which was sent to reinforce the women.[281] Some of the Amazons apparently did not fight at all but, continuing to act as bodyguards, positioned themselves behind the front where they protected their king.

How many female soldiers there were is not clear. Originally they are said to have numbered 'several hundred'.[282] At peak (1862), they may have numbered 10,000 in an army totalling 50,000 warriors. Of those 10,000 perhaps 2,500 were 'active' and the rest 'reservists'; all in a population of 250,000 or so. However, other sources claim that no Dahomean king ever commanded more than 12,000 troops and that most armies were much smaller. Perhaps part of the difference may be accounted for by assuming that many of the women (as well as the men) who went on campaign were not combatants but constituted a 'rabble' of porters, as one source claims.[283] If so they resembled the camp-followers of other armies – and indeed it is hard to see how 'reservist' women with little or no training could have done much more.

Be this as it may, there exists little doubt that some women were trained as soldiers and did fight: at Abeokuta in 1851 they are said to have been among the most intrepid warriors. By one French account: 'old or young, ugly or pretty, they were marvellous to look at. As strongly muscled as the black warriors, they were as disciplined and as correct in their attitude, aligned as if by rope. The commanders stand in front, recognizable by the riches of their dress, they carry themselves with a proud and resolute air.'[284] Particularly between 1879 and 1884 they took part in various campaigns, although the surviving sources seldom permit us to say with certainty when they were present and when they were not.[285] Like other troops they won some battles and lost others. When victorious, they would take the severed limbs, heads and even genitals of the defeated as trophies and display them. They enjoyed a reputation for ferocity and, when captured, refused to acquiesce in their fate; one surviving picture shows a female soldier killing a French soldier with her teeth as if she were a lioness and he some kind of zebra. Their enemies, as well as the population of Dahomey itself, are said to have regarded them with a mixture of respect and terror.[286]

Ferocious or not, the Dahomean warrior women were no more capable of saving the kingdom than the men. From the mid 1860s on repeated clashes with – exceedingly small, it should be said – French forces bit into its power. The final agony came in 1892 when Behanzin decided to risk everything and confront the French head-on. Between September and November there took place four small battles in which the Amazons formed anything between 7 and 30 per cent of the Dahomean force;[287] the official French account of the campaign does not even give them a single complete sentence.[288] Along with Behanzin they went down to defeat, or perhaps it would be more true to say that he went down with them. A new king, Ago-li-Agbo, was installed by the French and retained a small bodyguard, including a few Amazons.[289] Most went back to their villages and, if they could, married – often, being over-age, to husbands who already had wives and to whom they served mainly as drudges. A troupe of 'Amazons' – whether real or fake, as has been claimed – was brought to Paris and displayed behind the newly erected Eiffel Tower, performing exercises and martial dances. Their show must have been a success, for it was scheduled to be repeated in Brussels and Chicago. Some of their traditions survived in the form of songs, legends, and artefacts, and their exploits continued to be celebrated into the 1930s.

In all that regards the warrior women of Dahomey, separating fact from fiction is anything but easy. This is all the more true because there was nothing unusual in West African chieftains surrounding themselves with retinues of women – whether or not warrior ones. For example, when the British explorer and subsequent colonial administrator Frederick Lugard marched up the River Niger in 1894 he reached a place called Bussa where he encountered the king of all the Bassas. The latter was 'a specially dirty and mean-looking savage surrounded by … crowds of naked girls and semi-nude women';[290] a similar host of naked women was said to have attended the king of Kiama.[291] Likewise General Sir Garnet Wolseley reporting his victorious Ashanti campaign showered praise on the Fanti women who had acted as porters. The Fanti men, he said, were 'destitute of courage' and 'unmanly'; but the women's conduct had been 'admirable'. 'Seeing these characteristics of the two sexes it was not to be wondered that the King of Dahomey keeps up a corps of Amazons. The women have none of the indolence and cowardice of the men; they are bright, cheerful and hard working and we got excellent service willingly performed by them.' They were also 'most amenable to discipline', 'seemed to possess the instinct of order', had 'wonderful strength' but, alas, suffered from a 'lack of good features'.[292]

With that, we come to the crux of the matter. From biblical times on,[293] a well-known rhetorical ploy often used to humiliate male soldiers was to compare them with women; whatever the reality behind the Dahomean warrior women, plainly this was also the purpose of many of the nineteenth-century accounts of them. In explaining that the male tribal warriors whom they subdued were not even as good as their womenfolk,[294] the Europeans were asserting their own superiority. Their techniques were taken over by some modern scholars. For example, Harry Holbert Turney-High (1899–1982) was an anthropologist at the University of South Carolina.[295] He spent much of his academic career trivializing tribal warfare which, he claimed, took place below the 'military horizon', the goal being to contrast it with his own experience as a colonel in the US Army during the Second World War of which he was inordinately proud. Hence it is not surprising to find him writing that 'without casting any doubt on the competence or ferocity of these women, let the reader recall the type of action fought by the Dahomeans and he will suspect that women could do as well in them as men.'[296]

Moreover, the women paid a heavy price for their prowess. European observers always called them Amazons, but no group was further removed from the tribe of man-less, horse-riding, free-living, female warriors of ancient myth. Selected while still in their teens, the Amazons of Dahomey were taken into the Leopard's harem. Except for those who happened to catch his fancy, though, they did not enjoy the privilege of sleeping with him, and among all his 'wives' their status was the lowest. They were a special group that stood outside normal society, its members being destined to fulfil their biological destiny as mothers only, if at all, after they were released from their duty as soldiers. Amazons who followed their own inclinations and became pregnant by other men were put on trial and might, if they were unlucky, be executed.

The women themselves well realized their ambiguous status. They were considered men and saw themselves as men; they even had a sort of battle-hymn in which they celebrated themselves as 'strong men, very strong, with muscular busts'. 'Lets march together, let's march like men,' went another one of their marching songs. A third proclaimed that 'we are men, not women'.[297] As if to confirm that there could be no question here of female solidarity, they referred to their enemies as 'women' and were sometimes rewarded by presents of female slaves.[298] Their European conquerors often described them as 'furies', 'ugly', 'viragos' 'masculinized' and 'remarkable for stupendous steaopyga' (i.e. enormous buttocks).[299] One present-day female scholar has argued that those conquerors were shocked by the spectacle of female warriors and reluctant to admire their 'feminine beauty and grace'. However, it seems more likely that if the Dahomean women were really capable of standing up to male warriors in close combat they had to develop the appropriate physiques. Perhaps they looked like the women in some modern beefcake magazines.

In a society where women occupied a very low place,[300] whatever prestige the Amazons enjoyed derived solely from their royal master. Their sisters in the harems of Muslim rulers apart, it is hard to think of any other group of women who led a more secluded life, or enjoyed less independence, or were less able to realize themselves as women; so complete was their subordination that some were even selected to accompany their master on his journey to the afterlife.[301] As warriors they were always a minority – certainly no more than a quarter – in an army which, like all others throughout history, was made up mainly of men. Originally they constituted a royal bodyguard whose function, often enough, was to capture and execute other women. Later they developed into warriors. Collectively their military careers lasted for some fifty years. They ended up by going down to defeat along with their menfolk and their king, after which some of them were put on display 'like two-headed calves', as a contemporary French journalist put it.[302] To become warriors they had to surrender their womanhood, turn into men, and despise women, as they themselves said. To the extent that it is founded on fact, their fate was neither laughable nor enviable but simply tragic.

13 Revolts, Revolutions and Insurgencies

If true warrior women have been almost as rare as unicorns, the same does not apply to female participation in revolts, revolutions and insurgencies of every sort. A famous nineteenth-century picture by the French painter Eugène Delacroix presents Revolution itself in the form of a bare-breasted woman; she is shown storming forward, tricolour in hand, trampling over dead bodies while accompanied by a smallish, dark-faced, pistol-brandishing man. The present account is limited to those revolts, revolutions and insurgencies that involved an armed struggle. The type of struggle does not matter: whether it consisted of open clashes with 'the forces of order', or of guerrilla warfare, or of terrorism. On the other hand, episodes when change was achieved solely by political means, let alone mere 'revolutionary' writing and speechifying, are excluded.[303]

For some insurgencies quantitative information concerning the participation of women is available. After the Second World War a special committee determined that, from 1943 to 1945, 35,000 Italian women took part in 'at least three military operations' against the Germans; 4,653 were arrested whereas 2,750 died in action or were executed; 512 bore some kind of command responsibility; and 19 were decorated with the golden resistance medal.[304] Since the total number of officially recognized 'partisans' was 282,751,[305] women constituted about 12.3 per cent of the movement as a whole, a figure which as we shall see is in harmony with similar ones from other times and places. On the other hand, at one in seventy the number of those who exercised command functions of any kind is conspicuously low, given that in European armies during the Second World War approximately one in eight soldiers was an NCO and one in thirty or so an officer.

In Yugoslavia between 1941 and 1945 about one in ten of NOV (National Liberation Army, the military arm of the Yugoslav resistance) personnel were women, a figure that grew to one in eight towards the end of the war.[306] Women were among the first to join the resistance, and their numbers increased rapidly. Most were in their late teens or early twenties and unmarried. Patriotism apart, their motives are said to have included a desire for adventure, camaraderie, and equality with men; finally, fighting for Tito supposedly meant registering one's support for a post-war Communist Yugoslavia. If any women joined out of less lofty motives, such as the desire to escape from their families, then the Communist-inspired female author who did the research does not inform us of the fact.

Early on Yugoslav organization was unsystematic and haphazard as resistance fighters did what they could and learned by doing. Once the movement had become institutionalized and had succeeded in establishing a more or less secure base area, however, both women and men were given a one-month training period which turned them into fighters (*borac*). Next they were sent to the 'front'; those who survived often went on to more advanced courses including, in the case of women, communications and, above all, medical services. Women served as medics (*bolnicarka*) or fighter medics (*borac-bolnicarka*); indeed if there was one woman in a unit she was likely to be designated a medic, like it or not. A much lower number served as specialists in coding and decoding, and as artillery spotters. The latter in particular was a dangerous job since it meant operating well forward of the main forces.

Though 11 per cent of NOV women were NCOs and 8 per cent received a commission, they only filled 6 per cent of 'political' positions and no woman ever rose higher than major. On the surface this is balanced by the fact that even fewer are identified as service workers in traditional female occupations such as cooking, sewing, typing, and so on. The explanation is that those tasks were carried out by AFZ, or Anti Fascist Women's Organization, which allegedly numbered no fewer than 2 million and acted as the NOV's civilian infrastructure. In practice, of course, NOV and AFZ were often indistinguishable since 'combat', in the form of raids and bombardments by the occupation forces, often reached AFZ too. The total cost to the Yugoslav nation was about a million dead, though how many of those were female is unknown. It is claimed that among NOV dead, women were over-represented (25 per cent were killed, versus only 11 of the men). I can think of no other war in which the number of female killed in action exceeded that of men. If the figures are correct, then obviously the organization must have been using young and inexperienced women as cannon fodder. Another explanation is that women were more vulnerable to the extraordinary physical hardships which the struggle against the Wehrmacht often involved.

A third attempt to quantify the role of women in a revolutionary struggle involves the one waged by the Algerians against the French in 1955–62.[307] Like their Yugoslav sisters, Algerian women joining the FLN (Front de Liberation Nationale) tended to be very young and unmarried. Unlike their Yugoslav sisters, the vast majority were active in nursing and cooking (94 per cent of one sample). Some women also undertook liaison and intelligence work for which they were considered particularly suitable; like so many colonialists, the French lived under the illusion they could tell native women from French ones by their looks. However, women were rarely present at, or used in, open combat.

As in Yugoslavia, too, the 'official' FLN was only the tip of the iceberg. In the civilian sector, practically the whole population, including the female one, supported the uprising. The humble women, most of whom lived in villages and 98 per cent of whom were illiterate, 'repeated day in and day out their daily tasks: cooking, laundering, cleaning. Theirs was a monotonous and thankless task, bereft of military glory or heroism', and yet one that sometimes demanded exposure to danger during French raids or bombardments.[308] Depending upon the source one uses, the uprising cost the lives of between 300,000 and 1 million Algerians. We do not know how many of them were women, nor how female casualties stood to male ones. All we do know is that out of one sample comprising 10,949 FLN women 1,343 were imprisoned and 949 killed.

Of the above three, the Yugoslav and Algerian revolts in particular were among the most murderous in history, though the Italian one was not exactly a picnic either. They involved, on the part of the occupying powers, not just anti-terrorist operations but the destruction of entire villages and even

districts on a scale that sometimes approached, if it did not constitute, geno-
cide. By contrast, the struggle between the Jewish community and the British
authorities that took place in Palestine in 1945–7 was almost gentlemanly. The
British considered the Jews to be a 'semi-European race';[309] hence they did not
proceed nearly as brutally against them as they had against the Arabs in the
same country in 1936–9. On the Jewish side the organizations involved in the
struggle included PALMACH (3,000–4,000 members), PALMACH's par-
ent organization Hagana (30,000 members), ETSEL (7,000 members),
and LECHI (perhaps 700 members).[310] Figures concerning female mem-
bership are available only for PALMACH, where they made up between 15
and 20 per cent.[311] Accidentally or not, PALMACH was also the one whose
struggle was the least bloody. In the summer of 1946 it renounced terrorism
altogether, preferring to go into other kinds of anti-British activities such
as bringing in illegal immigrants and the like.

Of the three organizations Hagana was by far the largest. It was also the
only one that, thanks to the economic support provided by the kibbutzim,
was able to provide the members of its striking force with any kind of sys-
tematic training. PALMACH women did receive physical fitness, weapons
and combat training along with the men. Nevertheless, during the period
its units carried out so-called 'actions' against the British, such as blowing
up bridges or attacking army bases, the women were usually left behind.
Sometimes women acted in support. On one occasion a woman (and a man)
who had driven a party of PALMACH saboteurs to their objective and were
expected to collect them on their return were tied up and left with their
vehicle, the idea being that, should they be captured by the British, they
could plausibly claim to have been coerced.

Though there was no ban on female commanders, no PALMACH woman
seems to have commanded a unit larger than a squad. Much the same is true
of the two other fighting organizations for whom we have no figures but
which used women as medics, messengers, communicators and arms smug-
glers (this author personally knows one woman who smuggled hand-grenades
in her brassiere). A famous female LECHI member was Geula Cohen who
acted as an announcer on the organization's underground broadcasting

station. Making full use of her lugubrious voice, she directed blood-curdling threats at the occupation forces; much later she continued her histrionics as a right-wing Knesset member. All three organizations had in common that the number of women who lost their lives in the struggle was minuscule. Nor, for that matter, were there any women among those whom the British executed.

To be sure, these were not the only uprisings in which women took part. A few, nicknamed 'the Vesuviennes', probably fought for the 1848 revolutions in Paris. However, of eighteen articles published about them in the French press seventeen turned out to be fictional;[312] proof, if more were needed, that tales of warrior women often owe something to the titillating effect they seem to have upon men. The 'Red' Army that fought against the 'Whites' in 1918–19 included a number of female fighters as well as a few women political officers, or commissars. At least two of those, Rozalia Zemliachka and Evgenia Bosh, were as zealous as any of their male comrades, gaining notoriety for ordering their adversaries massacred.[313] As of January 1944, women formed a little under 10 per cent of 'operating partisans' in the Soviet Union: 26,707 out of 287,453, to be precise.[314] In the wake of the Second World War 250 Greek women were decorated for bravery in fighting against the Axis occupation.[315]

Outside Europe, approximately 3,000 women (as against 100,000 men) took part in Mao's Long March. Leaders' wives apart, most carried out the usual logistic functions; however, the leadership of the Red Army was monopolized by men.[316] Vietnam has a long history of female warriors who led uprisings against the Chinese. The tradition was continued in the twentieth century when many Vietnamese women participated in the revolts against the French and the Americans, undergoing extraordinary hardships which sometimes resulted in the loss of their child-bearing ability.[317] Though most formed part of the infrastructure, some actually fought weapon in hand. Their American opponents always insisted that these women were among the most 'vicious, ruthless, cunning' fighters,[318] as indeed they *had* to be if those opponents were to escape an even greater humiliation than the one they actually suffered. Other non-European insurgencies in which women participated included the Afghanistani Mujahedin as well as the Kurdish Liberation Movement (PKK). The same is true of countless Latin American liberation movements from the Peruvian *Sendoso Luminoso* down.[319]

These and other uprisings gave rise to many stories of individual heroines, some real, others not. The former included the Palestinian Leila Khaled. Along with some male accomplices, she tried to hijack an El Al plane, was overwhelmed by Israeli security, and extradited to Britain; released before long, she joined the 'Refusal Front' that declined to follow Arafat in renouncing terrorism and negotiating with Israel. The latter probably included Trieu, a 9 foot Vietnamese virago whose breasts were 3 feet long. With these slung over her shoulders, she is said to have ridden an elephant while leading an anti-Chinese uprising that took place around AD 240; she ended up defeated (and driven to suicide) when her enemies took advantage of her feminine daintiness and sent unwashed ruffians to fight against her.[320] Another legendary figure was the hard-riding, hard-drinking, gun-toting Adelita of the Mexican Revolution. Though she had a song named after her, like 'Molly Pitcher' she was probably either a composite character or a fictional one. The reality of female participation in the Mexican Revolution was described by the American journalist John Reed. Among the thousands of women he encountered over a period of several months, just one may have fought while another one carried military rank. The rest acted as camp-followers to their 'men' to whom they might or might not be officially married. As the latter died they were often unceremoniously passed from hand to hand.[321]

In the 'ideal type' insurgency, women probably formed about 10 per cent of the full-time revolutionaries, though on occasion they may have been a little more numerous. Whether as full-time revolutionaries or as part of the civilian infrastructure, the vast majority acted in a great variety of supporting roles from cooking to nursing to passing messages to gathering intelligence to carrying equipment to having 'involuntary sex' with their male comrades;[322] However, women fighters may have been proportionally more numerous in organizations that relied mainly on terrorism rather than engaging in semi-overt guerrilla warfare.[323] Male chauvinism apart, one reason for the dearth of female fighters was the fact that insurgents were normally short of arms and therefore allocated the few they did have to men. The relatively small number of women as well as their confinement to supporting roles may explain why they hardly ever rose to high rank in any of the movements in question. Or perhaps things worked the other way around and it was the dearth of women commanders that caused their sisters to be relegated to supporting roles.

Beyond doubt, participation in these and other insurgencies demanded extraordinary heroism on the part of men and women alike. In some ways, indeed, it demanded greater courage than did participation in open combat. One reason for this is that insurgents engaging in covert action are more likely to be alone and entirely dependent on their own mental resources. Second, unlike soldiers they have no rights under international law, therefore they are likely to be treated even worse when captured. Historically speaking, the catalogue of things that have been done to prisoners of war is a horrible one. The catalogue of things that have been done to rebels is much worse still.

On the other hand, captive female insurgents were often treated more leniently than men. For example, following the 1916 Easter Rising the British executed fourteen male leaders of Sinn Fein. Not so Constance Markievicz (1876–1927), also known as 'the Rebel Countess' who was reprieved 'due only to her sex'; later she joined the Irish parliament and became the first woman minister in any modern democracy.[324] In Nigeria in 1929 women engaged in violent demonstrations against the British authorities on the assumption – which proved wrong – that the latter would hesitate to fire on them.[325] That even the Germans in Russia hesitated to treat women as they did men is illustrated by an order issued by the pro-Nazi General Walter von Reichenau in October 1941. In it, he ordered 'draconian measures' to be taken against *male* members of the Russian population who could have prevented sabotage operations but failed to do so.[326]

If, in 1946–8, Palestinian Jewish women were able to hide arms on their bodies it was because British soldiers were not allowed to search them. Another example comes from the Seychelles. In 1982 the islands witnessed an attempted coup. After its failure the male perpetrators were sentenced to death, reprieved, and finally received stiff prison sentences. Not so the woman on the team, a South African national by the name of Sue Ingle; she only spent a single night under arrest before being released along with her pet cat.[327] To adduce one more example, one reason why the Palestinian uprising often saw women (and children) at the fore was because women being sprayed with gravel or beaten with truncheons looks bad on TV. On occasion the Israeli authorities released PLO women who had been captured and sentenced because, had they served their full terms, they would no longer have been capable of bearing children.

Thus, one reason why more women have participated in uprisings than in war is because they, and the men who usually commanded them, expected them to arouse less suspicion, and be treated less harshly, than men. However, there exists an even more important explanation. As we shall see, one of the cardinal functions of war is as an affirmation of masculinity. What distinguishes insurgency from war is the fact that, initially at least, the insurgents almost always find themselves faced by overwhelming odds, lacking numbers, training, experience, organization and resources. This lopsided balance makes all the difference. Contrary to the normal rules of social life, it permits men to fight alongside women – or, at any rate, a few women – without losing their self-respect.[328]

Similar reasoning may explain why, from antiquity on, women often participated in the kind of desperate home defence that still continued after everything was lost. For example, they might mount the roofs and throw down objects in cities whose walls had already been breached. During the last weeks of the Second World War even Hitler, for all his male-chauvinist ideology, agreed that German women might fight for the Reich,[329] though by then it was too late for the idea to be realized. Finally it explains why, in all cases without exception, no sooner did the insurgents or guerrillas or partisans or freedom fighters emerge from the underground than women were taken out of the fighting line and were retained, if at all, solely in supporting missions. This is what happened to 200 or so women who volunteered to fight for the Spanish Republic; to female Yugoslav 'partisans' who began being taken out of the line even before the Second World War ended; to

female members of the Israeli Hagana within one month of the establishment of the state; to Vietnamese women after the end of the Indochina War;
and to Eritrean women who, it is said, went straight back from the front to
the kitchen.[330]

In the future, women will undoubtedly continue to take part in insurgencies (as well as counter-insurgencies. Judging by its Vienna headquarters, no fewer than one third of Gestapo employees were female.[331] So were
10 per cent of concentration-camp guards; female members of various European resistance movements were likely to end up at Ravensbruck, which was
run mainly by women). Most will presumably serve in a very great variety
of supporting roles, but some will actually participate in operations and kill.
Given their physical limitations, most likely they will do so either in a covert
way: by planting explosives, as terrorists do, or else in self-defence when
about to be caught. If only because the vast majority of women end up marrying, having children, and looking after them, almost certainly the ratio
between 'active' male and female insurgents will continue to be as lopsided
as ever. Following the usual rules of social life, in few if any revolutionary
movements will the leading positions be occupied by women. Among them
again, experience suggests that the majority will probably lose their positions once the struggle has attained its ends.

In their capacity as insurgents, women will continue to prove that they
are as courageous, as determined, and as capable of withstanding the greatest stress, and the most gruelling conditions, as are men. For all the reasons
just adduced, however, insurgencies do not prove that war is a matter for
women. If anything, they are the exception that proves the rule.

14 The Age of Total War

As we saw, the gradual demise of camp-followers that began after the end of the Napoleonic Wars left late nineteenth-century armies more exclusively masculine than ever. By 1914 this had enabled them to develop a cult of masculinity; perhaps more than any other modern war, the First World War was regarded as a test of what men (as opposed to women) were and of what men (again as opposed to women) could do.[332] Alone among all the major armies the British one had a few thousand women in uniform, all of them nurses. Other armies also needed nurses, but preferred to employ them as civilians.

During the war itself the most restrictive policies were adopted by the German, Austrian-Hungarian, French and Italian forces. They did not consider women worthy of wearing uniform, though all four employed large numbers of civilian women;[333] in 1918 the Germans toyed with the idea of drafting women (unmarried ones) for obligatory labour service, but nothing came of it.[334] As to the Russians, they refused to set up a female auxiliary service but differed from all the rest in that they permitted a few women to serve in combat; after the revolution of February 1917 caused their armies to disintegrate they set up a few so-called female 'battalions of death' on which more below. This leaves two out of the six main belligerents: Britain and the United States. Accidentally or not, protected by water, in some ways they were less seriously affected and waged a less desperate struggle than the rest.

Britain at this time differed from its continental allies and enemies in that it did not have conscription. The government appealed for volunteers and got them by the hundreds of thousands; women, too, wanted 'to do their bit', and to satisfy them the Women's Emergency Corps (WEC) was founded during the autumn of 1914.[335] It acted as a sort of clearing-house for women, registering them, finding out what skills they possessed, and referring them to the forces which might or might not hire them *as civilians*. Usually they found themselves running canteens, or operating radio equipment at home, or acting as cooks and drivers. The largest single group consisted of nurses. However, the British military would not allow any women, including nurses, into war zones. Therefore some of them went abroad on their own initiative and served at the front with other forces, either in Belgium or in Serbia and Macedonia.[336]

In early 1917, having suffered brutal losses, the War Office was ready to put women in uniform and WAAC (Women's Auxiliary Army Corps) as well as WRN (Women of the Royal Navy) were formed; in 1918, after the Royal Air Force became an independent service, the WRAF (Women's Royal Air Force) was established. Some 100,000 women spent at least some time in these units (57,000 in the WAAC alone). Of them, some 12,000 who volunteered went to France; very few women accompanied the forces to other fronts such as the Middle East or Mesopotamia, and the majority went back to their own homes each evening. Women serving in France were restricted to the Communications Zone, which meant that, except for a very occasional air attack, they were out of harm's way. The army divided them into four categories: cookery (preparing and serving food); medical (nurses and doctors); clerical (typing, filing, operating telephones and the like); and 'miscellaneous'.[337]

From the forces' point of view, the main problem with women was not the quality of the service they gave – about which there were few if any complaints – but the need to prevent the public from perceiving the women's corps as dens of sexual licence. Such a perception might dissuade middle-class women, in which the forces were mainly interested, from enlisting; accordingly servicewomen were surrounded by strict rules of movement, dress and behaviour. Female uniforms were partly de-feminized, for example by removing the breast pocket which was thought to emphasize the bust. To reduce external sex differences, the salute and other forms of military comportment were introduced, and fraternization between male officers/ enlisted women, enlisted men/female officers prohibited. To assure parents and relatives that everything was proper, Queen Mary was made honorific

Commander-in-Chief, WAC. In April 1918 it was renamed QMAAC (Queen Mary's Army Auxiliary Corps) in her honour.

Though the women in these units were uniformed, billeted and paid by the military, there remained important differences between them and the men. When British men were made subject to conscription in 1916, women did not follow. Instead of officers they had officials who were called controllers and administrators, whereas at NCO level they were known as forewomen. Though they served in the military, recruitment was by way of the Ministry of Labour and women's organizations. Permitted to leave practically at will, the women were simultaneously in and out of the military; and the services, which knew better than to endanger their troops' self-respect by having too many in too many important positions, deliberately kept it that way.

Whereas the enlistment of British women must be seen against the background of very great manpower problems, this was much less true in the United States. No fewer than 10 million American men registered for the draft; therefore, to claim that the 34,000 women who passed through the United States Army and Navy were really essential is absurd. Like their British sisters, American women who signed up did so for patriotic reasons as well as the hope for adventure, camaraderie and, of course, in expectation of a well-paid job; some may have wanted to make a political statement in connection with female suffrage.[338] Since numbers were small, quality was extremely high; Navy women in particular were much better educated than the US population at large, male or female.[339] Most lived at home and commuted to work, as did many men. Once they had been sworn in and put into uniform they received little or no military training, passing straight from their civilian jobs to military ones. Most were active either in administrative and communication slots (following its positive experience, female telephone operators became a permanent feature of the US Navy) and as physicians or nurses in the medical corps; however, a smaller number performed a very great number of jobs from coding and decoding to fusing shells. Ten thousand went abroad, a few hundred were decorated, and thirty-eight died, mostly of flu.[340]

Neither in Britain nor in the US were women considered combatants.

The way the services saw things, the main danger to their welfare came from their own male comrades. That was one reason why neither country integrated women into the forces; instead they were kept in separate, all-female organizations. In Russia, things were different. Though it resembled other armies by making extensive use of female volunteers in hospitals and the like, the tsar's army never established a women's corps. By the early summer of 1917 incompetence and disorganization, for which that army was notorious, as well as the outbreak of the first Russian Revolution, had brought it close to collapse. Against this background, it was suggested to Alexander Kerensky as head of the provisional government that a female 'battalion of death' be raised and sent to the front.

The author of the proposal was one Maria Leontief Bochkareva. According to her autobiography, about which more in a moment, she was born in the city of Tomsk, Siberia. She grew up in extreme poverty, and at times had to support herself by working as a servant in a brothel. Twice she was married to, or lived with, abusive men of whom she was unable to rid herself; like Durova before her, she seems to have regarded the war as an escape from her marital difficulties. In November 1914, having discovered a desire to be 'in the boiling cauldron of war', she petitioned the tsar for permission to enlist. The proposal was accepted. During the next two and a half years Bochkareva served in the ranks, was wounded at least once, received no fewer than seven decorations, and did sufficiently well to rise to the rank of first sergeant. In this capacity she claimed to have been put in charge of a unit of twenty men.

At a time when the Russian Army still counted its troops in the millions, some 2,000 women heeded the call to arms.[341] Concentrated in a base in St Petersburg, most followed the example set by their male comrades and deserted. According to Bochkareva, this was because she would neither admit soldiers' councils nor compromise on discipline. In particular, she wanted to purge any forms of 'feminine' behaviour, to achieve which end the women had their hair shaved off in the manner of monks or Marines until they could barely be identified as women any more. Gigglers were treated with a slap across the face, and Bochkareva even claims that she once used her bayonet to run through a female soldier caught on the battlefield making love to a male comrade. In July 1917, having received five weeks' training, the remaining 300 women were reviewed by a distinguished visitor, Emmeline Pankhurst, who declared their enlistment to be 'the greatest event in world history'.[342] Next the battalion was formally awarded its colours by the commander-in-chief, General Kornilov, and was sent to the front. There it came under General Denikin. In his memoirs, he says the women had to be locked up lest they be raped by their male comrades.[343]

The battalion participated in one engagement, though whether 'on the northern front' (in the Baltic) or against the Austrians (which would place it further south) is not clear;[344] a third account places it at Smorgon in Belarus. Along with a male battalion, the women went on the offensive. Denikin says that they were very brave but, not knowing how to fight, suffered excessive losses and soon had their enthusiasm extinguished by the realities of the battlefield. His testimony is supported by that of a British Red Cross nurse, Florence Farmborough. She met Bochkareva soon after the event and found her 'brokenhearted' owing to her discovery that 'women were quite unfit to be soldiers'.[345] What little evidence we have from the other side of the hill also suggests that the Russian women's military performance did not command admiration.[346]

Unlike their commander, and in contrast to the majority of Russian male soldiers, most of the female warriors tended to be both literate and middle class.[347] This may be one reason why they were unable to accomplish their main mission, which was not so much to fight the Germans as to shame male soldiers into doing so by setting an example. Indeed Bochkareva's idea proved counter-productive: resenting the women's high patriotic tone, the troops regarded the presence of the battalion as proof that the situation was indeed desperate. After one episode during which the women were attacked by male deserters, machine-guns at the ready – possibly because they were confused with another type of 'battalion of death' whose mission was to catch and execute deserters behind the front[348] – Bochkareva's small force began to disintegrate. Units similar to hers are said to have appeared in Moscow, Odessa, Ekaterinodar and Perm. However, since none had a

Bochkareva to tell of their deeds information about them is hard to get and only the last-named one may have seen action.

Apparently the provisional government in St Petersburg did not trust its male soldiers any more than Ghezo did, for in October 1917 a force of female volunteers helped guard the Winter Palace; with what results is well known. The Bolshevik assault on the palace proceeded almost without blood-shed as the defenders, a troop of officer cadets known, since Petrine times, as 'the Junkers', were pushed aside by the crowd. Only six defenders, and no assailants, were killed. As the 'battle' raged the women, mistakenly believing a member of the government was besieged in a neighbouring building, tried to make a sortie and, as a result, were taken prisoner. Subsequently the most lurid stories were told as some of them claimed to have suffered a fate 'worse than death'.[349] However, sources sympathetic to the Bolsheviks claim that they simply went back to the camp from which they had come.[350]

Bochkareva herself returned to her native Tomsk, though whether to set up fresh women's battalions for fighting against the Bolsheviks, or in order to retire into private life, is not clear. By that time she was something of a celebrity and articles about her had appeared in the British and American press. Disguised as a Red Cross nurse, in April 1918 she left Russia for the US by way of Vladivostok. In New York she fell in with Emmeline (not Sylvia, as one source erroneously claims) Pankhurst. Regarding her as 'a Russian Jeanne d'Arc', Ms Pankhurst engaged a ghost-writer by the name of Don Levin to whom she dictated her memoirs.[351] Not knowing English and being practically illiterate in Russian as well, Bochkareva herself could neither read nor correct the book. It was published the next year and is composed in an operatic, not to say histrionic, style. It describes her adventures as 'Yashka' (the name of her second spouse, and the one she chose for herself during her service in the tsar's army) down to October/November 1917. At this time, after she had allegedly quarrelled with Lenin and Trotsky, they ordered her to be pushed from a moving train.

From New York Bochkareva went to Washington DC where she was intro-duced to President Wilson and tried to make him increase US aid to the Russian 'Whites'. Next she crossed the Atlantic to England where she met

King George V with a similar message. September 1918 found her back in Archangelsk. There she tried to raise another female 'battalion of death' to fight against the Bolsheviks, but apparently without success; in the end, to get rid of her, the British commander on the spot (and future chief of the Army General Staff, General Ironside) gave her 500 roubles and a ticket home.[352] In November 1919 she had just arrived in Omsk and was again trying to raise women soldiers when the town was occupied by the Bolsheviks. She was arrested by the Checka and accused of having worked for the White Commander Alexander Kolchak. To save her life, during her interrogation she minimized her military contribution to the counter-revolutionary cause, forgetting all about the train episode and claiming that the Whites had merely been using her name. On 16 May 1920, after an abridged 'trial', the thirty-one-year-old Bochkareva was executed.[353]

During the Russian Civil War female Communist Party functionaries, the most important of whom was Lenin's associate (and Stalin's reputed mistress) Alexandra Kollentai, had much to say concerning the need to reach out to women so as to make them join in the revolutionary struggle.[354] In practice, though, little came of these schemes and women only made up 2–3 per cent of the Red Army. Out of 50,000–70,000 who served, virtually all did so as nurses, secretaries and in food preparation;[355] yet some authors have claimed that the Bolshevik mobilization of women was 'a legendary success'.[356] After the Civil War ended the vast majority of Red women followed their sisters in other countries and went home. A few stayed on, but mainly for propaganda reasons and as symbols of what the new regime was prepared to do for the second sex.

Returning to the non-Communist world, during the inter-war period the various women's corps ceased to exist. This was not because they had not proven themselves; within the narrow limits that had been set for them, British and American women served faithfully enough and did at least as well as the men. As an American officer, Major Everett S. Hughes, wrote in 1928: 'if the need for women's service be great enough, they may go any place, live anywhere, under any conditions.'[357] He might have added that they can also do most jobs associated with modern armed forces. Unlike their predecessors until the middle of the nineteenth century, the latter are not simple and consist largely of vast 'tails'. This was carried to the point where, in the Second World War, only about 25 per cent of all the troops in the US Army were expected to fight, weapon in hand, as their primary occupation.

The problem, though, was that women were not needed. They were not needed in Britain and the US (and Germany), both of which did away with conscription and went back to small, all-volunteer, professional forces. They were even less needed in other countries which, thanks to conscription, had all the manpower they could use free of charge. Some, notably Italy, even suffered from a surplus of manpower since the under-developed state of their industries did not enable them to provide all their troops with modern weapons;[358] countries such as Poland, Romania, Yugoslavia and Greece also entered the Second World War with large, but badly under-equipped, infantry forces. These explanations are *ex post facto*. At the time nobody, least of all feminists, had hit on the idea that women could not be free and equal unless they served in the one human institution that is most hierarchical and which, prison apart, allows its members the least freedom.

In the Second World War, the country that made the most extensive use of women was Finland. The Finnish women's organization was founded in 1924; its members were known as Lottas, after the heroine (real or imaginary) of a famous patriotic poem who went under the name of Lotta Vraede and who assisted soldiers during the brief campaign of 1808. From the time the 'Winter War' broke out in November 1939 to Finland's surrender late in 1944, approximately 150,000 Finnish women served (compared with 600,000 men). Though excluded from combat, they were active as drivers, communicators, administrators, and also in relief work. A total of 681 of them died, including 113 who were killed by enemy action. So successful was the organization that Hitler summoned its leader, Ms Fanni Luukonen, to Berlin in order to present her with a medal for her 'outstanding contribution to the fight against Bolshevism'. Himmler, too, expressed his admiration for the Finnish women and sought to set up a similar organization to assist his SS. When Stalin finally forced Finland to its knees, he paid the Lottas the back-handed compliment of ordering their organization dissolved.[359]

Among the major powers, the leader was once again Britain where preparations for mobilizing women began as early as 1936. The French high command only recognized female 'auxiliary workers' on 21 May 1940, when its forces were on the verge of collapse;[360] later in the same year de Gaulle set up a female division of the Free French Forces, modelled on the British ATS.[361] Next came the USSR which, as the country with the largest population among the main belligerents, also mobilized the largest number of women. The United States followed soon after Pearl Harbor. Nazi ideology may explain why Germany acted slowly and hesitantly; in so far as this attitude pre-dated 1933, an even larger role was probably played by the German Army's exceptionally high social status and its leaders' reluctance to put that status at risk. In 1943–5 even Mussolini compromised his vaunted Fascist virility and tried to raise female soldiers to defend his German-dominated, much-truncated, *Republica sociale italiana*.[362] Finally, the Japanese were even more reluctant than the Germans to put women into uniform,[363] probably for similar reasons.

Though the numbers involved were much larger, on the whole British women served on terms similar to those of the First World War. As in the First World War, they were asked to volunteer. The response cannot have been too enthusiastic, for early in 1942 a proposal was made to conscript women aged twenty to thirty; however, it was never implemented.[364] Women comprised 2.27 per cent of all uniformed personnel in December 1939, 9.39 per cent in September 1943 (the peak) and 8.2 per cent when the war ended; the largest absolute number served in March 1944, when the forces had 450,500 women. This time women were able to receive commissions. Their status was that of non-combatants and they received two-thirds of men's pay; on the other hand, when they deserted they were simply allowed to go. Pregnancy proved a bigger problem than in the First World War, and pregnant women were given a compassionate discharge.

As in the First World War, each of the services had its own women's corps. The army divided its women into eighty MOS (Military Occupation

Specialities), including clerks, technicians, communicators, cooks, orderlies, drivers and anti-aircraft personnel – the latter a great innovation about which more in a moment. Air force women served in transport, mechanics, repair, communications, coding, parachute repair, cooking, photography and radar among others. Some women flew aircraft from one base to another inside Britain, an important job that could also be dangerous owing to difficult flying conditions and the fear of being shot at by friendly anti-aircraft batteries. Others served in anti-aircraft balloon units where they greatly outnumbered men; another branch dominated by women was the military canteen service.[365] Finally, Royal Navy women differed from the rest in that they did not enjoy military status. They were employed as drivers, clerks, housekeepers and communicators but were not allowed aboard ships, let alone combat ships. Of the total number of women in the British military 624 were killed, 98 went missing, 744 were wounded, and 20 were captured, most of them while serving as nurses in various theatres of war.

Even before Pearl Harbor, the US witnessed talk of some kind of obligatory service for women. However, the plans failed to make it through Congress. To quote Congressman Somers (D,NY): 'A women's army to defend the United States of America! Think of the humiliation. What has become of the manhood of America, that we have to call on our women to do what has ever been the duty of men?'[366] In the end it was decided to rely on volunteers, enabling each service to set up its women's corps. Once again, the women who chose to enlist were much better educated than the average American, male or female. Their motives are said to have included desire for escape, search of adventure, economic need and patriotism. As with male volunteers throughout the ages, on occasion patriotism probably served as a cover for other, less disinterested motives, but the extent to which this was true is not clear.[367]

This time there was no question of simply putting women into uniform and making them sit behind a military instead of a civilian desk. Instead each service established a regular, if separate, organization for women headed by a female commander and a female staff. Women's bases were established and the recruits given at least some instruction, starting with drill: one woman later commented that the army taught her that if she saw 'it' she should neither avoid 'it' nor try to skip 'it' but step straight into 'it'. Then came physical training, military courtesy and customs (if only because of the rules concerning fraternization, the women had to be able to tell an officer from an enlisted soldier and, if possible, a general from a lieutenant), and, of course, endless 'why we fight' type classes and films. Some women also received professional training in the fields for which they had been earmarked, and indeed it was in the hope of receiving such training that some of them enlisted.

Possibly because of the puritanical streak in the national character, the American public was less open-minded than the British one and less prepared to see its women wear uniform. To a greater extent than in any other country were the morals of servicewomen questioned and they themselves made the subject of sexual innuendo. The ridicule went on and on; much to the surprise of visiting British and Soviet female military personnel, who were sent over for propaganda purposes, press conferences tended to degenerate into questions concerning women's outerwear and underwear.[368] Military women got a bad name – through no fault of their own, as statistics concerning pregnancy clearly showed.[369] These attitudes translated into questionnaires which showed that, among male soldiers, a majority would not advise their own womenfolk to enlist. A greater majority thought women could make themselves more useful by working for the war industries; most disturbing of all, soldiers based in the proximity of women's corps were even less enthusiastic than the rest.[370]

These problems distracted the commanders of the various women's corps. They found themselves compelled to devote much attention to public relations and avoid anything that might reek of promiscuity or lesbianism, for example, while the military overlooked the promiscuity of men, women accused of it might be dishonourably discharged.[371] Bad publicity may help explain why, though America's population was three times as large as Britain's, both proportionally and in absolute terms the number of US women who wore uniform was much smaller. The total stood at 350,000. No more than 120,000 served at any one time, which means that turnover was high and wastage huge. At peak, women formed 2.3 per cent of all US military personnel.[372]

Of course, America's manpower needs were much less urgent than those of Britain. Thus, in early 1944, the pool of American males aged eighteen to thirty-eight was estimated at 22 million, whereas the armed services only numbered about 10 million.[373] These facts both explain why relatively few American women heeded the call to enlist and prove that they were not really essential. Even if they had been essential, they could have performed the vast majority of the jobs they did perform as civilians. For example, the German Wehrmacht and Waffen SS between them employed over 450,000 civilian female auxiliary workers on tasks roughly similar to those performed by British and American woman soldiers; some even served in the Reich's anti-aircraft defence system where their task was to direct fighter pilots to their targets. Most of the women in question were deployed inside greater Germany, but some were assigned to the occupied territories. Of the latter, at least some witnessed anti-Jewish and other atrocities and, to the extent that they handled the relevant paperwork, participated in them.[374] Since Hitler, as already noted, strongly opposed the recruitment of female warriors,[375] it was only in the last desperate days of the War that a few women were put in uniform. Ten years later, the fate that these and other German women suffered at the hands of the victorious Red Army persuaded the government in Bonn not to repeat the experiment when the Bundeswehr was formed.[376]

In the US Army, which also included the air force, 608 (out of approximately 800) Military Occupation Specialities were non-combat. Of these 406 were officially open to women; in practice women were concentrated in 146 MOS, a situation that was to be repeated in many post-1945 armed forces.[377] Some 800 women who had a pilot's licence flew aircraft (including combat aircraft) from one base to another. Many worked in maintenance, intelligence, logistic support, as flight instructors (in link simulators) or as parachute-folders.[378] As in other countries, the vast majority worked either in health care or in one of the countless offices without which no modern armed force can exist. As in other countries, too, women tended to be assigned to clerical work simply because they were women, regardless of any other qualifications they might have.[379] Some of the objections to the use of women in 'non-traditional' slots came from the women who, like US Army Colonel Oveta Hobby, were in charge of the women's corps. Having been a newspaper proprietor in private life, Colonel Hobby understood public relations. She feared, probably with reason, that putting women into such slots would make people question their femininity, which in turn might reflect on the number of volunteers.[380]

The largest single concentration of offices, and therefore of women, was in Washington DC. That apart, women were scattered all over the country. At peak, 17,000 women served overseas of whom about two-thirds were located in Europe and the rest in the Pacific theatre. No woman was permitted to carry weapons, but this did not prevent a few hundred from dying by air attack or after being torpedoed at sea; six died at Anzio when their hospital was bombed. Women caused few disciplinary problems – partly, no doubt, because those who did cause them were often discharged – and are said to have done well in all theatres.[381] However, they could also be a nuisance to commanders. Some complained that the services' 'no fraternization' policy put male officers out of bounds and condemned enlisted women to date a lower class of men than would otherwise be the case. When women were allowed to mix freely with the much larger number of men and suffered from sexual harassment, they complained. When they were secluded for their own protection, they also complained.[382]

This brings us to the vexed question of women in combat. According to one set of statistics,[383] 4.7 per cent of American servicewomen in the second World War had been 'in or near combat zones', 3.5 per cent had been fired upon, but only 2 per cent had been in 'serious combat', in other words were injured themselves and/or saw other Americans being killed and wounded. Except for the episode at Bataan early in the war, no women were taken prisoner. The explanation is that almost all women – including those who had been in 'serious combat' – were situated way behind the front. They got their experience by being subjected to bombing rather than to artillery or small-arms fire.

The only American women who came even close to handling weapons

were those who, in the middle of 1943, participated in an army-run experiment designed to see whether they could operate in anti-aircraft units. The
experiment is said to have been a great success as women actually did better than men. However, General Marshal as chief of staff agreed with Colonel
Hobby that American public opinion was not ready for 'masculine' women;
consequently the results of the experiment were classified as secret and the
unit itself disbanded.[384] The experience of other countries was entirely different. In Britain preparations for using women for anti-aircraft work started
in 1938 when General Frederick Pile, commander of Britain's ground anti-
aircraft defences, asked Caroline Haslett, an engineer and expert on women's
labour, to advise him on whether women could replace men in the gun
crews. She answered that they could do all tasks except the heavy work in
loading, manoeuvring, and firing the guns. Pile himself could see no reason why they could not fire the guns too; however, aware of the prejudices
to be overcome, he preferred to let the issue rest.[385]

Early on, the idea of using women to operate anti-aircraft batteries received
some negative publicity which was overcome when Winston Churchill
announced that his daughter, Margaret, would gladly serve in one. Next it was
necessary to overcome the opposition of the women who were in charge of
the ATS, or Auxiliary Territorial Service, as the women's corps was known.
No more than any other bureaucrats did they want to surrender their personnel, especially to male commanders; in Pile's words, they were prepared
to help the army, but only on their own terms and as they thought fit.[386] The
first mixed batteries became operational in August 1941 when one was stationed in Richmond Park, near London. It promptly became one of the
wonders of the world as gaping crowds came to see women marching, eating, drilling and working with men.[387]

The typical mixed battery consisted of 189 men and 299 women; eventually 70 per cent of all ATS recruits went to mixed batteries, with a peak
of 57,000 employed in operational duties in 1943. While there were some ups
and downs, by late 1944 Anti-Aircraft Command had more women than
men. They were employed as spotters, predictors, height finders, radio loca-
tors, radar and searchlight operators – in short, in every job short of loading

the guns and firing them; as the war went on even this difference largely disappeared since more and more batteries were fired by remote control. In point of camaraderie and cohesion the mixed batteries were as good as all-male combat units if not better. Some men griped, others tried and sometimes succeeded in having sex with the women, but it is said that neither phenomenon constituted a serious problem. Women worked with men, behaved as courageously as men, and, coming under attack, showed they knew how to die just like men.[388]

Like the remaining belligerents, during the Second World War the Soviet Union conscripted men but not women. As in other countries many Soviet women volunteered until the 'titanic figure'[389] of 800,000 was reached; to this should be added 200,000 uniformed nurses (and another 600,000 nurses who served without uniform),[390] giving a total of approximately 1 million. Now it so happens that, at the beginning of the German invasion in June 1941, the Soviet Union had 5.3 million men (and hardly any women) under arms.[391] During the next four years another 29.4 million people were called up or served as volunteers, which gives a total of 34.7 million[392] Thus, the Red Army that defeated Hitler (over 75 per cent of all German soldiers who died in the war lost their lives on the Eastern Front) was over 97 per cent male. Women's share in it was only slightly higher than in the US armed forces. It was also comparable to the German figure which stood at 2.3 per cent: 450,000 (civilian) women out of 19,150,000 people of both sexes. So much for the global picture.

At this point, the contradictions start. One researcher claims that 300,000 Soviet women served in anti-aircraft units where, as in Britain, they performed all tasks except loading and firing the guns.[393] Two others explain that 500,000 'actually served at the front either in combat or support roles' and that 'Komsomol women trained about a quarter of a million young women' in the use of various weapons.[394] Assuming there is no overlap, then these three categories must have comprised 31 per cent more female combatants than there ever were female soldiers (exclusive of nurses). If Soviet women did in fact participate in combat then their casualty rate must have been miraculously low, for when the war ended they still numbered

1 million.[395] To cut a long story short, judging from feminist-inspired Western writings about the subject one might conclude that, in Stalin's Soviet Union during what was probably the most murderous war in history, men sat behind typewriters while women fought.

The truth of the matter was apparently as follows. As we saw, the Russian Revolution resembled others in that women were relatively prominent both among the rank and file and among the so-called Commissars. Once the Civil War had ended and reconstruction got under way the regime, determined to show that the human personality is shaped by social factors rather than by biological ones, tried to 'solve' the woman question by eradicating the differences between them and men. To raise production it sent millions of women into paid work, including 'non-traditional' jobs such as driving tractors. Needless to say they also continued to do housework, which double burden eventually caused the birth rate to collapse.[396] Partly because of these policies, partly because of the desperate straits to which the country was reduced during the early years of the war, the claim that the Soviet Union trained many more women in the use of weapons than other belligerents rings true; pictures published during the inter-war years often showed heroic women, rifle in hand, prepared to defend the Socialist motherland. Still, even if 220,000 of them did in fact pass through 'sniper school'[397] this does not prove they actually saw combat. Hundreds of thousands of women serving in the Israel Defence Force also received some weapons training, as they still do. However, since the middle of 1948 hardly any of them have fought.[398]

In any case, the 220,000–250,000 'young women' who are said to have received weapons training only made up 0.7 per cent of all uniformed Red Army personnel; it is thus clear that, even if we count the 300,000 who served in anti-aircraft units as combatants, and assuming there was no overlap, women's share in the Soviet combat arms was absolutely minuscule. The relatively small number of women explains, and is explained by, the fact that the Red Army was not ready for them; at the start of the German invasion, it did not even have female underwear in store. Only in 1943 were the first gynaecological services established, and only towards the end of the war were suitable female uniforms designed and issued.[399] If women were often highly visible – a few were sent out on speaking tours in the West – this was due mainly to propaganda reasons.

As in all other armies, most Soviet women served in various logistic slots as cooks, laundresses (throughout the war, most laundry seems to have been done by hand), secretaries, communicators, drivers and the like. At a time when millions upon millions of men were driven into combat as a matter of course, women had to 'earnestly beg' to participate, or else 'earn the right in some other way',[400] which probably explains why, the anti-aircraft defence system apart, fighting women only formed a single regiment,[401] presumably of snipers. The Germans, who had previous experience with them from the First World War and also in their own country during the troubled years after 1918, called them *Flintenweiber*, literally 'musket-women', also meaning 'hard women'; not knowing whether to treat them as women or as soldiers, they hated their guts.[402] Some Soviet women acted as radio operators, and a few commanded tanks.[403]

Even so, in the entire Red Army there was only one woman who operated a heavy tank; among combat engineers, the presence of a female officer was considered sufficiently rare for her to be introduced to a visiting general.[404] Most of the women who did fight apparently received their assignments during the early years when people of both sexes flocked to volunteer and the prevailing chaos led units to take anyone they could. After 1942, except for partisan units, they largely disappeared. In part, this was because of the improving military situation; in part, it was because many of the original ones had been killed; in part, because the physical effort was so great that many of them became invalids. As one women recalled: 'we were all sick ... all of us are still [*c.* 1980] sick ... the female body is not built for such hardships ... the war not only robbed us of our youth, it has also kept many of us from having children as the greatest female happiness of all.'[405] In the end, out of 11,700 Heroes of the Soviet Union who emerged from the war, 86, or 0.7 per cent, were women.[406] Accidentally or not, this corresponds very closely to the number who had received 'weapons training'.

Finally, there was one aspect of the Soviet experience that had no equivalent in any other country: the use of women as combat fliers. Like so many of the sources on which the present book is based, the most important English-language account of this episode must be treated with caution.[407] It claims to be based entirely on interviews with ex-female pilots, which were conducted in Russia in 1990–92; however, internal evidence makes it clear that some of the 'interviewed' women had died decades previously. Other information came not from the women themselves but from reports about them in the Soviet press. Out of sixty-nine women whose accounts are given at first or second hand, some were not pilots but served as aircraft mechanics or else as parachute-folders and thus did work no different from those of their counterparts in the West. Yet there is no question that the USSR in the Second World War did have female pilots. Unlike their Western colleagues who (through no fault of their own, needless to say) only ferried aircraft behind the front, they did fly in combat.

The idea of training and using female pilots in war was first raised by a certain Marina Raskova, a famous pilot, holder of a non-stop distance flying record for women, and recipient of a medal at Stalin's hands. The time was October 1941; in the words of one veteran: 'I think that at that time we didn't need this women's detachment, because 1941 was an awful time for the Soviet army and people. The Fascist army was eighteen kilometers from Moscow … Even men pilots wasted their time because there were not enough aircraft for all of them [early in the War the Red Air Force had lost no fewer than 8,000 planes, amounting to perhaps one half of its strength; however, since most had been destroyed on the ground the pilots survived]. To some extent it was a kind of propagandist action, but still we were most happy that we joined the army.'[408]

The trainees themselves were a mixed lot. In the interviews they explained their reasons for wanting to become pilots. In most cases it was a question of studying for a profession, 'achieving something in life',[409] and doing something for one's country. Occasionally it was the country that selected them without further ado; particularly if they already had had something to do with aviation. Many had been active in the field before the war, maintaining aircraft or else gaining flying experience as radio operators and navigators. Some already held civilian pilots' licences and, to gain admittance into the Red Army's flying school, claimed many more flying hours than they actually possessed. Finally, most were single but a few were married and had children.

The upshot was three air regiments, 125th Bomber, 46th Guard Bomber, and 586th Fighter. Initially all three consisted of women only, but as losses mounted two out of the three became mixed.[410] Raskova herself commanded the first; however, after she was killed in an air crash in 1943 all three were commanded by men. As her successor, Major Valentin Markov, explained: 'during the war there was no difference between this regiment and any male regiments. We lived in dugouts, as did the other regiments, and flew on the same missions, not more or less dangerous. It's hard to fancy how difficult the conditions were for these women. There should be two toilets at least, for men and women. We had only one! All the crews had almost the same number of combat missions. Almost all of these women were shot down, and after hospitalization they came back to the regiment and flew bravely.'[411] However, Markov felt an injustice had been done as relatively few of his women were decorated; a feeling that several of them shared.

Were women fit for air warfare? The answer is yes, within limits. They certainly took part in it, flying all kinds of missions, running into anti-aircraft fire and sometimes enemy aircraft, shooting down some, and being shot down in turn; one source claims that casualty rates approached 75 per cent and that the women were considered expendable.[412] Like their male comrades, female pilots who were shot down and who reached the ground safely tried to make their way back to friendly lines and rejoin their regiments to fight another day. German records tell of a female pilot who shot herself to avoid capture;[413] another was wounded, captured, and sent to prisoner-of-war camp where she was apparently treated no differently from the rest.[414] Some women felt that, to avoid being looked down upon, they had to do better than any man.[415] One, Senior Lieutenant Nadezha Popova, once flew eighteen missions in a single night.[416]

On the other hand, there was no gainsaying the fact that the women were smaller than men and physically not as strong. They had trouble handling the controls of the Pe-2 light bomber that equipped two out of three regiments, forcing them to turn in some strange performances during take-off and landing.[417] More seriously, contemporary aircraft were not pressurized – some, in fact, had open cockpits – and pressure suits were unknown. This did not matter so much on bombing missions, at least as long as they did not come under attack and were not forced to engage in evasive manoeu-vring. However, the diving, turning and twisting of air-to-air combat would often cause blood to come out of the pilots' ears. Women suffered from the problem more than men did. On average they were able to fly fewer missions per twenty-four-hour period than did men, with the result that their aircraft remained under-utilized.

The women themselves had mixed feelings. One, Klaudia Pankratova, had piloted fighters and shot down a German JU-88. She had 'a strong belief that it doesn't matter whether it is a woman or a man at the controls; a woman can be a military pilot, she can fulfill combat missions if a misfortune like war falls upon the heads of the people of a country.'[418] Others were less sure. 'Our entire organism had to make such a rough adjustment that, throughout the war, we ceased being women. None of us had her period … and after the war not all could have children.'[419] 'The very nature of a woman rejects the idea of fighting. A woman is born to give birth to children … Flying combat missions is against our nature. Only the tragedy of our country made us join the army, to help our country, to help our people … To be in the army in crucial periods is one thing, but to want to be in the military is not quite natural for a woman. I think American women have the idea of romanticism connected with being in the military, and it leads them to want to be a part of it. That is probably because they have not fought a battle in their own country for a hundred years and don't know the nature of war.'[420] 'War is not a female profession, but we were defending the liberty and freedom of our country.'[421] 'I do not think women should make combat flights at all; I think a woman should remain a woman. Com-bat is not for a woman.'[422] 'When I was young … I was convinced it was a job for a woman to fly combat. In those times our only thought was to defend the motherland, to save the country. I didn't think of it as emotional and phys-ical pressure. I had become a pilot before the war and it was only natural for me to become a military pilot. Now I realize that the stress was very great and that it is not a female job.'[423] These reflections came forty-five years later. Their author, Captain Valentina Volkova-Tikonova, logged 518 combat flying hours.

Be this as it may, one thing the women did not do was press for feminist goals; they joined as Soviet citizens whose country was in danger, not as women seeking 'liberation'. Nor did they complain about sexual harassment. One pilot recalled how a general tried to bed her but was rebuffed.[424] Another said she was glad to serve with women because 'men are men and women are women; I was more comfortable.'[425] For the rest, 'everyone was so friendly, so helpful.'[426] Far from denying or concealing their sex, as so many female warriors did throughout history, the women did what they could to make themselves pretty and attractive; they all liked to knit and to embroider,[427] and indeed in the parcels destined for them the place of tobacco was taken by thread.[428] Once (only once?) a man put a hand to a woman's breast, but it was an accident.[429] Some commanders were hard, but they were hard on everybody.[430] Men watched their language when addressing women.[431] Amidst immense death and destruction, nobody had time to bother with 'gender issues'. Contrary to the present situation in many Western armed forces, there were no rules against fraternization. Many a love affair took place and was consummated. From Markov down, some men married women of their regiments. Others who were already married lived with so-called 'campaign wives' in liaisons that lasted as long as the war did.[432]

At the time he replaced the deceased Raskova, Markov himself was already a very experienced pilot. He took his assignment 'like a cold shower', and at first found it hard to discipline the women. Later, having learned everything possible about 'female problems', things improved and they came to admire and like him. 'Of course,' he said, 'there is a specific approach to the command of a female regiment, some peculiar features. You should be delicate when you are treating with the women, you should use your ears like radars.'[433] Apparently the fact that he had commanded women who in turn flew obsolescent aircraft did not damage his career, for after the war he remained in the air force and finally retired as a lieutenant general.

Once the two sides had become used to each other Markov grew as proud of his regiment as the women were fond of him. 'The women in my regiment were self-disciplined, careful, and obedient to orders; they respected the truth and fair treatment towards them. They never whimpered and never complained and were very courageous. If I compare my experience of commanding the male and female regiments, to some extent at the end of the war it was easier for me to command this female regiment. They had the strong spirit of a collective unit [due to being exceptional, no doubt] which is still manifested in our reunion day.'[434] When the war was over most of the women left the forces. Among the mechanics, 'all changed careers. None went back to it. They found it was too heavy work for women.'[435] Some stayed in civil aviation, some switched to other professions, and most got married. Apparently most of the women either left voluntarily or were invalidated for health reasons. However, at least one felt that '[when] it came to who should retire it was not the men, of course.'[436]

Allowing for the singularly desperate circumstances, in many ways the military experience of Soviet women in the Second World War was like that of their sisters in other countries. In proportion to the size of the armed forces neither more nor less of them served than was the case in the United States and Germany (where they did not wear uniform).[437] As in other countries the vast majority of Soviet women who were mobilized worked in administration, health care and food preparation. More than in other countries many of them were pushed into, or else volunteered for, field units.[438] The presence of Soviet women far forward probably both reflects and is reflected by the fact that some of them received at least some weapons training during their Komsomol days (elsewhere, none did). Some, however, went through Red Army training and participated in the fighting. They did so mainly at their own request, mainly as snipers, and mainly during the desperate early years when not only the fate of the Soviet Union as a state but the physical survival of its people hung in the balance. Finally, Soviet women formed about 10 per cent of the partisan units. Judging by analogy with other revolutionary movements such as the Yugoslav and Israeli ones, among them again probably only a minority fought weapon in hand.

A phenomenon unique to the Soviet Union was the use of female pilots in combat. However, they only numbered around a thousand. It therefore appears that, compared with the size of either the armed forces or the population, actually fewer Soviet women flew for the Red Army than did British and American ones for their respective armed forces; while other Soviet women may have ferried aircraft, I was unable to find a record of their doing so. What percentage of all Soviet pilots were women is unknown. However, the Soviet Union produced approximately 137,000 military aircraft during the war.[439] Supposing an absolute minimum of one pilot per aircraft, female ones probably amounted to about 0.7 per cent. Thus, in the air as well as on the ground, to claim that Soviet women performed a 'titanic' task in combat is going a little too far.

This was all the more so because, in the air as well as on the ground, physiological limitations meant that women's performance was not quite up to par. Possibly for this reason, the aircraft they were given to fly were obsolescent, made of wood and liable to be shot down by any German soldier with a rifle.[440] To escape the Luftwaffe's attention they were forced to operate mainly under cover of darkness,[441] which explains why their German enemies called them 'fly-by-night witches'. Operating by night, their aim was poor and they were substantially limited to *Stoerungsangriffe*, or 'harassment'. Conversely those women who, heroically, flew their obsolescent aircraft by daylight were sometimes turned into sitting ducks. At least two female pilots were told by their ex-enemies – Romanian pilots – that they would have been shot down; however, being recognized as women their lives were spared.[442] It is of course possible that the Romanians, who had just changed sides, were trying to ingratiate themselves with their new Soviet allies and masters. Yet the women in question, one Galina Burdina and one Nina Slovokhtova, would scarcely have told the stories forty-five years later if they had not believed them to have been true.

Within the above limits, and thanks in large part to the fact that the women considered themselves soldiers first and women second, the experiment was a success (though not such a great success as to prevent their regiments from being disbanded after the war). And why not?

15 The Weakness of Women

The above categories do not exhaust all the things that women have done in war. In particular, it is necessary to mention the use of women for intelligence purposes. Already the ancient Chinese military texts suggest that 'the tools for self-destruction – such as wine, women, and fascinating rarities' – be employed to bring down the enemy.[443] The story of the most famous female spy of all, Mata Hari, turns out to have been based on myth; the same is true of many other female agents who allegedly exchanged military secrets for sexual favours.[444] Still, from the British in Northern Ireland,[445] to Vietnam, where women working first for the French and then for the Americans often spied on them as well,[446] armies often used female agents. Most women (and many men) working for intelligence probably did so in perfect safety, by performing secretarial tasks, compiling indexes, or operating code-breaking machines at Bletchley Park during the Second World War; however, some probably had occasion to make use of the arms that they carried for self-defence. For example, in 1917 the Ottoman authorities in Palestine arrested a Jewish Palestinian woman, Sarah Aronson, for espionage. Between one torture session and the next she was given permission to go home and wash; getting there, she pulled out a pistol and shot herself.

Next it is necessary to consider situations in which women (along with men) endured sieges, as often happened from ancient times on; as well as others in which they (also along with men) came under air attack, as often happened in the last century. Perhaps the largest siege of all was that of Leningrad which lasted from 1941 to 1944 and cost the lives of up to a million people, including many women. From London during the Blitz to Hamburg and Dresden and Tokyo, air attacks sometimes turned entire metropolitan areas into seas of flame in which tens of thousands of women, as well as men, perished. Except for fighting in strict self-defence after everything had already been lost women seldom took an active part in defending besieged towns;[447] instead they supported their menfolk by bringing up supplies, dressing the wounded, and so on. In or out of uniform, women coming under air attack often helped organize civil defences, rescue and evacuation services, and the like. In these roles, there is no reason to believe that they endured and died less (or more) bravely than men.

To a large extent, the fact that most women did not actively participate in war was dictated by their life cycle. This is because, at most times and places, women were married off long before they reached military age. Arrian in his biography of Alexander claims that Indian girls were considered marriageable at the age of seven.[448] In Greece, Rome, Byzantium, China, Japan, ninth-century Provence, and fourteenth-century Ghent women were wedded during their early to mid teens.[449] Among Hindus and Muslims, teenage marriage persists to the present day; Iranian mullahs have even proclaimed that it is fit for a woman to have her first period in her husband's home.

Historically speaking, the only important exception to the rule is the so-called 'European marriage pattern'. In reality only Western Europe was involved; it did not include the Balkans, much of which was under Ottoman control between 1500 and 1900. How and why that pattern established itself is by no means clear; however that may be, even in the 2 or 3 per cent of the earth's land surface called Western Europe, and even according to those who date the change to the period before the Black Death, the vast majority of women were married during their late teens or early twenties (if they lived in the countryside); or their early to mid twenties (if they lived in the towns).[450]

Once a woman had been wedded pregnancy could be expected to follow quickly; after a mere two months in the case of upper-class French women during the second half of the nineteenth century.[451] Often the sequence was reversed and marriage took place *after* conception. It is estimated that, in England between 1550 and 1850, a third of all brides went to the altar while pregnant; in the US between 1760 and 1800 the proportion was similar.[452] Nor were these high figures necessarily due to lack of foresight. Particularly in rural settings, pre-nuptial sex was often deliberately engaged in and even encouraged as a form of trial marriage so as to see whether the couple would be fertile. In this connection it should not be forgotten that, until the onset and subsequent spread of the Industrial Revolution in the second half of the eighteenth century, well over 90 per cent of all people have always lived in rural settings.

At 350 extra calories a day pregnancy makes extremely heavy demands on the body. At 550 extra calories a day the demands of lactation are even heavier, approximating those of a female marathon runner in training[453] and ruling out heavy physical work. Lactation also acts as a natural contraceptive. Therefore it was often prolonged for as long as possible; once a child was weaned, another pregnancy could be expected after a short interval so that menstruation itself was a relatively rare phenomenon.[454] Being either pregnant or lactant, most women would be kept busy most of the time. Among hunter-gatherers, women used to breast-feed their children for as much as three years before becoming pregnant again during the fourth.[455] However, the advent of agriculture and permanent settlements caused the length of the cycle to be cut. Beginning in the Neolithic era, women could expect to give birth every second year,[456] as was still the case in the relatively advanced society of eighteenth-century America.[457]

Married women in early twentieth-century Russia were even more fertile than their American sisters, giving birth to two children every three and a half years on average.[458] In most Latin American countries (Argentina and Uruguay alone excepted) down to the mid 1960s a typical woman could expect to have five to seven children during her lifetime.[459] Other countries changed even more slowly. In 1976 the average Jordanian woman could expect to bear eight or nine children.[460] In Bangladesh, as late as 1985 a woman could expect to have two children by the time she was twenty-four, three or four by the time she was thirty, and five by the time she was thirty-five years old;[461] attempts to introduce contraception met with resistance by enraged husbands as well as the clergy. Assuming a woman had been married at fifteen, the normal age, this means that, at any one time during the next twenty years, she would have at least one child no more than four years old to look after.

In all mammalian species it is mainly the females who look after the young.[462] Human offspring require to be carried, fed, and looked after for a proportionally longer period than those of any other mammalians. Hence women found it hard to leave their children even for the comparatively short period needed to carry out a raid on a neighbouring tribe, let alone for an extended campaign. Having somebody else mind the children might solve the problem of individual women. Both because they could pay and because they often had more relatives suitable for the task, most of them belonged to the upper classes:[463] but substituting one woman for another could not change the fact that most of them remained tied to the home. Even in today's developed societies it is mostly women who look after small children, whether their own or, in day-care centres and kindergartens, those of others. Here and there attempts have been made to solve the problem by means of collective child-rearing. However, they only appeal to those who have not tried it by living on an Israeli kibbutz.[464]

The other reason why women have traditionally been absent from the battlefield is, of course, their relative physical weakness. From the time that humans first evolved[465] males have been considerably larger and stronger than females; indeed some biologists believe that nature has made them stronger in order that they may fight.[466] Over the last twenty years, studies found that the average US female army recruit was 12 centimetres shorter, 14.3 kilograms lighter, had 16.9 fewer kilograms of muscle, and 2.6 more kilograms of fat than the average male recruit.[467] She had only 55 per cent of the upper body strength and 72 per cent of the lower body strength of the average male. Since fat mass is inversely related to aerobic capacity and heat tolerance, women are also at a significant disadvantage when performing aerobic activities such as marching with heavy loads and working in the heat; as it happened, the very first woman ever to be admitted to the Citadel, a military school in South Carolina, soon dropped out because of heat exhaustion. At high altitudes, women's handicap is such that it may affect their ability to reproduce.[468] Finally, even when the experiments were controlled for height, women only had 80 per cent of the strength of men. Overall, only the upper 20 per cent of women can do as well, physically, as the lower 20 per cent of men.

Thanks to the 'superior ability of men to add muscle to their bodies',[469] intensive training, far from diminishing the physical differences between the sexes, tends to increase them still further.[470] After eight weeks of such training male plebes at West Point demonstrated 32 per cent more power in the lower body and performed 48 per cent more work at the leg press than female ones. At the bench press, the men demonstrated 270 per cent more power and performed 473 per cent more work than the women. One biologist claims that, if the hundred strongest individuals were to be selected out of a random group consisting of one hundred men and one hundred women, then ninety-three would be male and only seven female.[471] Another has calculated that only the upper 5 per cent of women are as strong as the median male.[472]

Morphologically, too, women are less well adapted to war. Thinner skulls, lighter bone ridges and weaker jawbones provide them with less protection against blows.[473] Many women develop large, pendulous breasts that impede movement and require special protection; as of early 1999 it was reported that the problem of designing brassieres which would be both attractive and comfortable to wear was preoccupying the British Army.[474] Shorter arms make it harder for women to draw weapons from their scabbards, stab with them, and throw them; to say nothing of the possibility that a different brain structure renders them less adept at guiding or intercepting projectiles.[475] Women's legs are also shorter and, being set at a different angle, less suitable both for sprinting and for running long distances; tests among ROTC cadets showed 78 per cent of men, but only 6 per cent of women, could run 2 miles in under 14 minutes.[476] All the above mentioned tests have been made on young, childless women. Once a woman has given birth the difference in pelvic structure becomes even more noticeable; in fact it is one of the characteristics that enable palaeontologists to differentiate male skeletons from female ones. The only relevant physical advantages that women possess is that they are apparently less subject to altitude sickness. Since they have proportionally more body fat, they also endure cold better.

Given these limitations, very few women were able to participate equally in military training and combat: 'to strike down an enemy, to mount guard ... to endure winter's cold and summer's heat with equal patience, to sleep on the bare ground and to work hard on an empty stomach', as Sallust, quoting Marius, puts it.[477] Ancient battles, particularly Greek ones, often consisted of shoving matches (*othismos*) when 'physical strength'[478] counted for everything. 'Set foot against foot, strain shield against shield, crest upon crest, helmet upon helmet, breast to breast close with your man and fight him, grasping your sword's hilt or long spear-shaft,' sang the Spartan bard Tyrtaeus in the sixth century BC; at Nemea in 394 BC, according to the Athenian writer Xenophon, Thebeans and Spartans 'set shield against shield, shoved, fought, killed and were killed'.[479] To suit their purpose, weapons and equipment were usually designed with large, powerful men in mind.[480] Sometimes even large, powerful men had to be accompanied by specially appointed shield-bearers. The Homeric *rhyton* or great shield may have weighed as much as 18–23 kilograms;[481] neither Ajax nor his biblical equivalent Goliath carried their own shields into battle.[482] The equipment of a Greek hoplite in classical times probably weighed 23–32 kilograms, of which the breastplates alone accounted for 11–13.5. Stooping, sitting or rising required Herculean effort. Thus it comes as no surprise that Greek (and Roman) sources bristle with complaints concerning the weight of equipment;[483] not for nothing do sculpture and painting often show soldiers stumbling, falling, or lying recumbent in their armour.

Of the various pieces of protective gear the shield was the most difficult both to carry and to fight with. A standard-issue Greek shield weighed between 7 and 9 kilograms. To be sure, its strongly concave form permitted it to be hung from the shoulder for much of the time, thus alleviating the strain;[484] still we possess hundreds of pictures in which shields are carried on the left arm as hoplites fight hand to hand. Finding their shields too heavy to run with except for the shortest distances, soldiers who were trying to escape abandoned them as a matter of course. Roman legionary shields were, if anything, even heavier, weighing around 9.5 kilograms exclusive of the leather sheath in which they were normally carried. Modern experiments made with replica have shown how hard they were to wield in combat for more than a few minutes.[485]

In view of this it is not surprising that, on those rare occasions when women were made to bear arms, they had to be provided with specially made ones. For example, Xenophon describes how a visiting Greek Army of which he was a member put on a show for the benefit of some Paphlagonian chiefs in Asia Minor. First a number of men, all wearing full armour, performed a series of complicated war-dances. Next an Arcadian officer presented a young woman in his possession. Instead of armour she was dressed in the finest clothes, carried a very light shield, and gave a fine performance that was greeted with loud applause on the part of the Paphlagonians who, being in a jocular mood, proceeded to ask whether Greek women also fought on their menfolk's side.[486] Similarly Alexander the Great at one point was presented with a troop of a hundred captive women said to be Amazons. Like the Paphlagonian dancing girl, they were provided with 'small targets instead of shields'.[487]

Passing to offensive weapons, the Homeric poems contain many descriptions of the extraordinary strength that the heroes required to hurl a 'long shadowed' spear, lift or throw a heavy rock.[488] Medieval and early modern lances and pikes, which might be used either from horseback or on foot, could be 5–6 metres long and weighed around 6.5 kilograms, with the result that pikemen had to be broad-shouldered men. In the late Middle Ages even some swords were so long (160–186 centimetres) and heavy that knights could wield them only by using both hands.[489] Military-type bows and crossbows, as distinct from the smaller ones used for hunting, could require a force of 35–70 kilograms to draw and fire. The Greeks even called the crossbow 'belly-bow', since to draw it a man had to put the weapon against his stomach and, using his back and leg muscles, pull with all his might[490] – not a procedure recommended for a woman. Relying on torsion that was generated by twisted skeins of rope, or else powered by counterweights that could weigh as much as 10 tons[491] and had to be pulled aloft by means of ropes and pulleys, ancient and medieval artillery pieces (ballistae, catapults, and trebuchets) were not designed for the weak of body either. Putting them into position and working them must often have been a back-breaking job; the same was even more true for other siege engines such as battering rams, towers, cranes, and the like.

Naval warfare did not require troops to carry heavy loads over long distances, but the physical demands it made were scarcely less. Before the advent of steam, the first requirement for warships, as opposed to merchantmen, was manoeuvrability.[492] Hence, even though they used sails for making longer voyages, during much of history they had to be propelled by oarsmen while entering combat and fighting. Often coming under the whip, an oarsman would find himself at the end of a 4-metre-long oar and could be required to develop one eighth of a horsepower or more.[493] Once the ships had drawn closely together, the weapons that their crews used for fighting each other were virtually the same as those employed on land and required the same bodily strength to use.[494] Thus, when the Romans first encountered the Carthaginians at sea they specifically adapted their ships so as to enable them to fight the enemy hand to hand.[495] Boarding remained the standard tactic throughout the Middle Ages, and a viable one until well into the seventeenth century.[496] After artillery duels had taken the place of hand-to-hand combat it still took parties of sweating, grunting men to load the guns (which could weigh as much as 2 tons),[497] haul them back into position after each round fired, and swab them clean. To say nothing of the sheer physical effort which, down to the present day, is needed to run a ship powered entirely by the wind.

Nor, in all that pertains to the physical effort that war demands, did the advent of firearms offer much relief. It is true that pulling a trigger did not require much muscle; however, apart from pistols – which were really suitable only for self-defence at close quarters – firearms during most of their history tended to be on the heavy side. Sixteenth-century arquebuses and seventeenth-century muskets were notoriously so, sometimes to the point that they required a fork so that they could be rested and aimed. In the eighteenth century there was some improvement. For example, the French 1777 pattern (which remained in service throughout the Napoleonic Wars) was a little lighter than most; even so, it weighed 4.5 kilograms, not counting the bayonet which was absolutely essential if infantry was to go on the attack or to withstand cavalry. At least until the advent of modern metallurgy during the last years of the nineteenth century, the only way to make weapons lighter was to shorten the barrels or thin them out. The latter might cause the weapon to explode whereas the former would reduce range and accuracy. A limitation which, if it was taken in stride, led to so-called 'ladies' guns'.

If firearms did little to diminish the sheer physical strength required by the infantry, the same was scarcely less true for the other two arms: the cavalry and artillery. Much longer than the infantry, which by and large had discarded it by the second half of the seventeenth century, heavy cavalrymen in particular continued to wear armour which could make it hard to mount a horse. Much longer than the infantry, too, they continued to fight with (or, at any rate, carry) edged weapons including swords, sabres, and lances, with the incidental result that many wounds sustained in mounted combat were to the right arm. The sword carried by Napoleon's cuirassiers was so long (96.5 centimetres) and heavy that even 'the strongest trooper' found it hard to fence with. Lances weighed around 3.5 kilograms and also required strong men.[498] In the hands of Dragoons, Uhlans, Cossacks, and the like both weapons remained in use throughout the nineteenth century; even as late as the early phases of the First World War, German cavalrymen invading France could be found sharpening the points of their lances each night.[499] On the Eastern Front, whose defining characteristics were wide-open spaces and a lower ratio of forces per square kilometre, cavalry lasted even longer.

Depending on horses to haul the guns as well as the ammunition for them, artillerymen on campaign could often hitch rides; a pre-First World War German military joke had it that, though they neither walked nor rode, still Our Father in Heaven enabled them to move. On the other hand, given the nature of pre-modern roads (it was only towards the end of the eighteenth century that any European roads began to be 'Macademized') moving the artillery was always hard: gunners often found themselves heaving and shoving, knee-deep in mud and water under driving rain, helping the straining horses drag guns and caissons through bog holes. Even if the weather was good, it was standard practice to unhitch the guns some 1,000 metres short of the enemy and rely on manpower to put them into the firing positions. For this purpose uniforms were provided with special hooks and rings to put ropes through.[500]

Nor did the difficulty end when the guns were finally positioned. Loading them, swabbing them out, and re-sighting them (it was only after the invention of recoil mechanisms in the very last years of the nineteenth century that guns no longer had to be re-sighted after each round) was extremely hard work; more often than not, it still is. It is true that the shells fired by field guns are now usually lifted by cranes and inserted into the barrel by a mechanical rammer. However, a 120 millimetre tank round, weighing 36 kilograms, has to be manhandled inside the cramped space of a turret. Substituting a mechanical loader, as in the Soviet T-72, eliminates that requirement but will reduce the crew from four to three. Which will make all the difference, for example, when it comes to repairing a cast-off track, a single link of which weighs around 50 kilograms.

In the age before mechanical transport soldiers often had to shoulder very heavy loads when marching. It is true that armies made extensive use of pack-animals and horse-drawn wagons, to the point that the 'tail' could exceed the 'teeth'. These, however, were regarded as obstacles to mobility; often they had to be abandoned at a moment's notice. Like their Greek predecessors, Roman legionaries – popularly known as 'Marius Mules' – carried a standard load weighing just under 30 kilograms which, in an emergency, could be increased to as much as 47 kilograms. Though medieval knights did not have to carry provisions on their backs, their arms and armour might weigh as much as 35–40 kilograms.[501] On occasion they might have to be worn while fighting not on horseback but on foot, as happened for example during the battle of Poitiers in AD 1356.

Beginning in the second half of the sixteenth century, the advent of firearms gradually caused armour to disappear. However, and depending on the period, mission and type, its place in weight was taken by 35–120 rounds of small-arms ammunition. For example, Prussian soldiers under Frederick the Great carried some 27 kilograms between hat, musket, ammunition, knapsack, spare clothing, tentage and tools.[502] One of them, Private Ulrich Braeker, described his experience during the 1756 invasion of Saxony in which, much against his will, he was made to participate. 'Everyone was loaded like a donkey ... we all believed we were going to suffocate under the burden,'[503] which was held in place by no fewer than five straps across the chest. His complaint failed to impress his superiors. Eighty years later, Prussian grenadiers carried 34 kilograms.

Nor did the advent of the railways change matters, given that they were used to carry troops during mobilization and deployment but not while campaigning in the field.[504] A German soldier of 1914 shouldered 28 kilograms and a Russian soldier of the same year 38; it was with these loads that they killed each other at the battles of Tannenberg and the Masurian Lakes. British soldiers attacking at the Somme in 1916 carried 32 kilograms, which would have prevented them from breaking into a run even if they had been allowed to try. Real relief from the burden of marching was only brought by the motorization of armies after 1918; but then it should not be forgotten that, in the Second World War, 75 per cent of the German Army covered the distance from the Polish border to Stalingrad (and the even greater one from Stalingrad to Berlin) on foot.[505]

During the 1982 Falklands War British paratroopers braved the atrocious weather and, carrying some 35 kilograms of equipment each, 'romped' the 80 kilometres from Port San Carlos to Goose Green. The standard kit of a German Panzergrenadier still weighs around 39 kilograms in summer and just over 40 kilograms in winter.[506] In June 1999 the American Marines moving into Kosovo looked as if they could barely move under the weight of their equipment; the backpack of a US soldier forming part of the futuristic 'Force XXI' and engaged in 'information warfare' weighs 29.5 kilograms, exclusive of the batteries.[507] As it happened, when researching this book in June 1998 I was visited by a young female television operative and took the opportunity to put her on the scales. She weighed 77 kilograms with her equipment, 58 without it. In other words, her equipment weighed one-third as much as she did; no wonder she had a hard time covering the few metres from her car into my street-level home and back.

Historically speaking, it is true that not all men who engaged in fighting were physically among the strongest. On the other hand, no other activity puts those who are physically not strong at so great a disadvantage as does fighting where the penalty for failure is both immediate and terminal. Thus exposing women to combat was little short of criminal even if, owing to the need for close co-operation with others usually standing shoulder to shoulder, it had not been counter-productive. Since armed forces neither recognized the distinction between 'front' and 'rear' nor included numerous non-combatants, there were few other positions that women could fill. During most of history up until the late twentieth century, so obvious were these considerations that the experiment was not even tried.

16 The Glory of Men

In the eyes of Clausewitz war is the continuation of policy by other means, a rational instrument towards attaining and/or defending some rational end. Whatever our view of this interpretation, and there is no doubt that it has much to recommend it, neither today nor at any other time or place has war ever been *only* an instrument in the hands of policy. Before it was anything else, war was an assertion of masculinity. When everything is said and done, an assertion of masculinity is what it remains.

Why masculinity should be in need of proof in the first place has become the subject of an enormous literature. Freud thought that men by virtue of being compelled by their fathers to resolve the Oedipus complex will develop a robust ego.[508] Turning his argument on its head, some of his followers claim that the male ego is fundamentally fragile: the reason being precisely that becoming and being a man is much harder than becoming and being a woman.[509] Like girls, boys start life under their mothers' care and in total dependence on them. Unlike girls, who can identify with their mothers and slip into the latter's role, at some stage they need to break away. This may be because the mother is seen as big and threatening;[510] or, as some feminists have argued,[511] because boys are bound to witness the sufferings their fathers inflict on their mothers and will do whatever it takes so as not to share them when they grow up. Either way they must discover a different role model that will clearly mark them as men.

Nor is nature of much help in the matter. The different phases in a woman's life are sharply marked by biological phenomena such as menarche, defloration, pregnancy, giving birth, and menopause. Not so men's transition from one stage to another which, being less obvious, has to be socially constructed.[512] As adults, males will find that they are less able than females to perform sexually and entirely unable to give birth. To quote

Friedrich Nietzsche: 'man is the unfruitful animal'. He is also the animal which is biologically superfluous, given that a single man can fertilize many women and that, having done so, his only remaining use is to sacrifice himself for them and their offspring.

Be this as it may, boys, having been born to women, must assert their masculinity by being set apart from women. By definition, it is only men who can engender men. Their method in doing this is to impose hardship and inflict pain, which must be withstood without flinching.[513] As carried out in countless societies around the world,[514] initiation rites start with the boys being separated from their mothers. They are then taken to some secret place located either outside the village or else in a house that no woman is allowed to enter. Next they may have their bodies tattooed or cut, circumcision included. They must endure hunger, thirst, cold and sleep deprivation, and may be confronted with unfamiliar noises and smeared with various unpleasant substances. They may also be severely beaten. In post-classical Sparta youngsters were made to walk around an altar and flogged until they collapsed, a ceremony which by Plutarch's time had lost its original meaning and degenerated into a tourist attraction. In Papua New Guinea some tribes had a rite in which men climbed a tower and were then dropped upside down with a rope tied to their legs, which is said to be the origin of bungee-jumping. Very often physical punishment was accompanied by various forms of humiliation, such as having one's hair – including one's pubic hair – shaved, being made to strike ludicrous poses and recite self-mocking formulae, stripping naked in front of one's elders, or assuming a sexually subordinate role by engaging in fellatio.

In fact, since the purpose of initiation is to reduce or remove the boys' 'female substance',[515] so long as women do not share in the rites their precise nature does not matter much. This is also evident from the fact that, at some point during the proceedings, the novices will be presented with male 'secrets' that they must never afterwards divulge even to the women who are nearest and dearest to them;[516] in some cases their foreheads are painted or tattooed to prevent those secrets from escaping.[517] Having graduated, youngsters are presented with special clothing, ornaments and implements – including, not least, weapons – that will henceforward mark their status as men.[518]

Though women may also have ceremonies of their own, the two are kept strictly apart. In particular, most female initiation rites lack the elements of pain and humiliation. Their main component is seclusion at the time of menarche; this is often followed by ritual purification and the presentation of female implements such as dress and ornaments. To the extent that the rite is painful, as in clitoridectomy, the initiates far from having to take it in silence are permitted, not to say expected, to scream with all their might so that male warriors are sometimes used to hold them down.[519] Should women start participating in men's rites, then the latter will lose interest and it will not be long before they are terminated. This is what happened to initiation ceremonies practised by the Munddugumor people in the 1930s.[520] This, too, is what may be happening to the bar mitzvah ceremony among non-Orthodox Jews at present.

Nor does the need to display masculinity come to an end when initiation is completed and the break with the mother accomplished. In view of women's above-mentioned superior sexual and reproductive qualities, men's existential problem – the question as to what, if anything, they are good for – continues to haunt them.[521] It demands that masculinity be asserted and reasserted throughout life, or at least until old age sets in, physical prowess declines, sexual activity diminishes, men and women become more like one another, and it no longer matters. To answer this question, certain fields, or activities, must be set aside as exclusively male and reserved for men. Assuming with Plato that the sexes overlap and that no activity is inherently suited only for men or only for women,[522] these considerations probably do more to explain the existence and persistence of the sexual division of labour than any others.

Of all the activities in which humans engage, obviously no other is nearly as suited for asserting masculinity than is war. All the rest are hedged in by more or less artificial limits on what may and may not be done; in war alone those limits do not apply. War allows, even demands, the most complete use of all man's faculties, physical as well as emotional and intellectual. It thus represents the one great opportunity for the human personality to unfold itself to the full, a fact that artists from Homer through Pindar and the authors of the *Nibelungenlied* all the way down to Nietzsche and Ernst Junger have always recognized and often extolled. Thus war is best understood as a particularly dangerous form of sport. However, war differs from other sports, such as mountain climbing, or white-water rafting, or big-game hunting, in that it enables those faculties to be employed against the most dangerous opponent: namely, another man who is as strong, and as intelligent, as oneself.[523]

Hence it comes as no surprise that, already in the biblical book of Exodus, as in many other tribal languages, the words for 'adult man' and 'warrior' are interchangeable;[524] the same is true for Old Latin where '*populus*' could stand for either 'people' or 'army'. Tacitus in *Germania* describes how, among the Germans of his time, a young male had to kill an enemy before he was allowed to marry;[525] in medieval Germany, 'to become a man' and 'to carry a sword' were synonymous.[526] Similar customs prevailed among many West African, East African and Polynesian tribes almost to the present day.[527] Among some tribes in North America, Cuba, Greenland and Micronesia, so strong was the link between masculinity and war that any man who for one reason or another could not or would not fight was classified as a woman and made to wear feminine dress.[528] Homer makes his favourite hero Diomedes speak of war as 'a man's glory', a phrase he later repeats through the mouth of King Agamemnon.[529] The citizens of Greek and Roman city-states could never praise *andreia* (courage; from *aner*, man) and *virtus* (prowess; from *vir*, man) highly enough; not only in militarist Sparta, but even in civilized Athens some form of military training was regarded as an indispensable prelude to manhood, citizenship and marriage. The same applied in many other civilizations, to the point that, in both modern Hebrew slang and ancient Greek, the same term can mean either 'killing an enemy' and 'having sex with a woman'.[530] In fact, as the statue of Nelson on top of his column in London's Trafalgar Square confirms, the idea of war as the highest proof of manhood is universal.[531]

Precisely because it has always been the supreme proof of masculinity, war resembles all other activities in that its social prestige depends on it being confined exclusively (or almost so) to men. As the twentieth century's most famous American anthropologist, Margaret Mead, once wrote:[532] 'men may cook, or weave, or dress dolls or hunt humming-birds, but if such activities are appropriate occupations of men, then the whole society, men and women alike, vote them as important.' More remarkably still, Mead's Law applies regardless of the 'objective' importance of the activities performed by each sex. For example, in tribal societies hunting, an almost exclusively masculine activity, is more highly regarded than gathering and gardening which are women's work, even though it is the latter that bring in more calories to feed on.[533]

Why men have always claimed that their own activities are the most important ones scarcely requires an explanation. In the words of a contemporary Dutch female poet, Chawwa Weinberg: 'if men were to bleed, how big and imposing the sanitary towels.'[534] What is harder to see is why women should, on the whole, agree with them.[535] As some feminists complain,[536] it is often women who have the highest regard for male activities; in other words, it is precisely they who are the most 'phallocentric' of all. Never in history has this fact been more obvious than in our own day as legions of women seek to jettison what one leading feminist has called their 'animal functions', such as 'caring for the young',[537] and join in male activities. Even if those activities are as unpleasant, as hard, and as dangerous as war; and even at the cost of denying or concealing their womanhood, as when American women Marines demand to be known simply as 'Marines'.[538]

Conversely, a female leader such as Margaret Thatcher is much less likely to make it to the cover of a women's magazine, such as *Cosmopolitan*, than to one that is read by members of both sexes, such as *Newsweek* or *Time*. Several studies show that women tend to rate the literary and artistic productions of women lower than those produced by men.[539] Others show that fewer women than men are prepared to work for female bosses; even though, which is much more surprising, they do *not* believe that men are better bosses than women.[540] When it comes to housewives nobody is as contemptuous of them as are other women, particularly college-educated ones, and indeed it is thanks to the votes of men, mainly married ones, that the occupation is able to command any respect at all.[541] A woman who is 'only' a housewife will still be able to get the respect of men owing to her sex, whereas members of her own sex will not even grant her that. Thus all the evidence confirms Friedrich Nietzsche when he wrote that 'on the whole 'woman' has hitherto been slighted most by woman herself ... I think it is a true friend of women who calls on them today, *mulier taceat de muliere'* (woman should be silent in regard to woman).[542]

Whatever the reasons, both men and women – but women even more than men – tend to reserve their highest regard for fields occupied largely or exclusively by men.[543] Normally the reason why women enter male occupations is because the pay is higher. While this may indeed benefit the pioneers, once the influx starts the occupation in question will be deserted by men and start losing both status and earning power. This process has now been documented for fourteen separate professions, including pharmacy, public relations, banking, systems analysis and insurance sales.[544] It may explain why, as the years from 1970 to 1990 saw one profession after another being invaded by women, the income gap between the sexes hardly closed; and why, to the extent that it did close, this was due more to the declining wages of men than to any gains made by women.[545] It may also explain why, even as the number of women working outside the home increased by leaps and bounds, men have remained on top of virtually every profession or organization. This even includes such 'feminine' fields as education and welfare, which, typically, are run by a handful of men lording it over vast numbers of badly paid, low-prestige women.

Which of the two processes is cause and which effect – whether it is the influx of women that causes a profession to lose prestige and earning power, or whether it is the loss of earning power and prestige that causes men to leave and opens the field to women – is moot. The available evidence is compatible with both interpretations; indeed it is possible that, depending on circumstances, either one could be correct.[546] So strong is the rule that feminization equals decline that it even applies to the most prestigious profession of all: government. It is almost certainly no accident that, out of seven countries with the highest percentage of women among their parliamentarians (Sweden, Finland, Norway, Denmark, the Netherlands, Germany and Austria) six belong to the European Union.[547] Thus female legislators are most prominent precisely in those states that are losing their sovereignty to a different kind of organization. Should present trends persist, then they may soon cease to be states.[548]

This brings us back to our original question: namely why, as far back into human history as we can look, women (even the relative handful who, physically and from a family point of view, were fit to do so) have rarely been permitted to join in war and combat. Judging by what happened to every other feminizing profession, including those which so long as they were exercised by men were among the most powerful and the most highly regarded, the answer appears simple. If women had entered war in any numbers and occupied positions that are at all prominent, then both the financial rewards which it could command and the prestige which it could have brought to its practitioners would have declined; the latter, not least in the eyes of women themselves. In other words, women must be excluded from war not so much because they are necessarily incapable of participating in it but in order that they may better appreciate the feats of the men who are engaged in it. Conversely men who fight alongside, or against, women will be caught on the horns of a dilemma. Should they lose, they are dishonoured. Should they win, then they are also dishonoured.

Except under very specific circumstances, such as last-minute defence or insurgencies, women's participation in war will take away one of the cardinal reasons why men fight, which is to assert their own glory. Once again, nobody has put the idea better than Aristophanes in *Lysistrate*. Here the male chorus sings:[549]

> These women! give them a handle howsoever small,
> And they'll soon outdo us in the manliest feats of all.
> They'll build them navies and they'll come across the sea,
> Come like Carian Arthemisia,[550] fighting against me.
> Or they'll turn their first attention to cavalry fights,
> If they do, I know the issue, there's an end of knights!
> Well a woman rides on horseback; lo and behold
> Where on Micon's[551] frescoes fight the Amazons of old!
> Shall we let these women, Oh my brothers, do the same?
> Rather first their necks we'll tighten in the pillory frame.

Part III 1945 and After

As will be clear from the above account, historically speaking women's relationship to war has undergone remarkably little change. Whatever the time and place to which we turn our gaze, some women helped instigate war whereas many others served as causes, objectives, victims and protégées. Whatever the time and place to which we turn our gaze, numerous women acted as camp-followers and provided a very great variety of essential, if usually low-prestige, supporting services. Here and there a few women, either inheriting their deceased menfolk's throne or (less often) usurping it by force and guile, ruled and commanded; here and there a few others fought weapon in hand, though seldom in the open and usually in disguise. Owing partly to their titillating effects, partly to other reasons, tales of warrior women have always enjoyed a certain popularity, with the heroines commanding the sort of admiration that freaks often do. Finally, in many times and places it is possible to find female deities acting as symbols of war and destruction, as they have continued to do almost to the present day.

Thus, our conclusion so far might well be that, judging by their respective relationship to war, the social roles of men and women are not nearly as flexible as some people believe or want others to believe. Not even the era of total war, when entire nations mobilized all their resources and waged a life-and-death struggle against each other, was able to change this relationship in any fundamental way. In 1914–18, and again in 1939–1945, the vast majority of women continued to do almost exactly the same things, and carry out almost exactly the same functions, as they had always done; the only difference was that the women of some countries, instead of acting as civilians and serving or following the troops on their own initiative, were also permitted to volunteer for the forces themselves if they wanted to. Then came nuclear weapons, and everything changed.

17 The Military Background

The military background to the influx of women into modern armed forces was formed by the retreat of major inter-state war, which during the closing years of the twentieth century was still under way. That retreat in turn was brought about primarily by the introduction of nuclear weapons. From the beginning of history, political organizations going to war against each other could hope to preserve themselves by defeating the enemy and gaining a victory; but now, assuming only that the vanquished side will retain a handful of weapons ready for use, the link between victory and self-preservation has been cut. On the contrary, at least the possibility has to be taken into account that the greater the triumph gained over an opponent in possession of nuclear weapons, the greater also the danger to the survival of the victor.[1]

Appearing as they did at the end of the largest armed conflict ever waged, it took a long time before the stultifying effects of nuclear weapons on future war were realized. During the immediate post-1945 years, only one important author seems to have understood that 'the absolute weapons' could never be used;[2] whether in or out of uniform, the great majority preferred to look for ways in which the weapon could and, if necessary, *would* be used.[3] As always, inertia and the 'lessons' of the Second World War played a part. So long as the number of available nuclear weapons remained limited, their power small compared to what was to come later, and their effects ill-understood, it was possible to believe that they would make but little difference. To those who lived during or shortly after the war the outstanding characteristic of twentieth-century 'total' warfare had been the state's ability to mobilize massive resources and use them for creating equally massive armed forces.[4] Hence it was not unnatural to assume that such resources, minus of course those destroyed by the occasional atomic bomb dropped on them, would continue to be mobilized and thrown into combat against each other.[5]

At first possession of nuclear weapons was confined to one country only, the US, which used them in order to end the war against Japan. However, the 'atomic' secret could not be kept for very long and in September 1949 the USSR carried out its first test.[6] As more and more weapons were produced and stored, there were now *two* states capable of inflicting 'unacceptable damage' on each other, as the phrase went. The introduction of hydrogen bombs in 1952–3 opened up the vision of unlimited destructive power (in practice, the most powerful one built was about three thousand times as large as the one that had demolished Hiroshima) and made the prospect of nuclear war even more awful. At the end of the Second World War there had been just two bombs in existence; but now the age of nuclear plenty arrived with more than enough devices available to 'service' any conceivable target.[7]

Even as the possible effects of nuclear weapons were becoming clear, the two leading powers were busily developing better ones. The original device had been too large and cumbersome to be carried in any but specially modified versions of the heaviest bombers of the time; however, during the 1950s smaller and lighter versions were built that could be delivered by light bomber, fighter bomber, artillery shell, and even a light recoil-less weapon operated by three men from a jeep. The acme of 'progress' was represented by ballistic missiles. Based on the ones developed by the Germans during the Second World War, within fifteen years after 1945 their range had been increased to the point where they were capable of delivering a hydrogen bomb from practically any point on earth to any other. The 1960s and 1970s saw missiles becoming much more accurate so that not only cities but pinpoint targets such as military bases could be aimed at and, with some luck, hit. Miracles of computerization led to the advent of Multiple Re-entry Vehicles (MRV) and Multiple Independent Re-entry Vehicles (MIRV). This permitted designers to put as many as ten warheads on top of a single missile and made the task of the defence even more difficult.

To focus on the US alone, the number of available nuclear weapons rose from perhaps less than a hundred in 1950 to some 3,000 in 1960, 10,000 in 1970, and 30,000 in the early 1980s when, for lack of suitable targets, growth came to a halt. The size of the weapons probably ranged from under 1 kiloton (that is, 1,000 tons of TNT, the most powerful conventional explosive) to as much as 15 megatons (15 *million* tons of TNT); although, as time went on and the introduction of new computers and other navigation aids permitted more accurate delivery vehicles to be built, there was a tendency for the yields of 'strategic' warheads to decline to as little as 50–150 kilotons. With some variations, notably a preference for larger warheads and a greater reliance on land-based delivery vehicles as opposed to air- and sea-based ones, these arrangements were duplicated on the other side of the Iron Curtain. At its peak between 1980 and 1985 the Soviet arsenal probably counted some 20,000 warheads and their delivery vehicles.

By basing them on the ground, at sea and in the air, as well as greatly increasing numbers, the nuclear forces themselves could be protected against attack, at any rate to the extent that enough of them would survive to deliver the so-called 'second strike'. However, the same was not true of industrial, urban and demographic targets. During the Second World War a defence that relied on radar and combined fighters with anti-aircraft artillery had sometimes brought down as many as a quarter of the bombers attacking a target; so, for example, in the case of the American raid against the German city of Schweinfurt in the autumn of 1943. Should the attack be made with nuclear weapons, though, even a defence capable of intercepting 90 per cent of the attacking aircraft would be of no avail, since a single bomber getting through was capable of destroying the target just as surely as Hiroshima and Nagasaki were.

In the absence of a defence capable of effectively protecting demographic, economic and industrial targets, nuclear weapons presented policy-makers with a dilemma. Obviously one of their most important functions – some would say their only rightful function – was to deter war from breaking out. Previous military theorists, with Clausewitz at their head, had seldom even bothered to mention deterrence; but now it became a central part of strategy as formulated by defence officials and studied in think-tanks and universities. On the other hand, if the weapons and their delivery vehicles were to be capable of exercising a deterrent effect then those delivery vehicles and those weapons had to be capable of being put to use. What is more, they had to be capable of being put to use in a 'credible' manner that would not automatically lead to all-out war and thus to the user's own annihilation.

In the West, which owing to the numerical inferiority of its conventional forces believed it might be constrained to make 'first use' of its nuclear arsenal, the search for an answer to this problem started during the mid 1950s and went on for the next thirty years. None of the ideas proposed by analysts ever showed the slightest promise of success; over time, however, a series of nuclear confrontations culminating in the Cuban Missile Crisis of October 1962 caused the superpowers to become notably more cautious. There followed such agreements as the Test Ban Treaty (1963), the Nuclear Non-Proliferation Treaty (1969), the two Strategic Arms Limitation Treaties of 1972 and 1977, and the cuts in the number of medium-range missiles and warheads achieved in the late 1980s by President Reagan and Chairman Gorbachev. Each was brought about under different circumstances, but all reflected the two sides' willingness to put a cap on the arms race, as well as the growing conviction that, should a nuclear war break out, there would be neither winners nor losers.

By the time the Cold War ended the number of nuclear states, which originally had stood at just one, had reached at least eight. From Argentina and Brazil through Canada, West and East Europe, all the way to Taiwan, Korea (both North and South), Japan, Australia and probably New Zealand, several dozen others were prepared to construct bombs quickly; or at any rate capable of doing so if they wanted to.[8] One, South Africa, preened itself on having built nuclear weapons and then dismantled them; although, understandably, both the meaning of 'dismantling' and the fate of the dismantled parts remained somewhat obscure. Meanwhile, technological progress has brought nuclear weapons within the reach of anybody capable of producing modern conventional arms, as is proved by the fact that states such as China, Israel, India and Pakistan all developed the former years, even decades, before they began building the latter.

The entry of new members into the nuclear club was not, of course, favourably received by those who were already there. Seeking to preserve

their monopoly, repeatedly they expressed their fears of the dire consequences that would follow. Their objective was to prove that they themselves were stable and responsible and wanted nothing but peace; however,
for ideological or political or cultural or technical reasons this was not the
case elsewhere.[9] Some international safeguards, such as the Nuclear Non-
Proliferation Treaty of 1969 and the London Regime of 1977, were set up,
the intention being to prevent sensitive technology from falling into
undesirable hands – which in practice meant those of Third World countries. However, the spread of nuclear technology proved difficult to stop.
If, at present, the number of states with nuclear weapons in their arsenals
remains limited to eight, on the whole this is due less to a lack of means
than to a lack of will on the part of would-be proliferators.

Looking back, the fears of nuclear proliferation proved to be greatly exaggerated. Instead of leading to war, let alone nuclear war, the world's nuclear
arsenals tended to act as an inhibiting factor on military operations. As time
went on, fear of escalation no longer allowed nuclear countries and their
major allies to fight each other directly, seriously, or on any scale. In fact, a
strong case could be made that, wherever nuclear weapons appeared or
where their presence was even strongly suspected, major inter-state warfare
on any scale is in the process of slowly abolishing itself. What is more, any
state of any importance is now by definition capable of producing nuclear
weapons. Hence, such warfare can only be waged either between or against
third- and fourth-rate countries.[10]

Given that, in the years since 1945, first-and second-rate military powers
have found it increasingly difficult to fight each other, it is no wonder that,
taking a global view, both the size of the armed forces and the quantity of
weapons at their disposal has declined quite sharply. In 1939 France, Germany, Italy, the USSR and Japan each possessed ready-to-mobilize forces
numbering several million men. The all-time peak came in 1944–5, when the
six main belligerents (Italy having dropped out in 1943) between them
maintained some 40–45 million men under arms. Since then the world's
population has almost tripled and international relations have been anything but peaceful. During over forty years of Cold War one 'crisis' followed

another; and yet the size of regular forces fielded by the most important states continued to decline.[11]

To adduce a more specific example, in 1941 the German invasion of the USSR, as the largest single military operation of all time, made use of 144 divisions out of approximately 209 that the Wehrmacht possessed; later during the Russo-German War the forces deployed on both sides, but particularly by the Soviets, were even larger. By contrast, since 1945 there has probably not been even one case when any state used over twenty full-size divisions on any single campaign, and the numbers are still going nowhere but down. In 1991 a coalition that included three out of five members in the Security Council brought some 500,000 troops to bear against Iraq, which was only about one-third as many as Germany, counting field forces only, used to invade France as long ago as 1914. As of the late 1990s, the only states that still maintained forces exceeding 1.5 million (for the US alone, the 1945 figure stood at 12 million) were India and China, and the last-named had announced that half a million men would be sent home. Of the forces of those two countries, most consisted of low-quality infantry, some of which, armed with the First World War rifles, was more suitable for maintaining internal security than for waging serious external war.

While the decline in the number of troops – both regulars and, even more so, reservists – has been sharp indeed, the fall in the number of major weapons and weapon systems has been even more precipitous. In 1939 the air forces of each one of the leading powers counted their planes in the thousands; during each of the years 1942–5, the US alone produced 75,000 military aircraft on average.[12] Fifty years later the air forces of virtually all the most important countries were shrinking fast. In 1998 the largest one, the United States Air Force, bought exactly 184 aircraft of which only forty were shooters. As a result, to wage a campaign against an opponent as small as Serbia, fully 44 per cent of the USAF's first-line order of battle had to be used;[13] the number of aircraft (if any) purchased by other countries was much smaller still.

At sea, the story has been broadly similar. Of the former Soviet Navy, on which fortunes were spent and which as late as the 1980s appeared to pose a global threat, little remains but rusting surface vessels and old, under-maintained submarines that allegedly risk leaking nuclear material into the sea. The US Navy is in a much better shape, but has seen the number of aircraft-carriers – the most important weapon system around which everything else revolves – go down from almost one hundred in 1945 to as few as twelve in 1995. The US apart, the one country that still maintains even one carrier capable of launching conventional aircraft is France; that apart, the carriers (all of them decidedly second-rate) owned by all other states combined can be counted on the fingers of one hand. Indeed it is true to say that, with a single major exception, most states no longer maintain ocean-going navies at all, and even the largest navy by far, the American one, has been cut by almost half since the late 1980s.

In part, this decline in the size of armed forces reflects the escalating cost of modern weapons and weapon systems.[14] A Second World War fighter-bomber could be had for approximately $50,000. Some of its modern successors, such as the F-15I, come at $100 million apiece when their maintenance packages (without which they would not be operational) are included; which, when inflation is taken into account, represents a thousand-fold increase. Even this does not mark the limit on what some airborne weapon systems, such as the 'stealth' bomber, AWACS and J-STAR – all of them produced, owned and operated exclusively by the world's sole remaining superpower – can cost. It has even been claimed that the reluctance of the US Air Force to use its most recent acquisition, the B-2 bomber with its $2 billion price tag, against Iraq, stemmed from the fact that there are no targets worthy of the risk.[15] Should one be shot down or lost by accident, then the storm of criticism would be hard to stop.

Even so, one should not make too much of the price factor. Modern economies are extraordinarily productive, and could certainly devote much greater resources to the acquisition of military hardware than they do at present. Thus, the cost of modern weapon systems may appear exorbitant only because the state's basic security, safeguarded as it is by nuclear weapons and their ever-ready delivery vehicles, no longer appears sufficiently at risk to justify them. In fact, this is probably the correct interpretation; as is suggested by the tendency, which has now been evident for decades, to cut the size of any production programme and stretch the length of any acquisition process almost indefinitely. For example, to develop the Manhattan Project – which besides involving the application of revolutionary physical science also included the construction of the largest industrial plant ever undertaken up to that time – and build the first atomic bombs took less than three years; but the designers of present-day conventional weapon systems want us to believe that a new fighter-bomber cannot be deployed in fewer than fifteen. The development histories of countless modern weapon systems prove that, in most cases, only a fraction of the numbers initially required are produced, and then only after delays lasting for years and years. The reason is that, in most cases, the threat – which would have made rapid mass production necessary and incidentally led to a dramatic drop in per unit costs – is no longer there.

At the same time, yet another explanation for the decline in the quantity of weapons produced and deployed is the very great improvement in quality; this, it is argued, makes yesterday's large numbers superfluous.[16] There is, in fact, some truth in this argument. Especially since precision-guided munitions have replaced ballistic weapons in the form of the older artillery and rockets, the number of rounds necessary to destroy any particular target had dropped very sharply; as the 1991 Gulf War showed, in many cases a one-shot, one-kill capability has been achieved. On the other hand, it should be remembered that for every modern weapon – nuclear ones only excepted – a counter may be, and in most cases has been, designed. However simple or sophisticated two opposing military systems, provided that they are technologically approximately equal the struggle between them is likely to be prolonged and to result in heavy attrition.[17] Expecting more accurate weapons to increase attrition – as, in fact, was the case both in the 1973 Arab-Israeli War and the 1982 Falkland War, each in turn the most modern conflict in history until then – logically late twentieth-century states ought to have produced and fielded more weapons, not less. The fact that this has not happened almost certainly shows that they are no longer either willing or able to prepare for wars on a scale larger than, say, Vietnam and Afghanistan;

and even those two came close to bankrupting the two largest powers, the US and the USSR respectively.

To look at it in another way still, during the Second World War four out of seven (five out of eight, if China is included) major belligerents had their capitals occupied. Two more (London and Moscow) were heavily bombed, and only one (Washington DC) escaped either misfortune. Since then, however, *no* first- or second-rate power has seen large-scale military operations waged on its territory, the reasons for this being too obvious to require an explanation. In fact, the majority of countries that did go to war – or against which others went to war – were quite small and relatively unimportant. For example, Israel against the Arab states; India against Pakistan; Iran against Iraq; the United States first against Vietnam and then against Iraq; and, for a few days in 1995, Peru against Ecuador before they decided to resolve their differences by setting up a national park. When the countries in question were not unimportant, as in the case of India and China during their pre-nuclear days, military operations were almost always confined to the margins and never came near the capitals in question.

Its ambitions curbed by nuclear weapons, strategy, which from Napoleon to the Second World War often used to measure its advances and retreats in hundreds of miles, could only operate on a much smaller scale. For example, no post-1945 army has so much as tried to repeat the 600-mile German advance from the River Bug to Moscow, let alone the 1,300-mile Soviet march from Stalingrad to Berlin. Since then, the distances covered by armies were much shorter still. In no case did they exceed 300 miles (Korea in 1950); usually, though, they did not penetrate deeper than 150 or so. In 1973 Syria and Egypt faced an unacknowledged nuclear threat on the part of Israel. Hence, as some of their leaders subsequently admitted, they limited themselves to advancing 10 and 5 miles respectively into occupied territory; to such lows had the formerly mighty art of 'strategy' sunk.[18] In other places where nuclear powers confront each other, as between India and Pakistan, what hostilities still take place (across the remote, and practically worthless, glacier of Siachen) do not involve any ground movements at all. Instead they take the form of artillery duels, skirmishes, heliborne raids, and the like.

As the twentieth century was approaching its end inter-state wars appeared to be on the retreat. In terms of numbers they were becoming as rare as dinosaurs; in terms of size neither the armed forces they involved, nor the magnitude of the military operations they witnessed, nor (in almost all cases) the threat they posed to the belligerent's existence even approached pre-1945 dimensions. From the Middle East to the Straits of Taiwan the world remains a dangerous place and new forms of armed conflict appear to be taking the place of the old.[19] Nevertheless, compared to the situation as it existed even as late as 1939 the change has been momentous.

18 Separate and Unequal

As major inter-state war began to retreat and the armed forces of developed countries entered a long decline, paradoxically women for the first time gained a permanent place in those forces. The various women's corps established by the belligerents during the First and Second World Wars had been intended as temporary expedients, and so it proved. After 1945 the vast majority of women – like the vast majority of men – were glad to go home. Three years later the only women left in the British forces for example were nurses, whereas in the US the various women's corps were on the point of being dismantled.

When the revival began, it had little to do either with feminist pressures or the desire of women to 'liberate' themselves. Instead it was the intensification of the Cold War, as demonstrated above all by the Berlin Blockade of 1948, which caused decision-makers on both sides of the Iron Curtain to have second thoughts. As already indicated, most people still expected the next war to be like the last; more modern and more destructive, to be sure, but likewise requiring the 'full use of the total personnel power of the nation'.[20] If women were to take part in the war effort, then one might want to have in place a small organization of trained female personnel. It could help call them up, select them, put them into uniform, train them, assign them to their various positions, and perhaps solve any problems arising from their employment.

In 1948 the US Congress held hearings on the subject. The star witness was General Dwight D. Eisenhower, then at the peak of his prestige as the man who had defeated Hitler and who, as everybody knew, was likely to run for president. The way he put it in his memoirs, prior to the outbreak of the Second World War he had been opposed to women in uniform. Later, however, coming to Britain and seeing them perform 'magnificently' in anti-aircraft batteries among other places, he changed his mind. Unlike their predecessors even as late as the American Civil War, he went on, modern armed forces were not simple organizations; they could scarcely exist, let alone operate, without the support of vast numbers of 'filing clerks, stenographers, office managers, telephone operators, and chauffeurs'. During the conflict that had just ended the women of many countries, including his own, had successfully performed all these tasks – he himself seems to have had a love affair with his own chauffeur, Grace Summerby – and there was no reason why they should not do so in the future too.[21]

Shortly thereafter Public Law 625 was enacted. For the first time, it authorized the US armed services to take in women on a permanent basis.[22] Partly because it wanted to protect women, however, and partly because it was aware of the threat their presence would pose to the male ego, Congress put strict limits on the positions they could fill, their numbers and their careers; the way the services interpreted the law, the limits became stricter still. Women were barred from combat, including sea duty (there were to be no women aboard any naval vessel except transports and hospital vessels) as well as flying duty. Women were prohibited from commanding men. Their number in the services was not to exceed 2 per cent of total strength; and no military woman was to carry any rank higher than colonel (navy captain). In comparison to men, women were also subjected to a whole series of petty restrictions that discriminated against them: for example, they could claim dependent husbands and/or children only if they could prove that these family members were in fact dependent on them for 'chief support'. Finally, to avoid bad publicity, attempts were made to control women's sexual behaviour by emphasizing the need for 'ladylike' comportment and by weeding out, as far as possible, both promiscuous women and lesbian ones.[23]

Under such circumstances it is perhaps not surprising that the attempt to recruit women was scarcely a resounding success. By 1950 there were only 22,000 of them, of whom one-third were in the health professions.[24] Attempts to recruit more women in order to meet the demands of the Korean War were only partly successful; by the end of 1952 there were only 46,000 instead of the target figure of 112,000. Once the Korean

Emergency had ended disinterest became even stronger and the numbers dropped to no more than 1.2 per cent of all uniformed personnel.[25] Among enlisted women turnover was so high that it was questionable whether they were worth having at all.[26] By the late 1950s American military women had become all but invisible. As air force recruitment posters of the period indicated, those who were still around seemed to have been born with a typewriter hung around their necks.

During this period uniformed women, trained in their own bases and disciplined by their own female commanders, acted as secretaries and telephonists for uniformed men. Uniformed women served cookies to uniformed men and, if they were so lucky as to be promoted to commanders' 'aides', were privileged to travel with them, carry their briefcases for them, and stand at their side during public appearances. Possibly in order that the best women should be able to serve as 'aides', very great emphasis was put on external appearance: the air force for example required that each applicant submit no fewer than four pictures of herself, each one taken from a different angle. Once inducted, women received no weapons training at all. Drill apart, they did receive some physical training, but only enough to keep them trim. Very great emphasis was put on various aspects of 'lady-like behaviour'. There were classes in comportment, the application of make-up, and so forth;[27] Marine Corps women were required to wear lipstick and nail polish while on duty. At a time when the 'feminine mystique' was at its height, the last thing the military wanted was for their women to look and act like men.

By the middle of the 1960s, fully 70 per cent of military women worked as secretaries whereas another 23 per cent were active in the field of health.[28] The air force excepted, each service had a women's director who carried the highest rank any woman could attain and who was assisted by a staff that was made up exclusively of women. In the words of one document issued by the Bureau of Naval Personnel, 'the Navy is still going to be made up of men – 98 per cent of it or more. If women recruits are to be able to fit into their own small niches, assuming their proper positions as working members of a very large outfit where there are many jobs which are beyond them physically, then it is necessary for them to recognize the ratings held by men only and to understand something of the basic responsibilities of these ratings.'[29]

By and large, the treatment women received in the armed forces of other Western countries was not dissimilar.[30] Following their experience in the Second World War Britain, France, Norway, the Netherlands and, on the other side of the world, Australia[31] all set up permanent women's corps for the first time. All had very small numbers of uniformed women, either such as were employed as medical specialists (nurses and doctors) or in a variety of, generally low-level, administrative positions. As in the US, military women served under a special commander who was herself a woman. As in the US, too, there were caps on their numbers, the ranks they could attain, and the positions they could hold. For example, in 1962 the active component of the French armed forces included 3,400 women as against 600,000 men; taking account of the reserve force (which was available in theory though less and less likely to be mobilized in practice) their share was much smaller still.[32] However, not all NATO armed forces agreed that women in the military were a good idea. In particular, those of Italy, Spain, Greece and Turkey remained stubbornly male.

Nor did the Soviet Union, which in the Second World War had been the only country to give at least some women weapons training and use them in combat, treat them differently. In the USSR, as in all other countries, the vast majority of women went home after 1945. Thirty years later there were only about 10,000 left in a force numbering just over 3.6 million,[33] a percentage even smaller than in the USA during the 1960s. While Soviet men were drafted and, depending on their arm of service, made to serve for two or three years, Soviet women could volunteer. As in other countries, most entered the medical services where they worked either as nurses (the majority) or as doctors. Also as in other countries, they served under their own female commanders. Women were barred from sea duty and from flying duty. Presumably because of fears for their safety, they were not even allowed to stand guard over their own separate quarters. Though pay, allowances, promotions and pensions were equal for both sexes, women could only be commissioned inside their own corps. Meanwhile Soviet psychology had performed a turn-about: in an effort to boost the falling birth rate, it now insisted – following a chance remark made by Karl Marx during a parlour game – that the chief quality of men was 'strength' and that of women, 'weakness'.[34] Thus, to claim that Soviet female soldiers during the Cold War were 'fully prepared by experience, organization, national expectations, and training programs to bring into service as many women as they might possibly need, and in whatever capacity – including the most violent kinds of combat'[35] seems a trifle exaggerated.

Other East Bloc countries followed the Soviet lead, more or less. In several of them, women had formed part of the anti-German resistance during the Second World War. After 1945 all set up women's corps, however small and however restricted in their functions. All used them to keep some women – mostly belonging to the medical professions, but with a few engineers and other experts thrown in – on the rolls with a view to future expansion; probably in none did the women in question even amount to 1 per cent of the forces. A peculiarity of the Communist system was that female (as well as male) star athletes and similar national treasures might be taken into the military by way of providing them with a living and enabling them to train and perform.[36]

Like other forces engaged in an uprising, the Chinese People's Army before 1949 contained a certain percentage of women.[37] Some Chinese women are said to have fought in Korea, though details about them are hard to get. Since then the PLA has recruited some 7,500 women annually, mainly as medical specialists or else for service in various administrative positions. They receive one month's basic training, including some weapons training; the navy also has them, but does not allow them to serve aboard ship. An unusual aspect of the Chinese experience is that, between 1950 and 1987, the air force trained 208 female pilots – a figure that nevertheless bears no comparison to tens of thousands of male ones. Though women do have access to higher military education, until 1988 there was only one female major general. Since then several more have been appointed, mainly in the fields of medicine, language training, and science and technology. On the whole, a military career is highly regarded in China and women in the forces are said to be doing better than most.[38]

Finally, before the advent of modern feminism around 1970 or so the army that received the greatest attention because of the way it treated women was the Israeli one. As we saw, women had served in the pre-state Hagana and PALMACH where their percentage was perhaps somewhat higher than is normal in organizations of this kind. PALMACH women received weapons training on an equal basis with men, and some were even taken on as squad platoon commanders; however, on the day the United Nations had voted in favour of the establishment of a Jewish state (which it did on 29 November 1947) a mixed patrol of Hagana men and women that was operating in the Negev was ambushed by Bedouin. Its members were all killed, their bodies mutilated. Next day an order from Hagana headquarters ruled that all women were to be taken out of combat units; no explanation was given or, it seems, required.[39]

Given the shortage of trained manpower, the order was not always obeyed. As a result, in February–April 1948 some women – probably no more than a few dozen – helped escort convoys on the way to Jerusalem, which was under siege; as before, the main reason why they were needed was because the British Mandatory troops would not search them for weapons.[40] A few women fought in the far north. At least one, Netiva Ben Yehuda, also saw combat at Latrun, in the centre of the country. There she may have become 'the blonde devil' of Arab myth – or rather the one that is attributed to Arab myth, since references to her are found mainly in Hebrew and English-language sources. However, even at this early stage in the war the role played by female combatants should not be exaggerated. Out of 1,200 PALMACHniks who died in action only nineteen were women, so that relative to their numbers in the force male dead stood to female ones at sixteen to one. To focus on one battle for which figures are available, out of about 300 Israelis who died around the Jordanian-held fortress of Latrun in May–June 1948 only three were women: of them, two were nurses and the third a wireless operator.[41] At that time, midway through the war, a typical PALMACH company operating near Jerusalem might consist of perhaps 140 men and three women.[42]

June 1948 saw the first UN-mandated truce between Israel and its Arab enemies. The young Israel Defence Force – it had been officially established on 27 May 1948 – used the breathing space in order to reorganize, bring in heavy weapons from abroad, and take the remaining women out of combat units. From then until the end of the war some 10,600 women continued to serve, forming just over 10 per cent of the force.[43] As in other armies, their main functions were medical and administrative, with the result that incomparably fewer of them were killed than men.[44] Even inside PALMACH units (before they were dissolved on Ben Gurion's order), women's main function was now to clean the men's rooms and serve them with meals when they returned from action. Used to greater equality, this was a situation which many of them resented and which caused some to leave the service by getting married.[45]

In 1949 Israel enacted its National Service Law. For the first time in history, it was decided to conscript women in peacetime, a decision made understandable against the background of the very great demographic disparity between Israel and its neighbours. Like men, women were drafted when they reached the age of eighteen. Like men, they originally served for two years. However, when men's period of service was extended first to two and a half and then to three years that of women did not follow; in practice, they now serve for about twenty-two months. Married women and pregnant women (including such as got pregnant while on active service) were exempt. So were women who declared themselves to be religiously observant, although they could serve as volunteers.

Once inside, the women formed part of their own corps, known as CHEN (an acronym for Chel Nashim, women's army, also happening to mean 'grace') and were trained in their own segregated bases. They received five weeks of basic training, later reduced to as little as ten days. During this training they might actually fire some shots; however, it was not until after the 1973 war that the IDF, originally a small army of a desperately poor country, obtained sufficient high-quality small arms for women to be issued with them. Some women might undergo additional training as psychological examiners, wireless operators, and the like, but the majority spent their time performing low-level administrative chores. For many years, the most any enlisted woman might look for was probably to fold parachutes, and, as her reward, to be kissed by heroic paratroopers.[46]

Women soldiers could, if they possessed the necessary qualifications and received their commanders' endorsement, be taken into officer school. Graduating as second lieutenants, they would spend the rest of their conscript service commanding other women; those of them who wanted to, and were acceptable to the IDF, could stay on as professionals. However, as in other armed forces, their career opportunities and prospects for promotion were strictly limited: women neither went to sea nor piloted aircraft – after 1956 even the ten female pilots the Israeli Air Force did train (of whom five graduated, and one flew a transport plane in the 1956 campaign) disappeared. Most female officers were active in administration, communications, social work and intelligence. No woman could be promoted beyond lieutenant colonel (later, colonel), and no woman was permitted to command men.

Though the IDF has never published figures on the number of women in its ranks,[47] it is possible to make some fairly accurate calculations. Most women were either destined for administrative slots or else spent their time in the military teaching, doing social work, and the like. Therefore the IDF demanded higher educational standards of them than of men, with the result that approximately 60 per cent of the females in each age class were drafted as opposed to 85 per cent of the males.[48] Since women also served for a shorter period than did men, and assuming the number of men and women in each age group is equal, at any one time they must have formed a little under 30 per cent of the conscript force. To this should be added the 10 per cent or so of officers who were female (1983 figure).[49] Women, however, rarely serve in the reserves which on paper at any rate make up as much as three quarters of the IDF's wartime strength.[50] As a result, their share in that strength is probably in the order of 7.5 per cent (43,300 out of 598,000). Less, be it noted, than during the 1947–8 war; and less also than in the Second World War British armed forces at their peak.

While the IDF was well aware of the publicity value to be got by putting armed women on display, sub-machine-guns at the ready, in practice whatever weapons training they got was largely symbolic; in 1998 some women posted to guard their own quarters were so badly trained that, for fear that they would shoot each other, their Uzi sub-machine-guns were taken away and replaced by whistles.[51] No Israeli woman was expected to take part in combat or even in combat support; in fact the first thing the IDF used to do whenever war broke out was to evacuate the female company clerks who, in peacetime, live with combat units (while occupying separate quarters) in so-called 'closed' bases. This explains why very few Israeli women soldiers have ever been killed in action since 1948. Of those who did die, most fell victim either to terrorist acts or to missiles that landed in their bases, far behind the front.

The legend of heroic Israeli women has been carefully cultivated by the IDF and, for reasons that Freud might explain, eagerly swallowed by its admirers abroad. Reality, though, is different. The model for CHEN was provided by the the Second World War British ATS in which many of its founding mothers, including its first head Colonel Stella Levy, had served. If only for that reason, the Israeli Army during the first three decades of its existence treated its women much as all others did. Like the rest, it inducted far fewer women than men and took various measures to limit the occupations in which they could serve and the promotions they could attain. Like the rest, it tried to control women's sexual behaviour so as to make sure it did not turn into a 'brothel';[52] the volumes upon volumes of regulations that CHEN headquarters has produced in order to deal with this matter have to be seen to be believed. With rare exceptions, it did not even consider their use in 'non-traditional' occupations, let alone in combat. Compared to their sisters in other post-1945 countries, Israeli military women differed in two aspects only. First they were *obliged* to serve, though in practice it was always much easier for a woman to gain an exemption than for a man. Second, being obliged to serve, they did so in greater numbers than elsewhere.

19 **Enter the Women**

While the armed forces of the developed world were slowly turning from war-fighting machines into deterrents and from deterrents into constabularies,[53] vast changes were taking place in civilian society. First, continuing urbanization caused fertility to decline. In much of Western Europe and North America the trend towards smaller families had started during the second half of the nineteenth century. The post-1945 baby boom led to a temporary reversal of the trend, making women retreat inside the home; during the late 1950s, however, it was accelerated by readily available information on birth control, better contraceptives, and, from about 1960 on, the pill.[54] In the so-called Eastern Bloc countries the decline in fertility was, if anything, greater still. Compared with their mothers – and also with their sisters in developing countries – women on both sides of the Iron Curtain spent a smaller and smaller part of what were becoming longer and longer lives either carrying children or looking after them.

Next, the introduction of the motor car caused millions to move from the inner cities into the suburbs. Particularly in the United States where distances are large, lots enormous by comparison, and community facilities often all but non-existent, the outcome was to condemn middle-class women to solitary confinement in what were, effectively, green deserts. The rising age at which people got married and the growing divorce rate compelled more and more women to look after themselves in an economic sense; finally, the post-1945 expansion of higher education meant that a much higher percentage of women than previously went to college and university. By the 1960s many of them were in their thirties and forties. Having witnessed their children go to school, they were beginning to wonder whether their education could not be put to better use than in cleaning bathrooms and waxing floors. Younger women, who could see the frustrating lives led by their mothers, were asking the same question.[55]

Given these changes, it was not surprising that many women decided to obtain work outside the home and that some of those who did so looked towards the military as a potential employer. Still, what really triggered the feminization of the forces was not any pressures that women brought to bear. As late as the mid 1960s, far from flocking to do their bit, women only formed 1.2 per cent of America's uniformed personnel, less than the figure authorized by Congress;[56] Israel apart, their proportion in the armed forces of other developed countries was even smaller. Instead, the decisive factor proved to be the war in Vietnam. The war had opened with the over-whelming support of the American people,[57] and in the summer of 1964 a *Newsweek* cover even celebrated 'the heroes of Tonkin'. But by late 1967 the war was turning sour as the Viet Cong and North Vietnamese Army, instead of cracking, mounted the Tet offensive. Faced with the services' insatiable demands for manpower, President Lyndon Johnson could antic-ipate the day when he would be forced to call up the reserves. Such a step would have been impossible to enforce and might have turned the anti-war protests into massive social unrest. Rather, the Department of Defense decided to see whether more women could be thrown into the breach.[58]

In the event, the first steps were taken by Congress just before Tet. In November 1967 the 2 per cent cap on the number of women was finally removed, though only in theory since not enough women volunteered to fill even that quota. So were the restrictions on the ranks that women could attain, with the result that it was only two years before the US Army acquired its first two female brigadier generals, Anna Mae Hays and Elisabeth Hois-ington.[59] These steps were too limited, and came much too late in the day, to have any appreciable impact on the war in Vietnam. If only because they consisted of volunteers, the total number of American women who served 'in country' probably amounted to 6,000–7,500 as opposed to approximately 2 million men.[60] As usual the great majority worked as nurses, it being their sad lot to do what they could for the large numbers of their countrymen who were being shot to pieces for no good purpose. Others were active on staffs, answered telephone calls, and fed punched cards into computers.

Almost 57,000 American men, but only eight American women, died in Vietnam, mostly by terrorist action or as the helicopters in which they rode crashed.[61] Yet this vast discrepancy did not prevent the soldiers of each sex from getting their separate monuments on the mall in Washington DC, with each monument comprising exactly three figures.

At this time the prestige of the US armed forces reached an all-time nadir.[62] Departing for East Asia, soldiers were greeted by demonstrators who gave them a flower and expressed the hope they might be killed; returning, they were often afraid to wear their uniforms for fear of being hassled or spat upon. To prevent a complete collapse, President Nixon announced the monumental step of abolishing the draft and returning to an all-volunteer, professional force such as the United States had had during most of its history. Needless to say, the new force was to be much smaller than the old: at one point there was talk of reducing the army to 500,000 men, about 30 per cent of its previous size.[63] Even so there were not enough male volunteers to be had, particularly college-educated ones. Willy-nilly – much more nilly than willy, because taking in more women in a greater variety of military occupation specialities was the last thing many senior commanders wanted[64] – the armed forces began looking at what women could, and could not, do; in the words of Lawrence Korb, under secretary for manpower during the first Reagan administration: 'no way [would we] ever leave a spot vacant rather than take a woman'.[65] Initially at any rate the women who entered the military were better educated than male recruits. On the basis of experience in the Second World War, they were expected to be more docile and to present fewer disciplinary problems.[66] They were also cheap: by taking up military slots men no longer wanted, some enlisted women in particular were able to *increase* their income by as much as 40 per cent.[67]

At the time the decision was made, scarcely anybody thought of using women in combat. On the contrary, the idea was to see which military posts could be occupied by women so that men – such men as were to be had – could be sent into combat units; women, in other words, were considered very much a second-rate substitute. A whole series of elaborate calculations were made and summed up in a Brookings Institute study of the subject;

within four years, the percentage of MOS open to women had more than doubled from thirty-five to eighty.[68] A few of the so-called 'non-traditional' fields were highly prestigious and involved work in science and engineering. The majority, though also 'non-traditional', merely gave uniformed women the right to join men in performing blue collar work in maintenance, logistics, housekeeping, and so on. By that time the percentage of women in the forces had more than trebled to about 7 per cent. If, in 1972, one out of thirty recruits had been female, in 1976 one in thirteen was.

To expand women's role in the military it was necessary to lift a whole series of restrictions on the things they could, and could not, do. Thus, by order of the Naval Chief of Operations Admiral Elmo Zumwalt,[69] women were allowed aboard ships, though not combat ships. Women were allowed to pilot aircraft, though not combat aircraft (later they were allowed to pilot combat aircraft too, but only on missions behind the front such as ferrying aircraft, testing them, and teaching their use to other pilots). For the first time, women began to receive at least some weapons training although what they received was not very serious. For the first time, too, women were allowed to command mixed units consisting of men and women. Women maintained aircraft, launched missiles, operated computers, ran construction equipment, refuelled tanks, and controlled air, land and sea traffic; as if to prove that they could do whatever men did, some women even drove forklifts around ammunition dumps.[70] In 1972 the separate officer training courses for women were abolished, and women were taken into Reserve Officer Training Course (ROTC) at civilian universities. In 1976, against much opposition, Congress forced the military academies to open their doors to women, with the result that the first class graduated in 1980.

Under Clifford Alexander, who was President Carter's under secretary for manpower, the shift toward equality accelerated.[71] In 1978 the position of commander, women's corps, was abolished and female soldiers were fully incorporated into the normal military chain of command.[72] Women's separate bases were also closed, and women's living quarters integrated with those of men, with the result that, instead of being largely segregated, members of the two sexes now often occupied separate floors in the same building. The aim was to create a unisex military, even to the point where unisex uniforms were tried; in the end, they turned out to fit neither men nor women and the experiment was quietly dropped. As I shall show, the attempt to integrate basic training caused women's drop-out rates to rise to dangerous levels whereas men no longer got any serious training at all. Integrated training, too, had to be abandoned, and the system of separate courses for men and women reinstituted.

By this time the US experiment had begun to be followed in, and imitated by, a number of other countries. Partly because of a falling birth rate, partly because of spreading pacifist sentiment that affected European NATO members in particular, many of them were also experiencing a shortage of males willing and able to serve; the more so because of the energy crisis which was causing their economies to falter and military budgets to be cut. Like any employer who cannot get the men he wants at the price he is prepared to pay, the armed forces of the countries in question turned to women. At one time or another this consideration applied to Japan, Australia, Sweden, Greece, Britain, the Netherlands, Belgium, and, as far as medical personnel are concerned, the Federal German Republic.[73] Israel, too, found itself taking a fresh look at what women could and could not do, though in this case the cause was not the growing reluctance of men to serve but the shortages that resulted from the vast expansion of the armed forces after the 1973 war.[74] All ended up either by taking in women for the first time, as Japan, Greece and West Germany did, or by opening additional MOS to them, as in most other NATO countries. All removed various restrictions on their use, though none as yet considered it necessary to have women in combat.

No sooner did many women begin to enter the armed forces during the 1970s than their presence started giving rise to endless, and continuing, trouble. In part, this was due to physical problems which prevented women from training as hard as men. Some standard training devices, notably monkey bars, proved too dangerous for women who did not have the requisite upper-body strength and had to be taken off them.[75] Women lagged behind on road marches and dropped out of group runs, so that some of the latter had to be abolished. They failed to negotiate obstacle courses (later modified to make them easier) and could not climb a rope. Nor could women throw a hand-grenade, that weapon *par excellence* of future urban warfare, to the minimum distance necessary so that they would not be blown to pieces, with the result that training with it either had to be cancelled or turned into a meaningless charade.

In the army, enlisted women lost their periods for months on end.[76] At West Point during the early 1980s women suffered ten times as many stress fractures as did men. A 1988 army study of 124 men and 186 women found that women were more than twice as likely to suffer leg injuries and nearly five times as likely to suffer fractures as men; injury also caused women to sustain five times as many days of limited duty as men.[77] At the Air Force Academy women visited doctors' clinics four times as often as men. They suffered nine times as many shin splints, five times as many stress fractures, and more than five times as many cases of tendinitis.[78] The Australian Army also found that, even after physical training standards had been sharply reduced, women continued to be injured twice as often as men; in Canada, only *1 per cent* of women who entered the standard infantryman's training graduated.[79]

In the years since then, the greater vulnerability of women both to orthopaedic trouble and to amenorrhoea (which if it persists can lead to sterility and osteoporosis) has been recognized by the world's most advanced female medical authorities.[80] Other female health experts have emphasized the connection between women's participation in many different kinds of competitive sport and eating disorders, such as anorexia and bulimia.[81] The list of diseases is topped by infections of the urinary and reproductive tract that result from rough living in the field as well as a 100 per cent increase in the miscarriage rate for female sailors serving at sea;[82] this author personally knows one woman who, ignoring physical limitations and straining to keep up with her fellow officers in the US Army during a forced march, lost her ovaries as a result.

In colleges and elsewhere, those responsible for devising physical training programmes for women's sports have long wondered how much is enough.[83] Having tried to train women together with men, and precisely

because they are *not* interested in differences between individuals, for the
first time in history the modern military have provided a clear answer:
keeping up with most men is too much for almost all women. Making women
measure up to the same standard as men is grossly unfair; worse, it will lead
to a massive waste of resources as a high proportion of women sustain injuries
and/or drop out.[84] Conversely, training all personnel to physical standards that
most women can meet means that the men will get hardly any proper training at all.

For example, during the period when the US Army engaged in the experiment the name of 'basic combat training' was changed to 'basic training',
whereas time previously devoted to marksmanship had to be dropped in
favour of classes in contraception.[85] During Israeli co-ed pre-military training closely observed by this author in 1998–9, the female runners present
always lagged so far behind their male comrades that the two groups could
not even see each other. If, as is usually the case, the training is carried out
in remote areas, this may present a threat to the women's safety and can
lead to lawsuits if anything goes wrong. Solving the problem by making
everybody run together means that the men are slowed down. Giving the
women a head start could be construed as sexual harassment, especially if
they are also used as bait to make the men run faster. The same reasons,
lack of physical strength on the one hand and fear of harassment on the
other, prevented the women from either carrying stretchers or being carried
on them. Yet teaching the trainees how to carry a wounded comrade was
among the main objectives of the exercise; at the time, hardly a week passed
without Israeli troops taking casualties in Lebanon. Briefly, whenever the
group included more than a few women, and whenever those women were
treated as anything other than a fifth wheel in a cart, the entire course began
falling apart.

In the US forces, and recently in those of Israel as well,[86] one solution to
these problems has been to put men and women through similar courses
while requiring separate physical standards from each sex. At Britain's Sand-
hurst Military Academy a compromise was adopted: in an unsuccessful
attempt to disguise the fact that women have an easier time of it, male and

female cadets begin and end their training at the same locations but follow a different course in between. Now training that is separate and unequal will lead to some of the personnel being qualified only within limits, which is why, in some international military publications, female soldiers are put in brackets. Moreover, unequal training – whether carried out in common or not – is unfair to the men; they will complain, rightly, that women are allowed to graduate without having to make the same effort and overcome the same obstacles.[87] Since all training standards are, in a sense, artificial the outcome is certain to be either an erosion of those standards or a situation where men's training is turned into a mockery and a humiliation; most likely, if they have the choice, they will prefer to drop out.

More troublesome still, the basic arrangements that governed the employment of women in the military had been set up in the years immediately after 1945, when both the prevailing social climate and the image most people had of the shape that future war would take were entirely different. The forces themselves had been designed very much with male soldiers in mind: now that the number and importance of the women who served in them was growing by leaps and bounds, numerous adjustments had to be made. Some of the regulations that discriminated against women were quietly dropped. Others gave rise to much controversy and only disappeared after lawyers acting on behalf of female soldiers took the military to court or threatened to do so.

To focus on the US experience as the most important one of all, in 1971 *Frontiero v. Richardson* struck at the rule that did not allow female soldiers to claim dependent pay unless she could prove she was the family's 'main breadwinner'. In 1976 *Cushman v. Crawford* enabled pregnant women to remain in the service and return to it after giving birth (a privilege, incidentally, that is neither required by American labour law nor granted by all of America's civilian employers). Two years later *Owens v. Brown* forced the navy to open additional ships to women.[88] At times the push for absolute equality took ridiculous forms and at others it backfired. For example, male crew members complained that females were allowed to keep stuffed toy animals in their bunks, causing the navy to prohibit both sexes from having them.[89]

According to Lawrence Korb, the issue of women took up more of his time than any other.[90]

During the decade that ended in 1981, the proportion of women in the US armed forces increased approximately sevenfold to 8.5 per cent of active strength. During the same period the number of troops went down from 2.7 million to 2,050,000, i.e. by 24 per cent. America's economic situation during this period was anything but easy. A vast federal budget deficit, combined with rising energy prices, was driving inflation into double digits. It also caused men's real incomes to fall for the first time in several decades; as a result, many women were being compelled to work outside the home.[91] Though the size of the military was falling, it still represented much the largest single employer outside the federal government. Hence it is scarcely surprising that some of them chose to work for the armed forces and that those forces became a butt for feminists seeking to expand employment opportunities for women.

Though women did score many points in their drive towards equality, in a sense they were caught on a treadmill. This, after all, was the area of 'more with less'. Even as more women entered the forces, those forces were becoming less important to national life both in terms of their own size and the number of troops per head of population. The less important the role of the services to national life, the harder they found it to attract suitable men and the greater therefore their reliance on women to fill the gaps. The unfavourable economic climate notwithstanding, by the late 1970s the US armed forces were facing such difficulties in attracting men – almost any men – that Secretary of Defense Harold Brown had plans prepared for bringing back the draft.[92] By that time military pay had deteriorated to the point where enlisted personnel in the continental US were often living on food stamps. Simultaneously, a sinking dollar meant that their comrades who were stationed in West Germany were almost literally starving and had become dependent on hand outs from the local population.

Early in 1981 the Reagan administration took office determined to reverse what was widely perceived as the decline in America's armed forces. Guided by Secretary of Defense Caspar Weinberger, it attempted to face the problem head-on by throwing money at the military. The defence budget was increased by as much as 40 per cent making possible, along with an unprecedented programme of rearmament, large rises in military pay. Coming at a time when the services were beginning to recover from the Vietnam débâcle, the changes made them more attractive to men. The feminization of the military came to a temporary halt. It has also been claimed that, in order to arrest the influx of women, the Department of Defense adopted 'anti-feminist' policies,[93] though the precise nature of those policies has never been specified.

Meanwhile the armed forces of other NATO countries, including those of Canada, Britain, France, Belgium and the Netherlands, were following the lead given by the US during the 1970s. Several, switching from conscription to voluntary service, found that they could not obtain enough men. All were squeezed by the new economic climate created by the energy crisis, and all responded by taking in additional women and busily conducting experiments to see what could, and could not, be done with them. As in the US, this led to limited female penetration of a very large variety of 'non-traditional' MOS ranging from technical and scientific work (France) to limited sea-duty (the Netherlands).[94] Here and there women began to receive weapons training, though initially it was only meant to prepare them for self-defence in case of an emergency. As in the US, servicewomen were sometimes compelled to resort to the courts in order to obtain what they regarded as their rights. Usually it was a question of opening additional MOS to women or else of equalizing their status with that of men in respect of pay, promotion, admission to service schools, and so on. Occasionally, though, the issues were bizarre, as when one Dutch female soldier insisted on piercing her tongue with a steel pin and was backed up by the soldiers' union.[95]

So long as the Cold War lasted and the forces still had an important role to play, the impact of change was limited. Thus, during the 1980s, women formed 8.4 per cent of the US forces; 7.7 per cent of the Canadian ones; 4.9 per cent of the British ones; 2–3 per cent of the French ones; 1 per cent of the Dutch and Norwegian ones; and 0 per cent of the West German Bundeswehr which, except for fifty physicians, had no women at all.[96] Skipping over NATO's so-called 'Southern Tier', made up of Mediterranean countries (including one that is Muslim), with their different cultural traditions, one fact stands out very clearly: namely that, the closer any member to the East-West border, the fewer the women its armed forces contained.

In 1988 Operation 'Just Cause' put some American servicewomen in harm's way for the first time. As they invaded Panama, a country well known for its military might, 18,400 US troops (of whom 800, or 4.3 per cent, were female) found themselves opposed by General Noriega's entire bodyguard. A few women were in 'combat support'. One of them, Captain Linda Bray, was said to have commanded a company that successfully attacked a kennel full of ferocious dogs.[97] At first Bray's exploits received much favourable publicity. Then, however, someone remembered that by commanding under fire she had violated the Pentagon's regulations which, at the time, barred women from combat. Whether for this reason or because the initial reports had been false, the official story was changed: the revised version claimed that, by the time she reached the spot in her jeep, the fight was over. Bray herself was understandably mystified by the system which glorified her one day and sought to minimize her role on the next. She ended up by leaving the army while suffering from stress fractures in both legs, injuries she blamed on the extra weight she claimed to have carried on road marches so as to prove herself to her doubting male comrades. Her feat, and the participation of women in general, caused Congresswoman Patricia Schroeder to propose that the ban on women in combat be lifted for an experimental period of four years. However, at this time the idea failed to make its way through Congress.

Once President Reagan had left office, the defence budget stagnated and started to decline. Under the Bush administration, the feminist conquest of the military was resumed. By 1991 the US services included 223,000 women who formed 12 per cent of strength. The greatest concentration was in the air force where they formed 14 per cent; not accidentally, the air force is also the service with the lowest ratio of 'teeth' to 'tail' by far since air-crew only form a minuscule fraction of all personnel. Next came the army with 11.5 per cent and the navy with 10 per cent. With 5 per cent, the Marines were at the bottom of the list. Probably the corps's reputation for toughness is partly responsible for the dearth of women in it. Another reason is because the Marines have part of their rear-echelon services provided for them by the navy; and because they spend much of their time aboard ship in forward deployment.[98]

Depending on one's point of view, women in the military had either made very great progress or none at all. To be sure, in the US military as that of other countries the percentage of women had grown. Many new MOS were opened to them, and they had made some steps towards equality with men. However, except in Canada which in 1987 became the first country to open all flying positions to women,[99] women continued to be barred from all forms of combat. Since combat forms – or is supposed to form – the true justification of any military, this exclusion had very serious consequences for women's careers; for example, out of thirteen US Army generals who commanded in the Gulf, twelve made their careers in units that are closed to women.[100] Along with the continuing opposition by men who often did everything to make their lives a misery,[101] more than any other factor it explains why women remained a subordinate minority. Even as they were achieving this much female soldiers, as well as male ones, often saw the social prestige of the organizations of which they were members eroded and the budgets allocated to those organizations cut. Then came the Gulf War, which presented women with their great opportunity.

20 Women into Combat

In the spring of 1990 the Cold War was at an end. Five years after Mikhail Gorbachev had taken power in the Kremlin and three years after his historic meeting with President Reagan at Reykjavik, disarmament in Europe – the so-called 'Central Theatre' – was under way. Having been defeated by the Afghanistani Mujahedin, the Soviet armed forces were in a bad way. The time was soon to come when the Red Fleet, which in 1976 had covered a Cuban landing in Angola, would rust at anchor in its ports; meanwhile Red Air Force fighters were being used to fly tourists as a means of earning hard currency. On the other side of the world President Bush, pressed by America's large and growing budget deficit, was preparing to cut the US armed forces by between one-quarter and one-third.[102]

Then, literally out of the blue, came the Gulf War. During much of the 1980s Saddam Hussein had fought against Iran, aided by a considerable part of the Western world which regarded him as the lesser of two evils and provided him with as many weapons as he could buy. That war having ended he turned against neighbouring Kuwait, a move which the West after some hesitation refused to accept. At the time Iraq, a Third World (though oil-rich) country of about 17 million people with a GNP perhaps 1–2 per cent of that of the United States, was said to be a leading military power – in fact some observers claimed that Saddam's army was the fourth most powerful in the world. Whether this was true or not, the Iraqi forces were certainly the only ones in their league that had not yet acquired nuclear weapons. From the point of view of the coalition that was formed against them, this fact turned them into ideal targets.[103]

The crisis also caught the US at an opportune moment. Though the Cold War was over, the forces that had been built up over decades in order to confront the Soviet Union in a possible Third World War had not yet been dismantled to any great extent. It thus proved possible to bring up over half a million American troops, plus about half as many again provided by other NATO countries and various Arab members of the coalition. In the air alone the coalition forces outnumbered the Iraqis by approximately three to one, not counting the heavy bombers that the US was able to deploy from bases as far away as the British Isles; at sea it was more like a hundred to one, the Iraqis possessing hardly any navy at all. To complete the US advantage in such weapons as stealth aircraft and cruise missiles and satellite communications the crack VIIth Armored Corps was brought over from Germany and deployed. Once it had become acclimatized its tanks, armoured personnel-carriers, heavy artillery and attack helicopters proved ideally suited for operations in the flat, featureless Kuwaiti desert.

At the time the crisis broke out, women formed 12 per cent of all American uniformed personnel and, except that they were still not allowed into combat, had become fully integrated. In the end 41,000 of them went to the Gulf, where they formed approximately 7 per cent of strength.[104] As so often in the past, many women worked in administration, communication, transportation (they served as drivers) and in the medical services. Unlike the past (or, at any rate, America's past), they also maintained and refuelled tanks, sited, directed and launched Patriot missiles, operated all kinds of sophisticated equipment, and gathered, collated and evaluated intelligence. Some were stationed aboard ship and others flew various kinds of aircraft and helicopters, sometimes over Iraq, but mostly over Saudi Arabia and the Gulf where they were out of reach of Saddam's air force. Contrary to all tradition, women were even used to stand guard. In fact the very first American woman to die in the Gulf was Army Staff Sergeant Tatiana Khaghani Dees of the 92nd Military Police Company. A divorced mother of two, she trained her weapon at a suspect while standing at the end of a pier at Daharein, 300 kilometres south of the Kuwaiti border. Backing off, she fell and drowned under the weight of her equipment.[105]

Compared with their male comrades, military women were considerably more likely to experience problems that prevented them from being deployed; one source puts the difference at almost four to one.[106] In some cases this was because they were pregnant (at any one time, about one in ten women in the services was likely to be pregnant);[107] in others, because they were seven times more likely than men to be single parents.[108] In theory, service personnel were supposed to make arrangements for such emergencies by having children taken care of by relatives and the like. In practice, though some heart-breaking stories did reach the media,[109] single parents were some-times let off the hook if they wanted to and knew which strings to pull.[110] Nor was deployability the only problem. Once female soldiers had reached the Gulf, they were more likely to be sent home because of illness or because they had become pregnant. In some cases, it is claimed,[111] women got preg-nant *in order* to be sent home. Others were not as lucky: 207 American female soldiers had to be evacuated from the theatre because of orthopaedic injuries, and two of them suffered amputation.[112]

After it was all over, Secretary of Defense Richard Cheney went on record as saying that 'women have made a major contribution to this war. We could not have won without them.'[113] Contrary to initial fears, the presence of women did not cause the Iraqis to fight harder. On the other hand, some problems did arise. Independent polls conducted among veterans – most of them male – showed that the presence of women caused some problems of unit readiness, cohesion and morale. They also showed that women's per-formance, while creditable, was rated somewhat lower than that of men.[114] Since the coalition forces in the Gulf enjoyed a vast surplus of everything from ammunition to hamburgers, it cannot be argued that these problems were very important or that they acted as a brake on operations. Still it remains true that, on a one-to-one basis, the American force that defeated Saddam Hussein was probably somewhat less cost-effective than it could have been had it consisted solely of men.

When the plans for Desert Storm were being drafted experts, basing them-selves on Iraq's performance against Iran, had calculated that the coalition forces might take as many as 10,000 casualties. In the event this proved to be a gross over-estimate; both in the air (after the first day or two) and on the ground, resistance was so light as to make the campaign look almost like a walk-over. The number of Americans who died in the war stood at 388, of whom thirteen, or 3.4 per cent, were women. Thanks largely to the fact that they were excluded from combat, women deployed to the Gulf were only half as likely to die as were men. Of the thirteen who did die eight were killed by enemy fire, including three who met their fate when a Scud missile hit their base. Two women were taken prisoner of whom at least one was sexually abused by her captors.[115] Later she claimed it had been 'no great deal'. What, if anything, this proves is not clear.

As interpreted by the feminist lobby in Washington DC women's participation in the war had been a resounding success. Major Everett's 1928 judgment that women could go anywhere and do anything appeared confirmed: according to Representative Beverly Byron (D, Md), chairperson of the House Armed Services Personnel and Compensation Subcommittee, the country had finally 'progressed' to the point where it was ready to see women taken prisoner or brought home in body-bags.[116] The body which had the greatest influence in the matter, and which received the greatest publicity, was DACOWITS, short for Defense Advisory Committee on Women in the Services. The founder of DACOWITS had been none other than General Marshal. In 1950, acting as secretary of defense to President Truman, he wanted to bring more women into the forces and sought to achieve this aim by enlisting the aid of prominent women. Eventually DACOWITS comprised around forty women, most of them professionals or academics, who were appointed by Congress for three-year terms.[117] Originally they included some women who had occupied key positions in the services' women's corps during the Second World War. Over time, however, the percentage of those who had any direct experience of the military declined.

During the Korean War DACOWITS failed to meet its mission, as is proved by the fact that, between September 1951 and July 1952, the Women's Army Corps actually lost personnel (it went down from 12,000 to 10,000). After the war was over the committee, reflecting the unimportant role played by servicewomen during the 1950s and most of the 1960s, languished. It sprang into life during the later stages of the Vietnam War when it was instrumental in lifting the restrictions on the number of women and the ranks they could attain.[118] The great days of DACOWITS were, however, still ahead. As the switch to the all-volunteer force led to a very great influx of women, throughout the 1970s and 1980s it actively promoted the interests of servicewomen in Congress, in the courts and in the media, causing the military to hate its guts. Then came the Gulf War which provided it with the greatest opportunity of all.

In the summer and autumn of 1992 the question of further expanding women's role was thrashed out by a Presidential Commission on the Assignment of Women in the Services which met in Washington DC. Dozens of experts were summoned and questioned as to their views; among them this author who was asked to testify based on his knowledge of the Israeli Army.[119] Some of the experts were women, but the majority were men. Some were in uniform, others not. Some were commissioned, others not: enlisted personnel who gave evidence included the senior NCOs of all four services. Some were on active service, others retired. The vast majority of witnesses firmly opposed the assignment of women to combat. Some argued that mixed units would suffer from morale problems (as, to some extent, was said to have happened in the Gulf);[120] others that women possessed insufficient physical strength to carry out many tasks. When the final analysis was made, it turned out that out of 133 'identifiable facts' only two were favourable to the integration of women on the basis of military effectiveness.[121] The commissioners ended up by voting 8:2 against women serving in ground combat units and 8:3 against women flying aircraft in combat. This, however, was election time. When a new Democratic administration took office in January 1992 the commission's recommendations were largely ignored.

Implementing the new policy fell to Secretary of Defense Les Aspin. He ordered the services to open all positions except ground combat to women, and even in this field their position was significantly 'improved' because they could now be deployed as far forward as brigade headquarters.[122] For the first time, women were allowed to fly aircraft in combat and were allowed aboard warships, submarines only excepted; two years later the aircraft carrier *Eisenhower* became the first to have them. To include 415 women in the crew (out of a total of 4,967) millions of dollars had to be spent making changes in accommodation, washing rooms, and so on. Gynaecologists were brought aboard to attend to female problems, and barbers taught how to do female hairdos. Menus were altered and a supply of contraceptives was taken aboard. Hundreds of orders were issued concerning all the things that male and female officers, male and female enlisted personnel, were and were not allowed to do separately, together, and to each other.[123] Yet none of this could prevent thirty-nine women – just under 10 per cent of the total – from getting pregnant during the cruise and, consequently, leaving the ship. If it is true that their absence did not affect operations, as the navy claimed, one might well wonder what they were doing aboard in the first place.[124]

As usual, American policy provided foreign feminists with the cue many of them had been looking for. The British, French, Canadian, and most other NATO armed forces all saw themselves constrained to abandon the last remaining regulations that prevented women either from serving aboard warships or flying combat aircraft. In January 2000 a ruling by the European Court finally forced the German Bundeswehr to open its ranks as well, which incidentally will force a shift from conscription to professional service since German women have already indicated their opposition to any kind of draft being applied to them. Going further than most, Norway and Canada now allow women to serve aboard submarines, and the former has already appointed its first female submarine commander. Another country, Britain, permitted women to join the Corps of Pioneers. As of the early months of 2000, about the only positions that remain formally closed to women are those involving ground combat forward of the brigade level.

Coming at the time it did, the exception was significant. As the end of the Cold War made major war much less likely, operations larger than those conducted on the brigade level virtually disappeared; indeed it became questionable whether, in an era of 'peace-keeping' and 'operations other than war', corps and divisions were still needed at all. The situation is paralleled in other fields. After half a century when not a single Dutch ship had fired a single shot in anger, Dutch women gained the right to serve aboard as equals.

At a time when the production of new artillery barrels for the British Army has all but ceased, British women gained the right to act as forward artillery observers.[125] At a time when demand for the new American F-22 fighter was down to only thirty a year,[126] that aircraft became the first ever specifically designed to accommodate both male and female pilots.[127] Even as the Soviet-Russian forces lost 97 per cent of their funding between 1989 and 1999, the share of women in them went up from near zero to 12 per cent, if only because, at the salaries offered, there simply were not enough men to be found.[128] And when the Italian and German armed forces are taking in women for the first time, the decision was made to reduce those forces from 270,000 to 190,000 and from 375,000 to 300,000 respectively.[129] The paradox is highlighted by the situation in France. Here women, on top of being barred from ground combat as is the case everywhere else, are excluded from the elite Foreign Legion. Not by accident, the Legion – 'the White SS' as it is sometimes known – is one of the few units that expect to survive the end of conscription and the ongoing savage reductions in the armed forces virtually intact.[131] Not by accident, too, it is the unit most likely to see action should there be trouble of any kind.

By the mid 1990s even the Israeli Army, long considered the sole shield that stood between the country and its Arab enemies and a bastion of male chauvinism, was beginning to feel the feminist heat. If only because the country's nuclear arsenal was growing all the time, over twenty years had passed since the country had fought its last major war against an Arab country; first its abortive invasion of Lebanon, and then the need to cope with the Palestinian uprising, were causing the IDF's social status to decline and its morale to falter.[132] By the later stages of the Lebanese adventure the IDF saw itself confronted with a serious problem. More and more male reservists were refusing to serve, and hundreds of them allowed themselves to be imprisoned instead.[133] Afraid lest any severe disciplinary measures might lead to still greater dissent, the General Staff hesitated. In the end it decided to replace the male reservists by less truculent female conscripts, though policy still prohibited them from crossing the border.[134]

In part, the growing feminist pressure reflected the fact that peace had been signed with the most important Arab country and that the threat presented by the rest was diminishing. In part it resulted from social change, since Israel was fast turning from a developing into a developed country with the attendant phenomena of a declining birth rate, better education and growing suburbs. Be this as it may, in 1996 the pressure bore fruit when the High Court compelled the air force to take on its first female pilot candidate.[135] As it happened, this was just the time when the IDF was being crucified by the media for the way it handled the Palestinian *intifada*; in the words of its own chief of staff, it had turned into 'the national punching bag'.[136] Now, to add to its troubles, the air force came under fire for allegedly discriminating against women.[137]

Yet in Israel as elsewhere 'progress' proved unstoppable. In 1997 the first women joined anti-aircraft units.[138] In 1998 the navy was forced to enrol female cadets. Other women were being trained as flight controllers, a position decreasingly attractive to men.[139] Late in the same year the first female pilot received her wings.[140] However, and if only because they may have feared being accused of 'sexual harassment', her fellow graduates would not embrace her during the graduation ceremony as they did each other; even as she listened to the force commander welcoming her, she stood alone. The final step was taken on 3 January 2000 when parliament decided to open all MOS to female soldiers. The Israel Defence Forces, as well as the media, took the decision very much in their stride. Perhaps this is because many Israeli women are showing that they are by no means as eager to risk their lives as their would-be leaders claim. Between 1994 and 1999 the number of those who obtained exemption by claiming to be religious grew from 20 to over 26 per cent of each class.[141]

By this time, the fashion for women warriors was spreading from the developed countries to at least some developing ones. For example, it would be difficult to claim that India has ever suffered from a shortage of male candidates to fly its combat aircraft; yet by the late 1990s, almost thirty years after it had fought its last serious war against Pakistan, and over twenty since it demonstrated that it, too, possessed a nuclear deterrent, the Indian Air Force had trained and deployed a few women pilots. The message that including women soldiers in one's armed forces constitutes a step towards modernization or at any rate is useful for propaganda purposes was even understood by some Muslim countries. Thus, ever since its establishment in 1922 the only country against which the Kingdom of Jordan has ever waged war in earnest has been Israel (1948 and 1967). Considered by many to be the best and most professional Arab force, throughout that turbulent period the Jordanian Army managed to do without women in its ranks. No sooner had peace with Israel been concluded in 1994, though, than it set up a women's corps, with a daughter of the late King Hussein at its head.

Like all large organizations, armed forces tend to be conservative and resistant to change. Like all large organizations, normally they will reform themselves only when faced by an extreme threat, good cases in point being the Prussian Army after defeat by Napoleon in 1806, the French one following its defeat by Moltke in 1870–71, and the British one after the Boer War. Alternatively, the willingness to reform may indicate that the organizations in question are no longer needed and that society can therefore afford to use them in order to conduct all kinds of social experiments. During the last decade of the twentieth century clearly there could no longer be any question of any developed state in North America, Europe, East Asia or Australasia facing a major military threat. According to French President Jacques Chirac, not for a thousand years had France found itself in a situation where neither it nor any of its allies could see an enemy within a thousand kilometres of its frontiers;[142] in Europe even more than the US, 'the will to defend' has disappeared and patriotism turned into a dirty word.[143] Thus the reality of the matter is that women's triumph in forcing their way into combat-related MOS was hollow. It was made even more hollow by the developments that accompanied it.

21 The Hollow Triumph

Even as the American feminist lobby in particular continued to push for women to be treated equally with men in regard to war, it was becoming more and more clear that being treated equally with men was the last thing most women wanted. Nor was this to be wondered at. In the Western world since the French Revolution the right to vote was often a direct outcome of, or at any rate went together with, conscription.[144] But women were able to obtain the former without being subjected to the latter; for them to be put on an equal footing with men would have meant an end to their greatest privilege. Conversely it was hardly by accident that, first in the US and then in other countries, the post-1970 feminization of the military coincided with the switch from conscription to all-volunteer forces.[145] Once the influx had started, it was pushed forward under the rallying-cry of equality. Unfortunately for the feminists, in 1979–80 the US armed forces were so short of volunteers that the Carter administration put the matter to the test by announcing its intention to bring back the draft. Polls were taken and the truth emerged: fewer than two out of every five women (as against more than three out of every five men) thought that conscription should be applied to them.[146]

At this point the debate concerning the draft started running at cross currents with the one surrounding the Equal Rights Amendment, or ERA. Originally proposed in 1971, in less than a decade ERA was ratified by thirty-five out of the thirty-eight states it needed to pass into law. By the late 1970s it seemed to have the wind blowing in its back; then the idea of reintroducing the draft made many women have second thoughts. Vainly did feminists try to save their handiwork by telling their followers that the Supreme Court (which is made up overwhelmingly of men) would never be so unchivalrous as to *oblige* the services to treat women as men in this respect.[147]

Perhaps it was to the credit of American women that most of them refused to follow the call of their would-be leaders and believe they could have their cake and eat it too. Faced with the choice between maintaining their traditional privileges and obtaining equality they preferred the former, causing ERA to be abandoned. Twelve years later the Presidential Commission took care to reassure women on this point. Not only would they not be conscripted, but even preliminary registration was out of the question.[148]

At this very time, a similar debate took place in West Germany. Unlike the US, the Federal Republic had (and, as of early 2000, retains) the draft. Like the US, during the late 1970s it was anticipating a shortage of military manpower, which, in this case, was brought about less by men's reluctance to serve than by a sharply declining birth rate during the previous ten years.[149] One way to solve the problem, it was suggested, was to conscript women; with that, the fat was in the fire. Right-wing, conservative women resisted the proposal because they considered women already made a sufficient contribution to the national welfare by giving birth to children.[150] Left-wing, feminist-inclined women resisted it because they detested the Bundeswehr as a bastion of male chauvinistic, patriarchal, capitalist, reactionary society and wanted to have it abolished.[151] As in the US, the idea that women share the burdens of equality as well as its rights got nowhere. In the end, all that happened was that the constitution was altered in 1989 in order to enable the Sanitary Corps, which was running out of male personnel, to recruit about 3,000 women to take their place.[152]

Within the military, too, the attempt to push women into 'non-traditional' MOS often met with resistance on the part of those concerned. Already in the US Army during the Second World War women only filled 146 out of the 406 MOS theoretically open to them.[153] By far the greatest number of women were found in a handful of MOS, such as nursing, communications and clerical work, from which they could not and would not be moved. The British Army during the same period discovered that the greatest obstacle to the opening of additional MOS to women consisted of WAC commanders.[154] In the Red Air Force, not one woman who had worked as a mechanic in 1941–5 remained in the field after the end of the war.[155]

During the late 1970s the attempts of the Israeli Army to make more extensive use of its female forces were also obstructed by CHEN commanders who did not want their charges to soil their hands.[156]

Since then, in most if not all of the Western armed forces that opened their ranks to them, women have drifted back into 'traditional' occupations;[157] the same, incidentally, happened in the Israeli kibbutzim which, between 1920 and 1950 or so, probably took the experiment further than any other human communities in history.[158] Often this is because many 'non-traditional' jobs involve difficult living conditions, shift work, the capability to respond to an emergency on a twenty-four-hour basis, and long separations from home, as in sea-duty, forward deployment, and the like. Others are dirty, unpleasant, and even dangerous as in maintenance, construction, and so on, as is also evident from the fact that, in civilian life, 93 per cent of all those killed on the job are men.[159]

What was true of 'non-traditional' MOS was even more true of the most unpleasant 'occupation' of all: combat. The first studies I could find on the subject date to the late 1970s and early 1980s: they showed that almost four times as many US enlisted men as women would do anything to get into combat (11 v. 3 per cent). Conversely, two and a half times as many enlisted women as men would do anything not to go (42 v. 16 per cent).[160] Similar results were obtained by Colonel David Hackworth, who had once been the army's most highly decorated officer in Vietnam, in a 1991 survey among 500 female soldiers at Fort Bragg. It turned out that these women – members of an airborne division and veterans of the Gulf War – well realized they had not been in serious combat. More remarkable still, having had their chance to see war at close quarters not a single one of them wanted to be.[161]

In 1996–8 the question was taken up once again by Laura Miller of Northwestern University. Her conclusions were similar to those just quoted: only 14 per cent of female officers, 13 per cent of female NCOs and 11 per cent of female enlisted said they would volunteer for combat.[162] Since enlisted personnel form the majority of all military women (and men), it appears that hardly more than one in ten of all military women was prepared voluntarily to enter the one field that justifies the organization they had joined;

what results are available for other countries point in the same direction.[163]
Both Hackworth and Miller also found that many enlisted women in particular felt uncomfortable with the pressure to open more combat positions
to females. The way enlisted women saw it, female officers did not grasp the
physical hardship that combat entailed on the enlisted level; this was even
more true for their supporters in the feminist lobbies, hardly any of whom had
ever spent a day in the military.[164] Thus it all boiled down to an attempt by
well-educated, well-to-do, successful women to advance their own careers
and political agendas – such as 'enrich[ing] the concept of citizenship'[165] – at
the expense of their poorly educated, less affluent, less successful 'sisters'.
Much in the way that, in civilian life, the standard way for professional women
to obtain the freedom to pursue a career is to hire other women to look
after their children and clean their houses for them.

To 'solve' the problem, it has been suggested that women be sent into
combat only if they volunteered.[166] Had the proposal been adopted – and
this may yet happen – it would have been entirely in line with the various
privileges that women have been granted since the first day they entered the
military. Thus, already in the First World War British servicemen, but not
British servicewomen, could be shipped overseas against their will. In the
US during the same period, no sooner had the first American women donned
uniform than Secretary of the Navy Josephus Daniels made it known he
took 'a dim view' of any attempt to court-martial them, insisting that '[one]
cannot deal with women as with men'.[167] The tradition was carried on into the
Second World War when the worst fate any female member of the US forces
might face after committing an offence was to be dishonourably discharged;
incidentally this may help explain how those women who did stay in the
service were able to gain their reputation for being more disciplined than
men.[168] In the Red Army during the same period to see a woman under arrest
was cause for surprise.[169] In the British forces women enjoyed better living
conditions, more leave,[170] and laxer discipline than their male comrades. To
say nothing of the fact that, as in all other armies, they were permitted to
desert almost at will.[171]

Not surprisingly, during the post-war decades all the forces that included

women continued to give them preferential treatment. Thus US servicewomen – but not servicemen – may keep their hair, wear some jewellery,
and so on. To protect their hair, female officers are allowed to carry umbrel-
las;[172] to protect their children, mothers of infants under four months old
were made exempt from deployment to some areas.[173] The situation in foreign military is broadly similar. For example, the Soviet Army was notorious for the harsh treatment it meted out to its male soldiers, to the point
that many of them were driven to suicide. By contrast, Soviet servicewomen
were exempt from the stricter forms of disciplinary action including arrest,
confinement to quarters, restriction to the unit area, assignment to extra
details, and transfer to punitive units; their accommodation was also superior,
and they were permitted to live with their parents if they wanted to.[174] Having started taking in women during the 1970s, the Greek armed forces provided them with better quarters and less harassment.[175] In Belgium female
soldiers were barred by law from carrying out dangerous and insalubrious
jobs such as trench-digging, handling lead-containing dies, and working in
pressure-chambers.[176] In Switzerland they had to do considerably less service
in order to gain promotion.[177] In Canada they cannot be sentenced to prison
because the forces do not have special facilities for female prisoners.[178]

In Israel women are conscripted for less than two years versus three for
men. Following some bad experiences (followed by equally bad publicity)
Israeli female conscripts are not made to guard bases as males do, with the
incidental result that they spend less time on duty and more at home. Certain
MOS considered particularly unpleasant or degrading, such as cooking, have
always been reserved for men, with the result that, in IDF slang, 'cook' and
'half-witted' have long been synonymous. As is also the case in Israel's civil
service, female officers who are mothers work shorter hours than men.
Unlike their menfolk who at the height of the Palestinian uprising during
the late 1980s and early 1990s might be called up for as much as ninety days
per year, Israeli women rarely serve in the reserves. Consequently they do
not incur the professional and financial penalties that such service often
entails for men; in all my thirty years as a member of the faculty at Hebrew
University not a single female student lost a single class because of reserve

duty. Finally, as feminist pressures took hold, parliament made sure that women retained their privileges by passing a special law that they would not be obliged to serve in a combat unit against their will;[179] now that all MOS have been opened to them, they can literally eat their cake and have it too.

In Britain military nurses are automatically commissioned.[180] In a force where officers continue to form less than 4 per cent of all personnel and where their status is accordingly high, this is not a small privilege; fortunately its impact on morale is limited because nurses have always been considered a class apart for which there are few, if any, male volunteers. In countries that conscript men but allow women to volunteer the latter are usually under-represented in entry-level slots and over-represented among NCOs.[181] Whether or not they are trained together with the men women tend to escape the more unpleasant aspects of military life, proceeding straight from a much-softened form of basic training to comfortable jobs and, if they can, sticking with them. In addition, whenever women enter such high-prestige, extremely demanding fields as pilot training, the physical requirements made of them are inevitably less, and the conditions under which they live invariably better, than those of the men.[182]

If all this were not bad enough, to compensate for women's physical weakness military men are often obliged to undertake additional hardship. For example, during the Second World War British anti-aircraft batteries were sexually 'mixed'. In practice this meant that the impending arrival of the women was often heralded by the men being asked to give up their quarters for them; a demand that they usually met, if not enthusiastically, at any rate with good grace. Once 'integration' was complete, somehow it was always the men who found themselves doing the heavier and dirtier work.[183] Since then 'social science' conducted by 'trained observers' has confirmed what anybody who has ever participated in a hike has always known. When mixed exercises are held the men will do women's chores in addition to their own. Whereas women, content to be helped along, become dependent on men for performing the hard work.[184]

In fact, had assignment been governed by physical strength alone, women would have been excluded from about 80 per cent of the MOS in which they actually served and which they could hold only because they were assisted by men.[185] As a result, one officially sponsored team reporting on the Gulf War used the euphemism 'teamwork' to disguise the fact that the presence of women in the US forces compelled the men who served with them to do more than their share;[186] this happened whenever there was a chore to be done, be it digging trenches or tearing down tents or loading boxes on trucks, causing the entire cycle of operations to be slowed down.[187] To round off the list of privileges, female service personnel could, and sometimes did, obtain a homeward ticket by neglecting to use contraceptives and getting pregnant. Meanwhile, men who voluntarily incapacitated themselves would be court-martialled.

To my knowledge, no armed force has gone further to humiliate its male personnel than did the Australian one, which in turn may not be unrelated to the fact that, among the almost two hundred states on this earth, Australia is one of those least likely to be involved in serious warfare of any kind. Like their counterparts in other countries, some Australian military personnel engage in SERE training. As part of that training they are routinely 'captured' and, among other things, subjected to body searches. During recent years the influx of women into almost every part of the service meant that some of them participated in the exercises. It goes without saying that for a male trainer to strip-search a female trainee is inconceivable and that any commander who allowed it would be court-martialled on the spot. Women, though, even such as are not medically qualified, do search the genitals and bodily apertures of men.[188]

Before the advent of modern feminism, men in and out of the military could often take a chivalrous attitude to women's privileges in the hope that living and working with them would not be without its compensations. Thus, as already noted, during the Second World War Soviet female air regiments provided the setting for many a love affair and even marriages. Mixed British anti-aircraft batteries provided a similar background for romance; in Israel, the fact that female conscripts have a much easier time of it than male ones does not prevent most youngsters from meeting their first sexual partners while serving in the IDF. But whereas in all of these cases the presence of women in the armed forces could be justified by a national emergency, this has not been the case in those developed countries which opened their militaries to women from about 1970 on. In them, the influx of women into the military was occasioned by the reluctance of men to enlist on the one hand and by the reluctance of governments to pay adequately those who did enlist on the other. Worse still, even as they demanded equality the women kept their privileges. Hence it is scarcely surprising that military men reacted like any other group whose position is undercut. They resented the women, often resorting to the most insidious methods to make their resentment felt.

First in the US and then in other countries as well, the forces were torn apart by a phenomenon known as 'sexual harassment'. As defined, for example, by Section 703, Title VII, of the US Civil Rights Act of 1964, sexual harassment referred to situations where superiors, who were usually male, used their power over subordinates, who were usually female, in order to obtain sexual favours for themselves,[189] a dastardly form of behaviour that no organization, military or civilian, can or should tolerate. During the 1970s and 1980s, however, the definition of 'sexual harassment' was stretched beyond recognition until it included anything that any woman might not like. 'Harassment' could exist even if there was no physical contact; even if it did not include pressure of any sort; and even if it did not damage her career.[190] At a time when military job opportunities are few and shrinking, this provided military women with a formidable weapon for use against their own side's military men.

In organizations that had always been noted for their coarse language – often used as a deliberate tool to humiliate recruits and make them amenable to discipline – all of a sudden for drillmasters to refer to a person's gender or bodily parts constituted 'sexual harassment'. In organizations where flamboyant displays of masculinity had always been tolerated if not encouraged as contributing to unit cohesion, suddenly anything that smelled of men's pride in themselves came to be construed as 'sexual harassment'. Traditionally cramped quarters and the frequent need to operate in confined places had always led to a certain amount of physical contact between soldiers; now anyone caught touching (or, under some interpretations, attempting to touch) a female soldier with the aim of straightening a tie or adjusting a belt while on parade put himself at risk of being accused of 'sexual harassment'. A male soldier who greeted a female comrade a little too effusively could be accused of 'sexual harassment'. A male soldier who did not greet a female soldier effusively enough could also be accused of 'sexual harassment'. In the US and Canada things reached the point where a male soldier could be court-martialled simply for looking at a female once too often, or for too long, or in the 'wrong' way. Even if the charge failed to stick, the man's career would probably be over. As happened, for example, in 1995 when President Clinton had a navy captain and admiral-designate who had just been acquitted taken off the promotion list.[191]

By the 1990s things had got to the point where the term 'sexual harassment', however inflated its meaning, could no longer be stretched to include all the forms of behaviour that some women claimed were 'offensive' to them. Accordingly it was supplemented by another, 'sexism'. Some forms of sexism originated in 'explicit sexist beliefs', others in 'sexist background stances and practices'. There was 'sexism by commission' and 'sexism by omission'. To 'categorize women' primarily in terms of 'sexual accessibility' counted as sexism; but doing the same in terms of 'nurturance' also counted as sexism. 'Objectifying' women constituted sexism, but then so did 'subjectifying' them. Since 'applying gendered attributes to women' (in plain words, believing or saying that women are women) also counts as sexism, men can be sexist simply for believing they are not women.[192] In theory, 'sexual harassment' and 'sexism' were a two-way affair. In practice the services tended to treat male complaints about them as a joke.[193] After all, a man unable to defend himself against a woman's advances, sexual or other, hardly deserves to be taken seriously as a soldier. This may help explain why such cases are reported much less frequently.[194]

As women entered other organizations besides the military, the services were hardly alone in their predicament; after all, the point has now been reached when a ten-year-old can be prosecuted for 'sexual harassment' and the school to which he went for failing to prevent it.[195] Still there are several reasons why 'the gender wars' probably took on a more insidious character inside the military than anywhere else. First, more than most other institutions the military are entirely dependent on public funding and thus on the whims of an electorate the majority of which is nowadays made up of women. Second, more than most other institutions they spend most of their time not so much carrying out their designated task as preparing and training for it. Since their main concern is input rather than output, the real impact that the influx of women has on the latter remains hidden. Conversely, the fact that it remains hidden permits more women to come in, and so on in a vicious cycle without either beginning or end.

Finally, more than most other institutions the military are subject to discipline. They can be made to perform almost like trained poodles as required by their political masters – or so those masters, ignoring growing bitterness both among the officers and among the troops,[196] appear to think. In an age when, in every developed country without exception, their place in national life was under assault and their budgets were being cut almost daily, nothing was more important to the military than avoiding bad publicity and litigation. This induced them to engage on an experiment in political correctness without precedent in history, one that some people, totally misreading the true situation, believe should serve as a model for other organizations.[197]

In essence female soldiers, while expecting and expected to be fully integrated into the organization, were put out of bounds. In one military after another, 'sexual harassment' was turned into a one-time offence that led to the immediate discharge of those convicted of it. Hundreds of regulations aimed at defining, preventing and punishing 'sexual harassment' were instituted; in Australia, for example, a major scandal (followed by a major investigation and the inevitable male casualties) on the subject may be expected every two years on average.[198] In one military after another, 'hot lines' were opened to enable female soldiers to inform on their male comrades behind the latters' backs. In one military after another, new prohibitions on fraternization were proclaimed. They were carried to the point where the US Air Force jailed a married couple because, during their period of courtship, the woman had been under the man's command. Any form of adultery also became a career-terminating transgression. Even if it has nothing to do with a person's military performance; and even if it had taken place decades previously. Thus soldiers who, from the time of Herodotus to the Second World War, regarded themselves and were regarded by others as the most manly of men were turned into eunuchs. To add offence to injury the services hired 'experts', many of them female, to mete out so-called 'sensitivity training'. As of early 2000, US Army recruits actually spend more time on this kind of training than in learning how to use their weapons; to say nothing of the implicit message that men are louts who do not know how to treat women properly.[199]

In the military, more than in any other institution, it is possible to prevent men from saying what they really think of their female comrades by simply ordering them to shut their mouths. For example, in October 1998 some American Marines criticized their commander-in-chief, President Clinton (the same who, three years earlier, refused to promote a navy captain accused, and acquitted, of 'sexual harassment') for engaging in the kind of behaviour with a woman for which they themselves would be dismissed from the corps; not only was the relationship with Ms Lewinsky adulterous, but she had worked for the president. Within days, they were officially silenced.[200] No wonder military men are often unwilling to discuss women even within four walls. Each time the subject comes up in a lecture the entire audience freezes.

In the military, as in any other institution, the influx of large numbers of women is both symptom and cause of declining social prestige.[201] In the military, as in any other institution, such a decline will be followed by falling earning power, which in turn will make men leave for greener pastures. As the 1990s were drawing to an end, military men in all developed countries had long started showing what they really think of serving along with women by voting with their feet. In the US, a growing population, a downsizing military and falling standards[202] still left the services so short of recruits that each one has to be paid a $6,000 enlistment bonus plus $50,000 in college money after four years in the service; to no avail, as is evident from the fact that, as of October 1999, all but the Marines were failing to meet their recruitment goals.[203] In Britain, more women were being inducted not because the forces wanted them or needed them but because 'many young men decided the services no longer offered a secure career'.[204] In fact, so short of men was the British Army in particular that it started considering foreign sources of recruitment.

On the other side of the world, Australia in 1998 saw as many as 20 per cent of all youths unemployed. Yet finding suitable men who are willing to become officers has become very hard indeed, with the result that their place at the Defence Academy is increasingly being taken by women. Israel, thanks to conscription, still has all the male manpower it needs. However, there too the influx of women during the last twenty years has probably contributed to the astounding decline in men's willingness to fight for their country;[205] as of 1999 even the vaunted air force was beginning to run out of male volunteers as pilots found that their jobs no longer commanded the same prestige as previously.[206] Returning to Europe, at the very time when the Bundeswehr had been ordered to open its ranks to women it was running out of male volunteers.[207] In the Netherlands between 1990 and 1996 the size of the military fell by no less than 40 per cent, and the process of downsizing still continues day by day as budgets are slashed, units disbanded, and purchasing programmes cancelled. Nevertheless, so strong has been the 'backlash'[208] to the women's perceived privileges as to make it all but impossible to recruit any men at all.[209]

22 The New World Disorder

If the influx of women is one symptom of the decline of the state-owned, regular military, the growth of irregular, non-state, armed forces of every sort is another. To quote a few figures only, the Russian Federation is supposed to have about 1,000 private security firms. In Britain between 1950 and 1976 the number of those active in the field of private security increased from 10,000 to 250,000.[210] In Germany between 1984 and 1996 the number of security firms more than doubled, whereas the number of personnel active in the field increased by 300 per cent;[211] by 2000 there were almost as many private policemen as state-employed ones.[212] In the US as of 1994 there were more people involved with private security than there were uniformed troops – 1.6 million to 1.4 million to be precise – and the relationship has continued to shift since then. Early in the 1970s the American defence budget stood to the turnover of the security industry at seven to one.[213] It has since gone down to between four and five to one, and if present trends persist the cross-over point is in sight.

While certainly not without its unique characteristics, in many ways the security industry is, like so many others, being heavily centralized at the top so that a handful of firms account for the majority of resources: for example, Wackenhut Ltd now operates in over fifty countries. Some firms are led by retired generals and admirals and employ the equivalents of entire divisions. Others run sophisticated organizations and possess every weapon up to, and including, machine-guns, all sorts of light anti-aircraft guns and missiles, light armoured personnel-carriers, and even some of the smaller gunship helicopters complete with rockets and anti-tank missiles.

Compared with the situation as it was only twenty or thirty years ago, the range of activities in which the firms in question engage is astonishing. It starts with the recruitment and training of individual guards to station in your local supermarket or protect a fancy wedding against gatecrashers. It progresses through research and development, both of equipment and of scenarios. It goes all the way to securing entire complexes from prisons (one of the largest firms, Wackenhut Ltd, alone owns and operates thirty prisons) to international airports; to say nothing of mounting so-called 'red' teams whose function is to test the defences of the complexes in question and suggest ways of improving them. Among the clients are individuals, neighbourhoods, municipalities and corporations, including such as operate in Third World countries or require protection against piracy on the high seas. Even governments are not above buying their services, given that private security personnel do not get the kind of fringe benefits to which regular policemen are entitled and can therefore be had at one-third of the cost.[214] Even in developed countries the firms in question sometimes engage – and, increasingly, are officially permitted to engage[215] – in so-called 'cowboy activities'. This includes detective work, debt-collection, bounty hunting, breaking up strikes, evicting squatters, patrolling neighbourhoods with or without their inhabitants' consent, arresting people and holding them until the arrival of the police, and much else.

Private security also hires some women, if only because, their average wage being about 60–70 per cent of men's,[216] they are even cheaper than the latter. For reasons that may not be beyond the comprehension of even the most avid feminist, by and large women are much less suitable than men for guard and patrol duty. At best they may accompany men; hence most are probably concentrated in support positions as secretaries, communicators, and so on. Take, for example, the aviation security business which in the US alone is worth approximately $2,000 million a year.[217] Secretaries apart, women are heavily concentrated at the bottom of the ladder where one can see them in various airports, manning electronic gates and checking bags; so boring is the task that the crews must be relieved every twenty minutes. Higher up, where the work can be extremely interesting but often demands irregular hours, the ability to respond to an emergency, and sometimes round-the-clock presence, there are few if any women.[218] To adduce another example, from Northern Ireland through Israel to Indonesia police teams specializing in crowd control and the like now often include a handful of helmeted, baton-carrying women. Like the fake Amazons of old, these women carry specially made small shields.[219] Since size is directly linked to the ability to protect against blows and rocks, this alone proves that they are not meant for serious work but for use – at the behest of men, needless to say[220] – against other women.

What is more, the services in question are capable of being exported. Long gone is the time when the governments of many developed countries felt responsible for the fate of their former colonies. The Cold War having ended, they are also much less worried about any 'gains' that the Soviet Union might make in the 'developing' world; they and their populations are becoming less and less willing to involve themselves in various 'peace-keeping' operations. The gap created by their departure is increasingly being filled by mercenaries. Mercenaries were banned by the St Petersburg Convention of 1864. During the first half of the twentieth century they had all but disappeared; their current return constitutes one of the more important, if less noted, phenomena of the modern world.[221] Ironically many of the personnel in question are themselves ex-members of the armed forces of the developed countries, meaning officers and men who, as the organizations to which they used to belong are being downsized, often find themselves on the streets with their skills no longer needed.

Most of the companies that employ mercenaries are based in the US, Britain, South Africa, and Israel. They have names such as BDM International, Brown & Root, Control Risks Group, Defense Systems Limited, Dyncorp, Executive Outcomes, Levran, Military Professional Resources Inc., Pacific Architects and Engineers, Rapport Research and Analysis, Saladin Security, Sandline, Saracen, Strategic Applications International, and Vinnel.[222] As in any other field of economic activity, not all of them have an all-round capability and some of them are rather specialized. Still, between them they will engage in the most varied activities starting with military analysis and threat-assessment through logistical support and procurement and training all the way to providing support for, or participating in, actual military operations.

Many of the firms in question operate with the full knowledge of their own governments. The latter regard them much as they would any other earners of foreign currency; the British Foreign Office for one even has a list of 'approved' defence companies open to anyone. In theory the more reputable among them will only contract with legitimate employers, i.e. governments; at least one, the South African Executive Outcomes, had that part of its turnover resulting from operations in Sierra Leone approved by the International Monetary Fund.[223] In practice very often they or their less reputable competitors will serve almost anyone, provided only that he can pay. For example, the Israeli firm Lava was accused of training private armies for drug-lords ('estate owners' was the euphemism used) in several Latin American countries.

'Mercs', as they are sometimes called, are active in many places around the world. In Eastern Europe, several ex-Soviet republics rely on them to train their forces and make the transition to Western methods. The war in Bosnia-Herzegovina alone saw the use of mercenaries from Afghanistan, Britain, Denmark, Finland, Italy, Sweden, Russia and the United States;[224] but they are even more conspicuous in Latin American, Central Asian, and African countries. For example, during Zaire's civil war both sides made use of mercenaries. Those fighting against President Mobutu were provided by the ubiquitous Executive Outcomes; they proved more capable than those hired to fight for him, most of them Croats and Serbs who found themselves unemployed as a result of the Dayton Accords which stopped them fighting in their own country.[225] In Angola and Sierra Leone it is mercenaries who protect the extraction of vital minerals such as oil and diamonds. From Papua through the Comoros Islands to West Africa other mercenaries have been involved in coups, either trying to topple governments or reasserting their authority.

What makes these developments possible is the fact that, outside North America, Western Europe, Japan and Australasia the five-sixths of the world often known as 'developing' are anything but peaceful. From Kosovo to Colombia and from Tibet and Sri Lanka through Afghanistan to the Sudan and throughout Central Africa, there are now numerous armed conflicts that involve open, if so-called 'low intensity', warfare. Much as the UN and other international bodies try to police these conflicts, neither their number nor their ferocity shows the slightest sign of diminishing. It is almost as if, each time one is extinguished, another one is waiting to take its place.

The preferred habitat of these conflicts is the land, possibly with some re-supply taking place by sea also as used to be the case in Vietnam and Northern Ireland and as is presently the case in the Philippines, Sri Lanka and East Timor. In order that heavy weapons not be brought to bear against them, invariably the kind of terrain in which they unfold is extremely complicated. Often it consists of mountains, as in Afghanistan and, most recently, Chechnia; or else of swamps and jungles as in much of South-East Asia and Latin America. Alternatively it may consist of the even more complex terrain presented by densely inhabited areas with their houses, roads, orchards, fields, power lines, factories and commercial establishments. So far from constituting 'stand off' and 'push-button warfare', combat often takes place at such close quarters that the parties can exchange insults. The physical demands that these struggles make on participants are enormous. Except perhaps for a handful of viragos, who are sometimes put on display in order to impress foreigners, in *none* of them do women carry weapons or fight in the open. For example, in Sri Lanka only one out of thirty-three Tamil organizations has female combatants.[226] In a Kosovo Liberation Army parade that was shown on CNN on 20 September 1999, the organization's flag was carried by a woman, but she seemed to be the only one present among perhaps a hundred armed men.

Confronted with these wars women, be they young or old, educated or not, 'liberated' or otherwise, are acting as women always have: as eggers-on, protégées, camp-followers (also as providers of sexual services) and, as events in Kosovo and East Timor showed once again, victims.[227] Partly this is because the belligerents regard these wars as a matter of life and death, as well they might; the last thing that enters their heads is to bow to the kind of social, political and juridical constraints that have compelled the armed forces of the developed world to take in women and treat them as if they were as fit for war as men. Partly it is because recruiters do not want them. In Sierra Leone in 1997–8 they preferred taking thirteen- to fifteen-year-old males; and the same is also true in other countries undergoing civil war such as Burma. Finally, and perhaps most important of all, the women themselves are under no illusions as to their suitability for the work at hand. Nor do they need fantastically elaborate (and costly) studies by 'trained observers' to be convinced of the fact.

Of all human activities war is by far the most nasty and the most danger-ous. It is also physically the most demanding, which means that, despite the claims of some feminists to the contrary, in no other activity are women as much at a disadvantage in relation to men. Under any but the most desper-ate circumstances involving home defence after everything has already been lost, to expose women to combat is little short of criminal: even if, since combat very often demands close co-operation between soldiers, it were not counter-productive. Unlike their sisters in the developed countries, who have enjoyed peace for over half a century on end and consequently no longer have the slightest idea of what war is really like, women in war-torn developing ones all over the world understand the score well enough. As best they can, the vast majority are staying away.

Conclusions **Change and Continuity**

Perhaps the first lesson of the present study is that pro-feminist scholars, attempting to prove that women can and should take an active part in armed conflict, have inflated the role played by women in the past out of all proportion. To adduce but four examples separated by over two thousand years, whatever our view of the function of the Amazon myth in Greek culture the decisive fact about them was that they never existed. Though a few female commissars did exist and committed atrocities with the best, on the whole the success of the Red Army in mobilizing women during the Russian Civil War was anything but 'legendary'. Nor is it true that Soviet women during the Second World War, or Israeli women serving in the IDF, played a much greater role than their sisters did elsewhere.

Many existing accounts are misleading and confused: for example, when they mix up real women with mythological ones or use the fact that some women have ruled and commanded to 'prove' that they can also fight. Very often, too, evidence is accepted or rejected as it suits the political needs of the moment. Thus most feminist writings about the First World War, seeking to show that women are peaceful by nature, present the reader with hardly a hint that most women welcomed the conflict as enthusiastically as did men.[1] When 'Russian general officers' informed the Presidential Commission for the Assignment of Women in the Military that Soviet female flyers in the Second World War had suffered very heavy casualties and were considered expendable they were believed; but when *the same* officers reported that women had served as pilots mainly for propaganda reasons their statement was dismissed out of hand as a 'new view'.[2] On occasion, so strident is the demand that women carry any hardship and share every danger that one cannot help but wonder whether Freud was right and penis envy really exists. For example, when one female author preens herself on the fact that women have earned the right to be called 'wimps' just as men are.[3]

Even disregarding the evidence provided by our closest living relatives, chimpanzees, it is clear without further ado that women's life cycle on the one hand and their weaker bodies on the other almost always prevented most of them from participating in war and combat. This may explain why, during most of history the exclusion of women from these activities was regarded as self-evident; most men and women took it for granted that such participation would be 'impossible' (Christine de Pizan) or 'bizarre' (Helene Deutsch). As late as the first decade of the present century one argument used by the suffragettes was that the world was becoming more peaceful, an idea they derived from male thinkers such as Herbert Spencer and Norman Angel. The supposed decline of war meant that future governments would be concerned mainly with good housekeeping; since women were as qualified for this task for as men, they deserved the vote.[4] The fate of ERA, as well as the debate that went on in the German Federal Republic during the late 1970s, are suggestive; had women been asked to share the burden of conscription as the price for citizenship most might well have preferred to do without. Even as this book was being written some Israeli feminists demanded that women, while retaining the vote and every other political right, should no longer share the burden of defence by being subject to the draft.[5]

The above considerations notwithstanding, there is reason to think that the real reason why women have so seldom participated in war on any scale is less their own disabilities than the psychological handicaps of men. Biologically speaking, women are superior to men in several ways, of which the most important one is the ability to have children. Well realizing their own dispensability, men seek to compensate; indeed it would scarcely be too much to say that much of human 'society' always has been and still is organized specifically in order to provide them with that compensation.[6] As Margaret Mead argues, and as much of the social reality around us confirms, provided only women are excluded from it the precise nature of that compensation does not matter much. At different times and places it has taken on an almost infinite number of forms from operating prayer wheels to deep-sea fishing and from rug-weaving through big-game hunting to playing certain musical instruments. Depending on one's point of view, some of those forms deserve being called ridiculous, others serious, and others still – involving as they do self sacrifice – sublime. Yet there is no denying that, of all human activities, war is in some ways the most suitable one for the purpose.

Even if women's bodies had not been weaker than those of men, and even if they had not been handicapped by their life cycle, this line of reasoning would explain why, historically, women – even those who were otherwise qualified – have very seldom been permitted to take an active part in war. To the extent that they participated, normally they did so in a very great variety of supporting roles; from administration and logistics and intelligence all the way to looking after what Voltaire once called 'the natural needs of heroes'. What all those roles had in common was that they did not threaten the men who engaged in war; by leaving almost all the killing and most of the being killed to the latter, they permitted male self-respect to remain intact. As noted, this consideration also explains why proportionally more women did participate in last stands, revolts and insurgencies of every sort. And why, in every single known case, no sooner did the uprising end than traditional attitudes reaffirmed themselves.

Here and there a few women were able to participate in combat by disguising themselves, while others found themselves in positions where they ruled and commanded. The former were without any historical significance save, perhaps, as freaks. The latter often did reasonably well, though seldom spectacularly so. Their existence proves, if proof were needed, that women, provided they get the chance, can command and rule just as well as men. Needless to say, far fewer women than men ever reached such positions. Partly this was because society did not give them the opportunity. Partly, one suspects, it was because on average they were less prepared to 'make the ... extraordinary sacrifices of personal happiness, health, time, friendship, and relationships in the pursuit and maintenance of power';[7] indeed the first of these factors may itself be an outcome of the latter. Be this as it may, in no field did women's relative lack of aggression and competitiveness confront them with greater obstacles than in war. The reason being that in war, as distinct from many other human activities, one either fights or dies.

Much to the surprise of many contemporaries who had not yet realized what a 'total' institution the military had become during the second half of the nineteenth century, between 1914 and 1945 the two World Wars saw women serving as soldiers for the first time. In reality, the change was smaller than most people believe and much smaller than some modern feminists, with their own agenda in mind, claim. In all armies, the vast majority of women who wore uniform continued to perform the same tasks as they had always done: to provide men with services of every kind. The various resistance movements apart, only very few women during either World War participated in combat, let alone ground combat. In 1941-5, some Soviet women did in fact participate in ground combat whereas others crewed combat aircraft. However, looking back, most female fighters did not think they were really suited for that role. After the conflict the majority were not unhappy to leave the forces and go home.

Whether in or out of uniform, female camp-followers were normally permitted, even encouraged, to retain their femininity. By contrast, those women who chose to exercise command or participate in combat usually found themselves forced to relinquish their femininity wholly or in part. As of late, females joining the palace guards of England and Denmark have been made to dress like men; it is as if, taking on male roles, women are obliged to *become* male. What is true of real-life women also applied to mythological ones. Most of them neither mated nor bore children, and some did not even have a father. At best such women would be called 'most manly', a dubious compliment and not one that many real-life women would wish to hear applied to themselves. At worst they were compelled to deny and conceal their sex. On occasion things seem to have worked the other way around, and women decided to participate in war and combat *because* they had problems with their sex to begin with.

The turning-point in the relationship between men, women and war, as in so much else, was brought about by the introduction of nuclear weapons in 1945. Politically speaking, nuclear weapons cut the link between victory and survival, thus ending the role of war as an instrument of politics and turning it into suicide. Even more important was their effect on masculine pride: precisely because there is no defence, they put an end to 'heroic action'. In this way nuclear weapons exercised a decisive influence both on those whose task it was to conduct war from their meeting-rooms and offices and on those whose job it was to risk their lives on the battlefield. Slowly but surely their proliferation around the world made war between states that possessed them, or which were suspected of possessing them, or which were even considered capable of producing them within a relatively short time, impossible as well as pointless.

Against this background it is no wonder that, in terms of both absolute size and relative numbers, the world's most important armed forces have entered a prolonged decline. Other things being equal, the less likely those forces were to fight serious wars against equal opponents the more women they took in. If only because the last thing most women wanted was to go into combat, the more women the armed forces took in the less capable they became of fighting serious wars against equal opponents. The chicken-and-egg game started some time during the late 1960s or early 1970s. As these lines are being written, it still continues; hardly a day goes by without the media reporting some further 'advance' by military women that is accompanied by further cuts. Along with nuclear weapons proliferation, the trend has long since reduced the world's most powerful armed forces into mere constabularies. If it continues then the day is in sight when the only mission left to most of them will be peace-keeping; even so, whenever peace-keeping gets under way in some remote Third World country (such as Sierra Leone in the spring of 2000) those who spearhead the effort are invariably men.

In all of this, the role played by women themselves was comparatively small. Contrary to the claims of some, it was not feminist pressures but the beliefs entertained by politicians, soldiers and scholars concerning the shape of future war that first enabled women to gain a permanent toehold in the military during the years after 1945; to say nothing of the fact that those expectations themselves, grounded as they were in a pre-nuclear world view, turned out to be completely wrong. Contrary to the claims of some, too, in most countries it was not feminist pressures but military requirements –

meaning a shortage of men – which triggered the growth of that toehold from about 1970 on. Often women, instead of freeing men for combat, simply took up positions men no longer wanted; in which respect the military are quite typical of other feminizing professions.[8] At most, feminist pressures as exercised partly by propaganda, partly by way of the political process, and partly through the courts helped open some additional MOS to women already in the services. They also brought about some improvements in the conditions under which they served.

Whatever the role played by feminism *vis-à-vis* other factors, and whatever also the implications of the process for women's position both in the military and in society as a whole, unquestionably the influx of women has caused the military to undergo the same processes as any other feminizing profession. To be sure, over time there have been some ups and downs. Given their widely differing structures and missions, the various units, arms and services did not feel the impact to the same extent. Depending on demographics, economics, cultural traditions and many other factors the situation varied somewhat from one country to another; thanks precisely to the fact that, during much of its existence, it faced overwhelming odds, one country – Israel – even managed to mobilize women *and* avoid the consequences of Mead's Law. Yet even in Israel, once the worst emergency had passed, the more women signed up and the greater their prominence the less attractive the military as a male job. The less attractive the military as a male job, the more women signed up either on their own initiative or because the Services deliberately targeted them as a means of filling the gap.

Meanwhile, the world has not stood still. Since 1980 or so in most developed countries the state has been in retreat and privatization the order of the day. Nor did this trend skip the armed forces. Most of them are even now fast hiving off and privatizing those parts of themselves where women are most likely to be found: namely, rear services of every kind.[9] As also happens in other feminizing professions,[10] the remaining women are usually better educated than the men whose places they take. Particularly at the enlisted level, joining the military may often entail entering some rough company and even experiencing actual downward social mobility. Nor are the women themselves unaware of this fact. It helps explain why, for all the talk about equality and in *every* military organization for which data are available, they tend to drift back into 'traditional' – read safe and usually desk-bound – jobs.

Last not least, military women are often absolutely detested by the male majority. As a result, the more determined and the more successful their quest for equality the more their special privileges were taken away and the more exposed they felt to 'sexual harassment', both real and imaginary. This has been carried to the point where, in 1998, some American servicewomen demanded that the process be put into reverse gear. They want a return to a separate chain of command for women, separate living quarters for women, separate dining facilities for women (given that pre-meal queues are said to provide males with some of the best opportunities for 'sexist' behaviour), and separate training courses for women.[11] By this view, women's attempt to improve their social position by joining the military has not only failed but backfired. Instead of showing they are equal to men, it has proved they cannot do without special protection.

What the bottom line ought to be depends on one's vantage-point. A man who reads this study might feel confirmed in his belief that women in the military do indeed present a problem. For example, it may be galling to see that, back in 1985, *Life* magazine's commemorative issue on the Second World War carried the pictures of seven female 'heroes' and ten male ones.[12] The fact is that, in 1941-5, over 15 million American men were conscripted of whom over half were sent overseas and almost 300,000 died. Meanwhile 99 per cent of American women stayed home: as to those who volunteered, such were the privileges they enjoyed that they could not even be sent abroad without their consent. Thus to pretend that the members of two sexes risked their lives, or shed their blood, to roughly equal extent is to devalue the very meaning of heroism; no wonder the supply of potential heroes, in other words men willing to enlist, is drying up. Still, and if only because those rare women who *are* successful and *do* reach the top invariably identify not with their weaker sisters but with their male comrades, women do not threaten to end the dominance of men either in the field of war or in any other.[13] Thus such a man – in fact, the great majority – might conclude that, so long as one stays out of trouble and is not accused of 'sexism', the problem is manageable. Since proving 'sexism by omission' is harder than proving 'sexism by commission', his best course is to play it safe by ignoring his female co-soldiers as far as he can. Which, very often, is exactly what happens.

Another male interpretation might be that the military are being split. In the US as of late 1998 soldiers in 221,000 male-only slots performed or prepared to perform difficult and dangerous jobs, mainly in ground combat and in small-unit action behind enemy lines. Soldiers in 1,180,000 slots open to both sexes often had little to do with war at all. At best (if that is the term) they might fire cruise missiles at unresisting Iraqis hundreds or thousands of kilometres away. At worst (if that is the term) they worked in an environment that is as safe as, though a good deal less uncertain than, most civilian ones.[14] Presumably a man who wants to 'use his prowess... [to] prove his valour and the vigour of his body for the honour of himself and his dependents'[15] would go for the first kind. In that case he should choose the Marine Corps which provides one-fifth of the positions in question; also, it is the only one that has refused to integrate basic training. It cannot be an accident that, over the last thirty years, the Marines have been most successful both in expanding their position *vis-à-vis* the remaining services (from 9.2 to 12.5 per cent)[16] and in attracting and retaining personnel. As of late 1999 they were the only service capable of meeting its recruitment targets.[17] Still, given the waning of major war on the one hand and the danger of being accused of 'sexual harassment' on the other, such a man might perhaps be excused for regarding the entire military as a waste of time. Having been trained, he might consider joining the rapidly growing 'security industry'. Or perhaps he should enlist as a mercenary and go to some developing country in which war is still war and men are still allowed to be men. For good or ill, of such countries there is no shortage.

Thus, both a man who considers his career in the military merely as another job and one who wants to see action would find little reason for taking his female colleagues as a serious threat. By contrast, a woman inclined towards radical feminism who reads this study might conclude that men are hopeless. Whether for biological or psychological reasons, the desire to prove themselves – if necessary, by the use of violence – so as to gain the approval of women among other things is built into their system. By this view women who join the military, so far from being heroes or pioneers or revolutionaries, are renegades to their sex; instead of weakening 'patriarchy' they reinforce it.[18] What women should (if they only could) do is break with men and start a society of their own. Only in a society without men will women be safe from the latter's greater aggression and physical strength. Only in such a society will the biblical command that 'unto him shall be thine passion, and he shall rule thee'[19] cease to apply. It is even possible, as some feminists claim and hope,[20] that a society made up solely of women will no longer engage in war. On the other hand, we saw that most women are as susceptible to the excitement of war as men. Moreover, some female leaders are as aggressive, as competitive, and as bent on exercising dominance as any males. For these reasons, and also because war is – among other things – a competition for limited resources, I doubt whether a world consisting exclusively of women would be noticeably more peaceful than the one we actually have.

Finally, a woman who is neither a feminist nor a moderate might conclude that the members of her sex neither can nor should try to beat men at their own game; that there are certain fields, of which war is far and away the most important, that had better be left for men to run. After all, to do so constitutes sound strategy: given a choice, and as some feminists belonging to a previous generation saw clearly enough,[21] deliberately to play in the opponent's court is little short of madness. Physically speaking the only thing women who try to compete with men can expect is injuries, some of them crippling and others dangerous to their ability to bear children. So long as the fighting takes place in the open, they do not stand a chance. Worse still, regardless of whether they fight as co-soldiers or as opponents they will make themselves hated by men. The best they can expect from men is every form of harassment. The worst, being 'tamed' by them just as the Amazons were by the Scyths.[22]

As the number and importance of wars between states, particularly developed ones, continue to decline it is likely that more women will enter the armed forces of those states. As more women enter them, the armed forces in question will become both less willing to fight and less capable of doing so. Meanwhile, masculine pride as the real engine of war has not disappeared. Like the devil who after being driven out through the door returns by way of the window, it is certain to be with us as long as men remain men and the differences between them and women persist. Prevented by nuclear proliferation from fighting in the name of states, increasingly men look for, and find, other organizations in whose name they can and do fight. In many developing countries this scenario is unfolding even now; however varied they may be in other respects, in *none* of the thirty or so wars currently being fought around the world is women's role any different from, or greater than, it has always been. What is more, just as the influx of women into boxing is spurring men to invent even more violent forms of competition, so future wars, by obliterating the customary distinction between soldiers and civilians, will very likely be even more atrocious than the old, causing women (and men) to be victimized by the hundreds of thousands if not millions.

As to developed countries, at the turn of the second millennium they appear less threatened by war than at any point during their history. With no opponent more powerful than Serbia or the militias of East Timor, they can afford to trample on male pride. They can use the little that remains of their armed forces for indulging in all kinds of social experiments, some of them curious indeed. However, should they ever again come under a *real* threat then almost certainly the expanded role of women in the military will vanish like the chimera it is. The bugles will sound, the banners will unfurl, and, it is to be hoped, men will answer the call; and women, heeding the advice that the young Freud once gave to his bride,[23] will again seek the protection of men.

Notes to the Text

INTRODUCTION

1 Cf. Michael D. Feld, 'Arms and the Woman', *Armed Forces and Society*, 4, 4, August 1978, pp. 557–8, 564; Leisa D. Meier, *Creating GI Jane: Sexuality and Power in the Women's Army Corps during World War II*, New York, Columbia University Press, 1996, pp. 1–2, 5; Cynthia Enloe, *Does Khaki Become You? The Militarization of Women's Lives*, London, Pluto, 1983, pp. 16–17.

2 See most recently and vehemently Brian Mitchell, *Women in the Military: Flirting with Disaster*, Washington DC, Regnery, 1998; also Stephanie Gutman, *The Kinder, Gentler Military: Can America's Gender-Neutral Armed Force Still Win Wars?* New York, Scribner, 2000.

3 Carl von Clausewitz, *On War*, Michael Howard and Peter Paret, eds., Princeton, Princeton University Press, 1976, p. 97; Leo Tolstoy, 'The Raid', in *Tales of Army Life*, London, Centenary Edition, 1933, vol. 4, p. 3.

4 Some women think otherwise: see in particular C.H. Enloe, 'Women in NATO Militaries – a Conference Report', *Women's Studies International Forum*, 5, 3/4, 1982, pp. 329–34.

PART I

1 Sandra Baxter and Marjorie Lansing, *Women and Politics: The Invisible Majority*, Ann Arbor, University of Michigan Press, 1980, p. 59.

2 Tacitus *Germania*, London, Heinemann, Lob Classical Library, 1980, 7–8.

3 James Fraser, *The Golden Bough*, New York, MacMillan, 1955 [1922], pp. 31–2.

4 See Harry Turney-High, *Primitive War: Its Practice and Concepts*, Columbia, University of South Carolina Press, 1971 [1949], p. 152ff., and the vast literature there cited.

5 Ibid., pp. 156–7

6 Ibid., pp. 157–8, 162; Lawrence H. Keeley, *War Before Civilization: The Myth of the Peaceful Savage*, New York, Oxford University Press, 1996, p. 102.

7 *Vinland Sagas*, Baltimore, Penguin, 1965 p. 69.

8 Keeley, *War Before Civilization*, p. 102.

9 All these examples from *Moralia*, 240ff.

10 J. Krige, *The Social System of the Zulus*, London, Longmans, 1936, p. 279.

11 On this subject see Jan van der Dennen, *The Origin of War*, Groningen, Origin, 1996, vol. I,

p. 423; also Napoleon A. Chagnon, 'Kin Selection and Conflict: An Analysis of a Yanomamo Ax Fight' in Napoleon A. Chagnon and W.G. Irons, eds., *Evolutionary Biology and Human Social Behavior: An Anthropological Perspective*, Situate, Duxbury, 1979; Robert Lowie, *Primitive Society*, London, Routledge, 1921, pp. 295–9.

12 Keeley, *War Before Civilization*, p. 145.

13 For her story see Judges 4–5.

14 According to Alice Buchan, *Joan of Arc and the Recovery of France*, London, Hodder & Stoughton, 1948, p. 59.

15 Quoted in J. Calmette, *Jeanne d'Arc*, Paris, Presses Universitaires, 1950, p. 54. See also Valerie R. Hotchkiss, *Clothes Make the Man: Female Cross Dressing in Medieval Europe*, New York, Garland, 1996, pp. 52–3, for what is known about the origins of the quote.

16 Julien Quicherat, ed., *Process de condemnation et de Réhabilitation de Jeanne d'Arc, ditte la Pucelle*, Paris, Renouard, 1841–9, vol. 3, p. 101.

17 Margaret Sommerville, *Women in the First Capitalist Society: Experiences in Seventeenth Century England*, Urbana, University of Illinois Press, 1988, p. 28.

18 Antonia Fraser, *The Warrior Queens*, New York, Vintage Books, 1994, pp. 248–9.

19 Magnus Hirschfeld, *Sittengeschichte des Weltkrieges*, Leipzig, Schreibner, 1930, vol. 1 p. 32.

20 See Sara Friedrichsmeyer, 'The Diary of Kaethe Kollwitz', in Helene Cooper and others, eds., *Of Arms and the Women*, Chapel Hill, University of South Carolina Press, 1989.

21 Roland Stromberg, *Redemption by War: The Intellectuals and 1914*, Lawrence, University of Kansas Press, 1982, p. 233.

22 Angela Woollacott, 'Khaki Fever and its Control: Gender, Class, Age and Sexual Morality in the British Home Front in the First World War', *Journal of Contemporary History*, 29, 2, 1994, pp. 325–47.

23 Charles E. Montague as quoted in Noel T. St Williams, *Judy O'Grady and the Colonel's Lady*, London, Brassey's, 1988, pp. 173–4.

24 Quoted in Johanna Alberti, *Beyond Suffrage: Feminists in War and Peace, 1914–1928*, New York, St Martin's Press, 1982, p. 50.

25 Quoted in Lynne Layton, 'Vera Brittain's Testament(s)', in Margaret R. Higonnet and others, eds., *Behind the Lines: Gender and the Two World Wars*, New Haven, Yale University Press, 1987, p. 72.

26 Avner Offer, 'Going to War in 1914: A matter of Honor?' *Politics and Society*, 1995, p. 232.

27 James Williamson as quoted in Joanna Burke, *Dismembering the Male: Men's Bodies, Britain and the Great War*, Chicago, University of Chicago Press, 1996, p. 158.

28 For what follows see Jean Bethke Ehlstain, *Women and War*, Chicago, University of Chicago Press, 1995 [1987], pp. 111–12, 16l also Françoise Thebaud, 'The Great War and the Triumph of Sexual Division', in Françoise Thebaud, ed., *A History of Women in the West*, Cambridge, Bellknap, 1994, vol. 5, pp. 57–60.

29 Thebaud, 'The Great War and the Triumph of Sexual Division', p. 37; Sandra M. Gilbert,

'Soldier's Heart: Literary Men, Literary Women, and the Great War', in Higonnet and others, eds., *Behind the Lines*, pp. 204–12.

30 Eleanor Roosevelt, *This is My Story*, New York, Harper, 1937, p. 260.

31 Ehlstain, *Women and War*, pp. 137–8.

32 The text may be found in Robert Graves, *Good-bye to All That*, New York, Cape, 1929, pp. 271–4.

33 Helene Deutsch, *The Psychology of Women, a Psychoanalytic Interpretation*, London, Research Books, 1947, vol. 1, pp. 300–1.

34 Helene Swanwick, *I Have Been Young*, London, Gollancz, 1935, p. 34.

35 See Barbara Spackman, *Fascist Virilities: Rhetoric, Ideology and Social Fantasies in Italy*, Minneapolis, University of Minnesota Press, 1996; also Victoria de Grazia, 'How Mussolini Ruled Italian Women', in Thebaud, ed., *A History of Women*, vol. 5, pp. 120–48.

36 Gisela Bock, 'Nazi Gender Policies and Women's History', in Thebaud, ed., '*A History of Women*', p. 149, claims that the Nazis 'deceived' women into voting for them.

37 John Donne.

38 Adolf Hitler, *Mein Kampf*, London, Pimlico, 1992 [1925], pp. 146, 148–9.

39 First promulgated by Robert L. Trivers, 'Parental Investment and Sexual Selection', in Bernard G. Campbell, ed., *Sexual Selection and the Descent of Man*, Chicago, Aldine, 1972, pp. 1136–79.

40 Van der Dennen, *The Origin of War*, vol. 1 pp. 421–3; see also Keeley, *War Before Civilization*, p. 125, and Turney-High, *Primitive War*, pp. 162–3.

41 Napoleon A Chagnon, *Yanomamo: The Last Days of Eden*, San Diego, Harcourt, 1992, pp. 106–7, 150, 183, 218–9.

42 Margaret Mead, *Blackberry Winter, My Earlier Years*, New York, William Morrow, 1972, p. 204.

43 Judges 19.

44 E.g. Homer, *Iliad*, London, Heineman, Loeb Classical Library, 1947, VI.410ff.

45 Jenny Jochens, *Women in Old Norse Society*, Ithaca, Cornell University Press, 1995, p. 40.

46 Snorre Strualson, *Heimskringla, or the Lives of the Norse Kings*, New York, Dover 1990, part I, chapter 33.

47 Gerard A. Zegward, 'Headhunting Practices of the Asmat of Netherlands New Guinea', in Andrew Vadya, ed., *Peoples and Cultures of the Pacific*, Garden City, Natural History Press, 1968, p. 433.

48 Keeley, *War Before Civilization*, pp. 86–7.

49 E.g. in pre-colonial Dahomey a man was worth 32 heads of cowries, a woman 26; Archibald Dalzel, *The History of Dahomey, an Inland Kingdom of Africa, Compiled from Authentic Memoirs*, London, 1793, Frank Cass reprint, 1967, p. 213.

50 See on this episode Arlene W. Saxonhouse, *Women in the History of Political Thought, Ancient Greece to Machiavelli*, New York, Praeger, 1985, pp. 122–3.

51 Herodotus, *The Histories*, London, Heinemann, Loeb Classical Library, 1975 VI.9.

52 Susan Brownmuller, *Against Our Will*, New York, Simon & Schuster, 1975.

53 See most recently Mary Kaldor, *New and Old Wars: Organized Violence in a Global Era*, Oxford, Polity Press, 1998, p. 8; Claudia Card, 'Martial Rape', in Charlotte Annerl and others, eds., *Krieg/War: Eine philosophische Ausseinandersetzung aus feministischer Sicht*, Munich, Fink, 1997, pp. 32–3, 36.

54 Keeley, *War Before Civilization*, appendix, table 6.2.

55 Julius Caesar, *Bellum Gallicum*, 7.47.

56 Modern edition, Honoré Bonet, *The Tree of Battles*, Liverpool, Liverpool University Press, 1949.

57 See Peter H. Wilson, 'German Women and War, 1500–1800', *War in History*, 3, 1996, p. 129.

58 See on these changes Martin van Creveld, *The Transformation of War*, New York, Free Press, 1991, chapter 2.

59 Emmerich Vattel, *The Law of Nations*, London, Clarke, 1811 [1758].

60 Arrian, *Anabasis*, London, Heinemann, Loeb Classical Library, 1978, II.12.3–8; Livius, *The History of Rome*, London, Heinemann, Loeb Classical Library, 1976, XXVI.50.

61 Alberto Pinelli, 'Il "picciol vetro" e il maggior vaso': I due grandi cicli profani di Domenico Beccafumi in Palazzo Venturi', in A.A.V.V., *Domenico Beccafumi e il suo tempo*, Milan, Electa, 1990, pp. 626–7.

62 Luigi Lenzi, 'Fanti e cavalieri nelle prime guerre d'Italia, 1494–1527', in *Richerche Storice*, VIII, 2, 1978, Club Cooperative Editrice Universitaria, Florence, 1978, p. 359.

63 The numbers of victims in Berlin alone is put at 100,000, forming some 7 per cent of the entire female population: Barbara Johr, 'Die Ereignisse in Zahlen', in Helke Sander and Barbara Johr, eds., *Befreier und Befreite, Krieg, Vergewaltigungen, Kinder*, Munich, Kunnstman, 1992, pp. 54–5.

64 See Wayne E. Dillingham, 'The Possibility of American Women Becoming POWs: Justification for Combat Exclusion Rules?', *Federal Bar News and Journal*, May 1990, p. 228.

65 *Annale Uladh: Annals of Ulster*, William H. Hennessey and Brian MacCarthy, eds., Dublin, A.Thom, 1887–, vol. 1, pp. 482–3, as quoted by Matthew Strickland, *War and Chivalry: The Conduct and Perception of War in England and Normandy, 1066–1217*, Cambridge, Cambridge University Press, 1996, p. 306.

66 Leon Degrelle, *Die Verlorene Legion*, Oldendorff, Schuetz, 1972, p. 93.

67 For their ordeal see Helen Rogan, *Mixed Company, Women in the Modern Army*, Boston, Beacon Press, 1981, p. 266; also Linda H. Francke, *Ground Zero; The Gender Wars in the Military*, New York, Simon & Schuster, 1997, p. 83ff.

68 Cited in R.H. Bainton, *Christian Attitudes towards War and Peace: A Historical Survey and critical Re-Evaluation*, New York, Abingdon, 1960, p. 207.

69 Aristophanes, *Lysistrate*, London, Heinemann, Loeb Classical Library, 1979, 168–70.

70 Clausewitz, *On War*, p. 75.

71 Homer, *Iliad* XIX. 282–300.

72 Simone de Beauvoir, *The Prime of Life*, Harmondsworth, Penguin, 1962, pp. 452, 454.

73 200,000 children: Johr, 'Die Ereignisse in Zahlen', p. 71; 10 per cent: on the assumption that 90 per cent of women in the occupied territories did what 90 per cent of their German sisters did, i.e. abort children who were the fruit of rape. Ibid., p. 58.

74 'Down by the Banhof/American Soldat/da gibt's Zigaretten/und auch Schokolat. Wieviel, Lili Marlene? Wieviel, Lili Marlene?'

75 For this entire line of thought I am indebted to Nany Huston, 'Tales of War and Tears of Women', in Judith Stiehm, ed., *Women and Men's Wars*, Oxford, Pergamon, 1983, pp. 271–82.

76 Homer, *Iliad*, VI.445–60.

77 Josephus Flavius, *The Jewish War*, London, Heinemann, Loeb Classical Library, 1926, VII.8.7.

78 See Glenda Riley, *Women and Indians on the Frontier, 1825–1915*, Albuquerque, University of New Mexico Press, 1984.

79 Hirschfeld, *Sittengeschichte des Weltkrieges*, vol. 2, pp. 298–305.

80 Edith Hall, 'Asia Unmanned: Images of Victory in Classical Athens', in John Rich and Graham Shipley, eds., *War and Society in the Greek World*, London, Routledge, 1993, pp. 111–12.

81 Ruth Harris, "The Child of the Barbarians": Rape, Race and Nationalism in France during the First World War', *Past and Present*, 141, 1993, pp. 170–206.

82 Irene C. Willis, *England's Holy War: A Study of English Liberal Idealism during the Great War*, New York, Garland, 1972 [1928], pp. 131–3.

83 Susan Gubar, '"This is my Rifle, This is my Gun": World War II and the Blitz on Women', in Higonnet and others, eds., *Behind the Lines*, pp. 231–40.

84 Jay W. Baird, *The Mythical World of Nazi War Propaganda, 1939–1945*, Minneapolis, University of Minnesota Press, 1974, p. 247ff.

85 Meiron and Susie Harries, *The Last Days of Innocence: America at War, 1917–18*, New York, Random House, 1997, p. 173; also Marilyn Yalom, *A History of the Breast*, New York, Knopf, 1998, p. 128ff.

86 E.F. Ziehlke and others, *Sittengeschichte des Zweiten Weltkrieges*, Hanau, Nueller&Kiepenheuer, n.d., pp. 357–40.

87 Quintus Snyrnaeus, *Ta met' homeron*, Leipzig, Teubner, 1891, 659–74.

88 See Sarah Fishman, *We Will Wait: Wives of French Prisoners of War, 1940–1945*, New Haven, Yale University Press, 1991, particularly pp. 136–7.

89 For details see André Kaspi, *La Libération de la France, Juin 1944–Janvier 1946*, Paris, Perrin, 1995, pp. 198–200.

90 Kari Helgessen, 'Viewed as the Germans "Wenches"' [Norwegian], *Historisk Tidskrift*, 69, 3, 1994, pp. 285–310.

91 Horrace, *Satires*, London, Heinemann, Loeb Classical Library, 1996, 1.3.107–8.

92 Virginia Woolf, *A Room of One's Own,* New York, Harcourt, Brace and Jovanovich, 1957, pp. 35–6.

93 Aristophanes, *Lysistrate*, 554–64.

PART II

1 For example, in Terry Maple and Douglas Matheson, *Aggression, Hostility and Violence*, New York, Holt, Reinhart & Winston, 1973, women are not even mentioned.

2 Deutsch, *The Psychology of Women*, pp. 4–5, 177, 187, 221, 254–5, 281, and, above all, 299–303.

3 Christine de Pizan, *The Book of the City of Ladies*, New York, Peresa, 1982, p. 31.

4 Helene Swanwick *The War in its Effect Upon Women*, 1916, Garland Reprint, London, Garland, 1971, pp. 3, 28.

5 Mary Wollstonecraft, *Vindication of the Rights of Women*, London, Unwin, 1792.

6 See 'Women's Liberation Movement', *Encyclopaedia Britannica*, Chicago, Britannica, 1989, vol. 12, p. 735.

7 Cora Kaplan, 'Wild Nights: Pleasure/Sexuality/Feminism', in Nancy Armstrong and Leonard Tennehouse, *The Ideology of Conduct, Essays in Literature and the History of Sexuality*, New York, Methuen, 1987, p. 174.

8 See Moira Ferguson, *First Feminists: British Women Writers, 1578–1799*, Bloomington, Indiana University Press, 1985.

9 Flavius Renatus Vegetius, *Epitome of Military Science*, N.P. Milner, ed., Liverpool, Liverpool University Press, 1993, p. 12.

10 Sun Tzu, *Art of War*, Oxford, Oxford University Press, 1961, pp. 57–8.

11 For example Caius J. Caesar, *The Gallic War*, London, Heinemann, Loeb Classical Library, 1946, I.1.

12 E.g. JoAnn McNamara, 'The Herrenfrage: the Restructuring of the Gender System, 1050–1150', in Clara A. Lees, ed., *Medieval Masculinities: Regarding Men in the Middle Ages*, Minneapolis, University of Minnesota Press, 1994, p. 3.

13 Robert Ardrey, *The Territorial Imperative*, New York, Atheneum, 1966.

14 See Jan van der Dennen, *The Origin of War*, Groningen, Origin, 1996, vol. I, pp. 148–9.

15 See above all Evelyn Shaw and Joan Darling, *Strategies of Being Female: Animal Patterns, Human Choices*, Brighton, Harvester, 1984.

16 Bettyam Kevles, *The Female of the Species: Sex and Survival in the Animal Kingdom*, Cambridge, Harvard University Press, 1986, pp. 97–8 describes a species of Mexican marsh-birds whose females treat males like 'serfs ... in pre-Revolutionary Russia'.

17 For a description see Erich Hoyt, *The Earth Dwellers: Adventures in the Land of Ants*, New York, Simon & Schuster, 1996, pp. 196–236.

18 van der Dennen, *The Origin of War*, vol. 1, pp. 155–7.

19 A.M, van Hoof, 'Intergroup Competition and Conflict in Animals and Man', in Jan M.G . van der Dennen and V.S.E. Falger, eds., *Sociobiology and Conflict: Evolutionary Perspectives on Competition, Cooperation, Violence and Warfare*, London, Chapman & Hall, 1990, pp. 23–54.

20 See J. Itani, 'Intraspecific Killing among non-Human Primates', *Journal of Social and Biological Structures*, 5, 4, 1982, pp. 361–8; Richard Wrangham and Dale Peterson, *Demonic Males: Apes and the Origins of Human Violence*, Boston, Houghton Mifflin, 1996, pp. 5–6, 16–8.

21 van der Dennen, *The Origin of War*, vol. 1 pp. 164–5, 186; M.P. Ghiglieri, 'War among the Chimps', *Discovery*, 8, 111, 1987, pp. 67–76; Meredith F. Small, *Female Choices: Sexual Behavior of Female Primates*, Syracuse, Cornell University Press, 1993, p. 49.

22 Lila Leibowitz, 'Perspectives on the Evolution of Sex Differences', in Caroline B. Brettel and Carolyn F. Sargent, eds., *Gender in Cross-Cultural Perspective*, Englewood Cliffs, Prentice Hall, 1993, p. 9.

23 J.H. Manson and R.W. Wrangham, 'Is Human Aggression Nonbiological? Problems with the Statement on Violence', *Human Ethnology Newsletter*, 5, 2, 1987, pp. 3–4.

24 Jane Goodall, 'Life and Death at Gombe', *National Geographic Magazine*, 155, 5, May 1979, pp. 592–621.

25 For the evidence see Barbara B. Smuts and R.W. Smuts, 'Male Aggression and Sexual Coercion of Females in Nonhuman Primates and Other Mammals', in P.J.B. Slater and others, eds., *Advances in the Study of Behavior*, New York, Academic Press, 1993, pp. 1–63.

26 Wrangham and Peterson, *Demonic Males*, pp. 166–7.

27 See Richard W. Wrangham, 'The Significance of African Apes for Reconstructing Human Social Evolution', in Warren G. Kinzey, ed., *The Evolution of Human Behavior: Primate Models*, Albany, SUNY Press, 1987, pp. 51–71.

28 Umberto Cassuto, *The Goddess Anath*, Jerusalem, Magnes, 1951, p. 58.

29 Homer, *Iliad*, XIV.170.

30 Miriam R. Dexter, *Whence the Goddesses, a Source Book*, New York, Pergamon, 1990, p. 102.

31 Tikva Frymer-Kensy, *In the Wake of the Goddesses: Women, Culture and the Biblical Transformation of the Goddesses*, New York, Free Press, 1992, pp. 64–5.

32 Ibid., p. 67.

33 Judith Ochshorn, *The Female Experience and the Nature of the Divine*, Bloomington, Indiana University Press, 1981, p. 122.

34 Dexter, *Whence the Goddesses*, p. 30.

35 Details from C.M. Brown, 'Kali, the Mad Mother', in C. Olson, ed., *The Book of the Goddess Past and Present*, New York, Crossroads, 1994, pp. 110–23. See also *Encyclopaedia Britannica*, Chicago, Britannica, 1993, vol. 6, p. 692.

36 Cassuto, *The Goddess Anath*, p. 65.

37 Hesiod, *Theogeny*, M.L. West, ed., Oxford, Clarendon, 1966, 925–6.

38 Homer, *Iliad*, VIII.415ff.

39 Ibid., V.880.

40 Homer, *Odyssey*, XIII.291–9.

41 Homer, *Iliad*, XXII. 224–305.

42 See Sue Blundell, *Women in Ancient Greece*, Cambridge, Harvard University Press, 1995, pp. 7, 28–9; also K. Kerenyi, *Athene, Virgin and Mother in Greek Religion*, Dallas, spring 1978, pp. 14, 25, 26. An older version of the myth presents Athene as born to Zeus from one of his many wives, Metis: Hesiod, *Theogeny*, 877ff.

43 Aeschylus, *Eumenides*, London, Heinemann, Loeb Classical Library, 1921, 737–8.

44 Homer, *Iliad* IV.242, 11.384–95; Sophocles, *Ajax*, London, Heinemann, Loeb Classical Library, 1951, 1120–2; Eurypides *Hercules Furiosus*, London, Heinemann, Loeb Classical Library, 1950, 188–203.

45 Homer, *Iliad*, XXI.481ff.

46 Ovid, *The Art of Love*, Bloomington, University of Indiana Press, 1957, p. 113, line 261.

47 Michael Grant, *Gladiators*, Harmondsworth, Penguin, 1967, p. 99.

48 Homer, *Iliad*, VI.428.

49 For Artemis see Blundell, *Women in Ancient Greece*, p. 45; also H. King, 'Bound to Bleed: Artemis and Greek Women', in A. Carnera and A. Kuhrt, eds., *Images of Women in Antiquity*, Detroit, Wayne State University Press, 1983, pp. 122, 123.

50 Dexter, *Whence the Goddesses*, p. 90ff.

51 Ibid., p. 65.

52 Ibid., p. 103.

53 Peter Berresford Ellis, *Celtic Women: Women in Celtic Society and Literature*, London, Constable, 1995, p. 32.

54 Barbara Ehrenreich, *Blood Rites*, New York, Metropolitan Books, p. 97ff.

55 Mary Condren, *The Serpent and the Goddess: Women, Religion and Power in Celtic Ireland*, San Francisco, Harper and Row, 1989, *passim*.

56 Ellis, *Celtic Women*, p. 35.

57 Joseph Needham, *Science and Civilization in China*, Cambridge, Cambridge University Press, 1994, vol. 5, part vi, p. 92.

58 Reproduced in Jean Bouret, *Henri Rousseau*, London, Oldbourne, 1961, plate 73.

59 *Punch*, 19 August 1914.

60 Blundell, *Women in Ancient Greece*, p. 175; also Ken Dowden, *The Uses of Greek Mythology*, London, Routledge, 1992, p. 140ff.

61 Phyllis Chesler, *Women and Madness*, New York, Harcourt, 1972, p. 286. Another modern feminist is said to have burst into tears upon learning that they did not exist: William B. Breuer, *War and American Women: Heroism, Deeds, and Controversy*, Westport, Praeger, 1997, p. 124.

62 Strabo, *The Geography*, London, Heinemann, Loeb Classical Library, 1917, 11.5.3; Palaiphatos, '*Peri Amazonoon*', fragment 32, in Richard Wagner, ed., *Mythographiai Graeci*, Stuttgart, Teubner, 1965.

63 Diodorus, *Bibliotheca Historica*, London, Heinemann, Loeb Classical Library, 1946, III.53.1.

64 See M.R. Lefkowitz, *Women in Greek Myth*, New York, Duckworth, 1986, p. 20.

65 The following analysis is based on Josine H. Blok, *The Early Amazons: Modern and Ancient Perspectives on a Persistent Myth*, Leiden, Brill, 1995, pp. 155ff., 167, 173, 223ff.

66 Homer, *Iliad*, III.184.

67 On the change see Thomas H. Carpenter, *Art and Myth in Ancient Greece*, London, Thames & Hudson, 1991, pp. 125–6.

68 See the reproduction in Fraser, *The Warrior Queens*.

69 See the reproduction in Blundell, *Women in Ancient Greece*, No. 10.

70 See the reproduction in Michael Avi Yonah and Israel Shtazman, *Illustrated Encyclopaedia of the Classical World*, New York, Harper and Row, 1975, p. 344.

71 See William B. Tyrell, *Amazons, a Study in Athenian Mythmaking*, Baltimore, Johns Hopkins University Press, 1984, pp. 44–5.

72 Xenophon, *Anabasis*, 1961, 4.4.16.

73 Lysias, *Funeral Oration*, London, Heinemann, Loeb Classical Library, 1930, 4–6.

74 Herodotus, *The Histories*, London, Heinemann, Loeb Classical Library, 1946, 4, 113.

75 Ibid., 4, 117; *Airs, Waters, Places*, G. Gundermann, ed., Bonn, Marcus &Weber, 1911, 17; Plato, *Laws*, London, Heinemann, Loeb Classical Library, 1952, 804–805a. Arrian, *Anabasis*, VII.13.2 says that the Amazons who were presented to Alexander had asymmetrical breasts, the right one being smaller than the left.

76 Blok, *The Early Amazons*, pp. 23–7, 36.

77 Tyrell, *Amazons*, pp. 44–5.

78 Blok, *The Early Amazons*, pp. 440–1.

79 Diodorus, *Bibliotheca Historica*, 2.45.3.

80 Strabo, *Geography*, 11.5.1–2.

81 Carl Mueller, ed., *Fragmenta Historiorum Graecorum*, Paris, French Typographical Institute, 1848, 14 F2, 33 F2.

82 Diodorus, *Bibliotheca Historica*, XVII.77.1.

83 Fraser, *The Warrior Queens*, p. 125.

84 E.g. Jessica A. Salmonson, *The Encyclopedia of Amazons, Women Warriors from Antiquity to the Modern Era*, New York, Paragon, 1991.

85 Giovanni Boccaccio, *Concerning Famous Women*, New Brunswick, Rutgers University Press, 1963.

86 See below, p. 71.

87 Virgil, *Aeneid*, London, Heinemann, Loeb Classical Library, 1960, XI.539ff.

88 See Margaret L. King, *Women of the Renaissance*, Chicago, University of Chicago Press, 1991, p. 188ff.

89 The following is based on H.C. Heaton, *The Discovery of the Amazon, according to the Account of Friar Gaspar de Carvajal and Other Documents*, New York, AMS, 1970.

90 *Time*, 27.12.1971. The anthropologist in question was one Jesco von Puttkamer.

91 See Dianne Dugaw, *Warrior Women and Popular Balladry, 1650–1850*, London, Cambridge University Press, 1989; also (for the Netherlands), Rudolf M. Dekker and Lotte van Pol, 'Wat Hoort Men Niet al Vreemde Dingen', *Spiegel Historiae*, 17, 10, 1982, pp. 486–93.

92 Dugaw, *Warrior Women*, p. 41.

93 Rudolf M. Dekker and Lotte C. van de Pol, *The Tradition of Female Transvestism in Early Modern Europe*, New York, St Martin's, 1989, pp. 70–1.

94 *The Tain*, Thomas Kinsella, trans., Oxford, Oxford University Press, 1950, p. 250.

95 Ellis, *Celtic Women*, pp. 71–4.

96 Qingyun Wu, *Female Rulers in Chinese and English Literary Utopias*, Syracuse, Syracuse University Press, 1995, pp. 19, 31–2.

97 Royall Tyler, 'The Woman Warrior', in Chieko I. Mulhern, ed., *Heroic with Grace: Legendary Women of Japan*, Armonk, East Gate, 1991, pp. 129–50.

98 Salmonson, *The Encyclopedia of Amazons*, p. 234.

99 For women warriors as they appear in comics see Sherri A. Inness, *Women Warriors and Wonder Women in Popular Culture*, Philadelphia, University of Philadelphia Press, 1999, chapter 8.

100 Inness, *Tough Girls*, pp. 37–8.

101 See Ferry D. Luckett, 'Military Women in Contemporary Film, Television and Media', *Minerva: Quarterly Report on Women and the Military*, VII, 2, summer 1989, p. 11.

102 Blundell, *Women in Ancient Greece*, p. 62.

103 'Sin', by Ritual.

104 See C.T. Wright, 'The Amazons in Elizabethan Literature', *Studies in Philology*, 37, 3, July 1940, pp. 433–56; P. Dubois, *Centaurs and Amazons: Women and the Pre-History of the Great Chain of Being*, Ann Arbor, University of Michigan Press, 1982, pp. vii, 32; Pierre Vidal-Nacquet, 'Slavery and the Rule of Women in Tradition, Myth and Utopia', in R.C. Gordon, ed., *Myth,*

Religion and Society, London, Cambridge University Press, 1981, p. 190; M. Merck, 'The City's Achievements. The Patriotic Amazonomachy in Ancient Athens', in S. Lipshitz, ed., *Tearing the Veil: Essays on Femininity*, London, Routledge, 1978, p. 96.

105 For example, Ellen in *The Quick and the Dead*; see Inness, *Tough Girls,* pp. 79, 81.

106 William Shakespeare, *Henry VI* in *Complete Works*, London, Oxford University Press, 1957, part III, act 1, scene iv.

107 L. McMaster and R.J. Green, *Women at War*, New York, Doherty, 1995.

108 Lefkowitz, *Women in Greek Myth*, p. 22.

109 Tadeusz Sulimirski, 'The Scyths', in I. Gerschevitsh, ed., *The Cambridge History of Iran*, London, Cambridge University Press, 1985, vol. 2, pp. 190, 195.

110 See Martin van Creveld, *Command in War*, Cambridge, Ma., Harvard University Press, 1985, chapter 1; also Everett L. Wheeler, 'The General as Hoplite', in Victor D. Hanson, ed., *Hoplites: the Classical Greek Battle Experience*, London, Routledge, 1991, pp. 121–72.

111 For a short survey see Martin van Creveld, *The Training of Officers*, New York, Free Press, 1990, pp. 7–18.

112 Plutarch, *Flamininus*, London, Heinemann, Loeb Classical Library, 1968, I.3.

113 Fraser, *The Warrior Queens*, pp. 136, 148.

114 An excellent recent discussion is Dvora Gera, *Warrior Women: the Anonymous Tractatus de Mulieribus*, Leiden, Brill, 1997, who kindly presented me with a copy of her book.

115 According to Demetrius, *Fragmenta Graeciae Historica*, F5. 34. 3.

116 Hellanicus, *Fragmenta Graeciae Historica,* 4 F167c.

117 Herodotus, *The Histories*, I.214.

118 Ibid., VIII.103.

119 Gera, *Warrior Women*, pp. 60–1.

120 Ibid., p. 75.

121 A recent example is Salmonson, *The Encyclopedia of Amazons*. See also David E. Jones, *Women Warriors: A History*, London, Brassey's, 1997; and Fraser, *The Warrior Queens*.

122 See on this episode S.A. Cook and others, eds., *The Cambridge Ancient History*, Cambridge, Cambridge University Press, 1965, vol. 8, p. 239.

123 Mary R. Lefkowitz, 'Influential Women', in Averil Cameron and Amelie Kuhrt, *Images of Women in Antiquity*, Detroit, Wayne State University Press, 1985, p. 57.

124 C. Julius Caesar, *De Bello Alexandrino*, London, Heinemann, Loeb Classical Library, 1955, 2.

125 On the military role played by Hellenistic queens see Grace H. Macurdy, *Hellenistic Queens: a Study of Woman-Power in Macedonia, Seleucid Syria, and Ptolemaic Egypt*, Baltimore, Johns Hopkins Press, 1932, pp. 232–3.

126 For a somewhat fanciful account of her exploits see Ellis, *Celtic Women*, p. 85ff.; also Fraser, *The Warrior Queens*, chapters 3–7.

127 Dio Cassius, *Roman History*, London, Heinemann, Loeb Classical Library, 1968, LXII,7,2. There is a similar story told of a twelfth-century French female commander: *Recueil des historiens des Gaules et de la France*, M. Bouquet and others, eds., Paris, Plon, 1869–, vol. 19, p. 98.

128 Tacitus, *Annales*, 35.

129 Ellis, *Celtic Women*, pp. 41, 106, 119.

130 Fraser, *The Warrior Queens*, p. 114.

131 For Zenobia's story see above all Fraser, *The Warrior Queens*, chapter 8.

132 China: Salmonson, *The Encyclopedia of Amazons*, p. 187; India: A.S. Attekar, *The Position of Women in Hindu Civilization*, Benares, Motilal Banarsidas, 1956, p. 22; the Maya: David Freidel and Linda Schele, 'Maya Royal Women: a Lesson in Precolumbian History', in Brettel and Sargent, eds., *Gender in Cross-Cultural Perspective*, pp. 59–63.

133 Eirik's Saga, in *Vinland Sagas*, Harmondsworth, Penguin, 1965, pp. 75–6.

134 Jacques Contamine, *War in the Middle Ages*, Oxford, Blackwell, 1984, pp. 241–2.

135 Taken from Marty N. Williams and Anne Echols, *Between Pit and Pedestal: Women in the Middle Ages*, Princeton, Wiener, 1994, pp. 173, 174, 175–6.

136 See Fraser, *The Warrior Queens,* pp. 197–9.

137 Antonia Fraser, *The Weaker Vessel*, New York, Random House, 1984, p. 166ff.

138 Niccolò Machiavelli, *The Prince*, Harmondsworth, Penguin, 1965, chapter 20.

139 In the words of Megan McLaughlin, 'The Woman Warrior: Gender, Warfare and Society in Medieval Europe', *Women's Studies*, 17, 1990, pp. 193–209.

140 Athenaios, *Deipnosophists*, London, Heinemann, Loeb Classical Library, 1961, XIII, 560ff.

141 According to Tacitus, *Annales*, 37.

142 On this entire episode see Douglas D.R. Owen, *Eleanor of Aquitaine, Queen and Legend*, Oxford, Blackwell, 1993, p. 148ff.

143 Froissart, *Chronicles*, London, Macmillan, 1931, ii.144–6 and iii. 9.

144 Ibid., xvi, 290.

145 Niccolò Machiavelli, *Discourses*, London, Kegan Paul, 1950, book 3, chapter 6; Fraser, *The Warrior Queens*, p. 198. For a similar story see Jenny Jochens, *Women in Old Norse Society*, Ithaca, Cornell University Press, 1995, pp. 76–7. A picture of a Polish woman who scares away German soldiers by exposing herself is reproduced in Klaus Theweleit, *Male Fantasies*, Cambridge, Polity Press, 1987, p. 200; in seeing this and similar phenomena simply as the product of an over-excited male imagination, though, Theweleit misses the mark.

146 According to Fraser, *The Warrior Queens*, pp. 176–7.

147 See L.S. Marcus, 'Shakespeare's Comic Heroines, Elizabeth I, and the Political Uses of Androgyny', in M.B. Rose, ed., *Women in the Middle Ages and the Renaissance*, Syracuse, Syracuse University Press, 1986, pp. 113–34.

148 Quoted in Simon Shepherd, *Amazons and Warrior Women: Varieties in Feminism in Seventeenth-Century Drama*, New York, St Martin's, 1981, p. 22.

149 Eugène d'Auriac, *Thamar Reine de Georgie*, Paris, Renouard, 1892, pp. 9, 12; Jean B. de Nervo, *Isabella the Catholic*, London, Smith & Elder, 1897, p. 203.

150 See on these developments Martin van Creveld, *The Rise and Decline of the State*, Cambridge, Cambridge University Press, 1999, part 2, chapter 5.

151 E.g. Evelyne Accad, *Sexuality and War, Literary Masks of the Middle East*, New York, New York University Press, 1990, p. 11ff.

152 To date the only country to have had a female minister of defence is Finland (Maria E. Renn, 1990–95). In a conversation in St Petersburg on 25.2.1999, she explained how she suffered under her work-induced neglect of husband and family.

153 F.G. Burwell and Meredith R. Sarkes, 'Women and National Security Policy', in Ruth H. Howes and Michael R. Stevenson, eds., *Women and the Use of Military Force*, Boulder, Riener, 1993, p. 133.

154 According to the *Encyclopaedia Britannica*, vol. 1, p. 427, this was due to her 'intellectual limitations'.

155 Eytan Haber, *Ha-yom Tifrots Milchama* [Today War Will Break Out], Tel Aviv, Idanim, 1987, pp. 16, 28.

156 On her role see Stuart Cohen, 'Operational Limitations of Reserve Forces: The Lessons of the 1973 War', Bar Ilan University, BEZA Center, 1998, unpublished, p. 17.

157 Phrase used of Queen Elizabeth of England by Fraser, *The Warrior Queens*, p. 225.

158 Macurdy, *Hellenistic Queens*, p. 234, quoting Demosthenes.

159 Herodotus, *The Histories*, London, Heinemann, Loeb Classical Library, 1930, viii. 8.

160 According to Fraser, *The Warrior Queens*, p. 209.

161 *Encyclopaedia Britannica*, vol. 3, p. 282.

162 Peter Petschauer, *The Education of Women in Eighteenth Century Germany*, Queenston, Mellen Press, 1989, pp. 535, 542, 554; Zoe Oldenbourg, *Catherine the Great*, New York, Random House, 1965, pp. 182, 220.

163 As Jean-Paul Sartre and Simone de Beauvoir discovered when they visited Israel in the spring of 1967; Claude Francis and Fernande Gontier, *Simone de Beauvoir*, London, Mandarin, 1986, p. 318.

164 *Ms.*, April 1973, pp. 26–7.

165 Mithan Shoksi, *India's Indira*, Bombay, Orient Longman, 1975, p. 20. To embellish the tale, she explained how even during her childhood she had been attracted to boy-like activities such as playing soldiers and climbing trees.

166 See Fraser, *The Warrior Queens*, pp. 318, 319.

167 *Spare Rib*, August 1982, editorial.

168 Clausewitz, *On War*, pp. 85–6.

169 Grant, *Gladiators*, p. 93.

170 Kevin McAleer, *Dueling: the Cult of Honor in Fin-de Siècle Germany*, Princeton, Princeton University Press, 1994, pp. 125–7, 145–6, 158ff.

171 See Michael D. Poliakoff, *Combat Sports in Classical Antiquity*, New Haven, Yale University Press, 1987.

172 Blundell, *Women in Ancient Greece*, p. 134.

173 John K. Evans, *War, Women and Children in Ancient Rome*, London, Routledge, 1991, pp. 130–1; Grant, *Gladiators*, pp. 34–5.

174 See Dominique Briquel, 'Les femmes gladiateurs', *Ktema*, 12, 1992, pp. 87–93.

175 Tacitus, *Annales*, 15.32.

176 Juvenal, *Satires*, Harmondsworth, Penguin, 1974, VI.247–69, p. 136.

177 The floralia took place from 28 April to 3 May. It was a time for games and farces, with all kinds of liberties permitted and prostitutes playing a large part in the proceedings.

178 Cassius, *Roman History*, LXVI.80.

179 For hunting as preparation for war see van Creveld, *The Training of Officers*, pp. 8, 12.

180 On the history and evolution of tournaments see Steven Pederson, *The Tournament, Tradition and Staging*, Ann Arbor, UMI Research Press, 1987.

181 See the description in Johan Huizinga, *The Waning of the Middle Ages*, Harmondsworth, Penguin Books, 1965 [1924], p. 81.

182 For another case of this kind see Vern L. Bullough, 'On Being a Male in the Middle Ages', in. Lees, ed., *Medieval Masculinities*, p. 37.

183 Ian Dunlop, *Palaces and Progresses of Elizabeth I*, New York, Taplinger, 1962, p. 85.

184 Salmonson, *The Encyclopedia of Amazons*, p. 201.

185 Quoted in Dugaw, *Warrior Women*, pp. 125–6.

186 Mary Wollstonecraft, *A Vindication of the Rights of Women*, p. 33.

187 ZDF 3, 10.10.1999.

188 CNN, 21.10.1997.

189 *Yediot Acharonot* [Hebrew], 31.10.1997, p. 7.

190 Australia TV, channel 9, 10.10.1998.

191 *Yediot Acharonot*, Weekend Magazine, 12.2.1999, pp. 34–7.

192 Homer, *Iliad*, XXII.261.

193 Arrian, *Anabasis*, VIII.17.4.

194 The little we know is summed up in Margaretha Debrunner Hall, 'Eine reine Maennerwelt? Frauen und das roemische Heer', in Maria H. Dettenhofer, ed., *Reine Maennersache? Frauen in Maennerdomaenen der antike Welt*, Munich, Deutscher Taschenbuch Verlag, 1996, pp. 207–28.

195 Herodotus, *The Histories*, 9.81; Maria Brosus, *Women in Ancient Persia*, Oxford, Clarendon, 1996, p. 87ff.

196 Xenophon, *Anabasis*, I.10.2.

197 See Charles Hindley, 'Eros and Military Command in Xenophon', *Classical Quarterly*, 44, 1994, pp. 365–7.

198 Euripides, *Iphigenia at Aulis*, London, Heinemann, Loeb Classical Library, 1912, 821–6.

199 Homer, *Iliad*, XIX.176–7, XXIV.676; Homer, *Odyssey*, 9.39–42.

200 Plutarch, *Alexander*, London, Heinemann, Loeb Classical Library, 1926, 48–9.

201 Arrian, *Anabasis*, 7.4.8.

202 Appian, *Roman History*, London, Heinemann, Loeb Classical Library, 1987, ix.3.

203 Appian, *Roman History*, London, Heinemann, Loeb Classical Library, 1964, 6.85.

204 George R. Watson, *The Roman Soldier*, Ithaca, Cornell University Press, 1969, p. 133ff.

205 Tacitus, *Annales*, 2.55.

206 Ibid., 3.33–4. On this episode see also Saxonhouse, *Women in the History of Political Thought*, p. 114.

207 Herodian, *Historia Augusta*, London, Heinemann, Loeb Classical Library, 1968, 3.8.5.

208 Lactantius, *De moribus persecutorum*, Oxford, Clarendon, 1984, I.88.

209 See Contamine, *War in the Middle Ages*, p. 241.

210 F. Gabrieli, *Arab Historians of the Crusades*, Berkeley, University of California Press, 1969, pp. 204–6.

211 Williams and Echols, *Between Pit and Pedestal*, p. 97.

212 P.H. Wilson, 'German Women and War', *War in History*, 3, 1996, pp. 127–40.

213 Johann J. von Wallhausen, *Kriegskunst zu Fuess*, Oppenheim, de Bry, 1615, p. 16.

214 Jakob Heinrich, *Gesetze fuer die K.u.K Armee in Auszug*, Vienna, n.p., 1785, p. 182.

215 St Williams, *Judy O'Grady*, pp. 11–12.

216 L.I. Cowper, *The King's Own (4th Foot), the Story of a Regiment*, Oxford, Oxford University Press, 1939, vol. 1, p. 57.

217 See the description in B. Farwell, *For Queen and Country*, London, Allen Lane, 1981, p. 229.

218 For a graphic description of punishments, complete with pictures see Christopher Duffy, *The Army of Frederick the Great*, London, Purnell, 1974, p. 62ff.

219 John R.Elting, *Swords around a Throne*, New York, Free Press, 1988, pp. 608, 613; *Reglement fuer die saemmtiliche Kaiserliche=Koenligliche Infanterie*, Vienna, Trattnern, 1769, p. 103.

220 St Williams, *Judy O'Grady*, pp. 49–50. On women in Wellington's army see also G. Bell, *Soldier's Glory: Rough Notes of an Old Soldier*, London, Bell, 1956, pp. 61, 74, 75.

221 Carl E. Warnerey, *Des Herrn Generalmajor von Warnerey saemtiliche Schriften*, Hanover, Helwing, vol. 2, pp. 26–7.

222 Linda Grant de Pauw, 'Women in Combat: the Revolutionary War Experience', *Armed Forces and Society*, 7, 2, winter 1981, p. 214.

223 William H. Blumenthal, *Women Camp Followers of the American Revolution*, Philadelphia, McManus, 1952, pp. 66, 80–1.

224 See David Chandler, *The Campaigns of Napoleon*, New York, MacMillan, 1980, p. 369.

225 Elting, *Swords around a Throne*, p. 609.

226 St Williams, *Judy O'Grady*, p. 15.

227 For some contradictory evidence concerning her true identity see L.K. Kerber, '"History Can Do it No Justice"': Women and the Reintepretation of the American Revolution', in R. Hoffman and P.J. Albert, eds., *Women in the Age of the American Revolution*, Charlottesville, University Press of Virginia, 1989, pp. 11–19; Grant de Pauw, 'Women in Combat,' p. 210; Blumenthal, *Women Camp Followers of the American Revolution*, pp. 69–70; and, above all, Carol Klaver, 'An Introduction to the Legend of Molly Pitcher', *Minerva: Quarterly Reports on Women and the Military*, xii, 2, summer 1994, pp. 100–5.

228 F.C.C. Pages, *Following the Drum: Women in Wellington's Wars*, London, Deutsch, 1986, p. 32; Elting, *Swords around a Throne*, pp. 610, 614.

229 See Suzanne J. Stark, 'Women at Sea in the Royal Navy in the Age of Sail', *American Neptune*, 57, 2, spring 1997, pp. 101–18.

230 John Charteris, *At GHQ*, London, Cassell, 1931, pp. 208–10.

231 See, for the British Army, Myna Trustram, *Women of the Regiment: Marriage and the Victorian Army*, Cambridge, Cambridge University Press, 1984, pp. 3, 91.

232 Blumenthal, *Women Camp Followers of the American Revolution*, p. 68.

233 Glenda Riley, *The Female Frontier; a Comparative View of Women on the Prairie and the Plains*, Lawrence, University Press of Kansas, 1988, pp. 160–3.

234 Linus P. Brockett, *Women at War: A Record of their Patriotic Contributions, Heroism, Toils and Sacrifice during the Civil War*, Philadelphia, Zeigler, 1867, 1993 reprint, p. 19.

235 John Reed, *Insurgent Mexico*, New York, International Publishers, 1969 [1914], p. 202.

236 Quoted in R. Th. Ulrich, 'Daughters of Liberty: Religious Women in Revolutionary New England', in Hoffman and Albert, eds., *Women in the Age of the American Revolution*, pp. 214–17.

237 Dekker and van de Pol, *The Tradition of Female Transvestism, passim*.

238 St Williams, *Judy O'Grady*, pp. 10–11.

239 Dekker and van de Pol, *The Tradition of Female Transvestism*, p. 98; for more French transvestites see Rudolf Dekker and Lotte C. van de Pol, 'Republican Heroines: Cross-Dressing Women in the French Revolutionary Armies', *History of European Ideas*, 10, 3, 1989, pp. 353–63.

240 Brigitte Holt, *Die Frau im Krieg*, Vienna, Heeresgeschichtliches Museum, 1986, vol. 1, pp. 45–7.

241 St Williams, *Judy O'Grady*, p. 10.

242 Diane Dugaw, *The Female Soldier: Or, the Surprising Life and Adventures of Hannah Snell*, Los Angeles, University of Los Angeles Press, 1989 [1750]; Blumenthal, *Women Camp Followers of the American Revolution*, p. 70.

243 Dugaw, *The Female Soldier*, p. 34.

244 Nadezha Durova, *The Cavalry Maiden: Journals of a Female Russian Officer in the Napoleonic Wars*, London, Paladin, 1990. The introduction provides the rest of what we know about her.

245 Durova, *The Cavalry Maiden*, p. 52.

246 Ehlstain, *Women and War*, chapter 3.

247 Blumenthal, *Women Camp Followers of the American Revolution*, p. 68.

248 Riley, *The Female Frontier*, p. 108.

249 Figures from John W. Chambers, II, *To Raise an Army: The Draft Comes to Modern America*, New York, Free Press, 1987, p. 290 fn. 3.

250 Hirschfeld, *Sittengeschichte des Weltkrieges*, vol. 1, pp. 249–50.

251 Ulrich, 'Daughters of Liberty', pp. 236–7.

252 A picture of the Revolutionary Nancy Hart is said to be at the Library of Congress and is reprinted in Carol R. Berkin and Clara M. Lovett, *Women, War and Revolution*, New York, Holmes Meier, 1980. The information about the Civil War-vintage Ms Hart comes from *Encylopaedia Britannica*, 11, p. 385, entry 'Summersville'.

253 Elting, *Swords around a Throne*, p. 611.

254 My account of the Brazilian Amazons is based on Heaton, *The Discovery of the Amazon*.

255 See C.T. Wright, 'The Amazons in Elizabethan Literature', *Studies in Philology*, 37, 3, July 1940, p. 444.

256 A.L. Herisse, *L'ancien royaume de Dahomey*, Paris, Larose, 1911, p. 90.

257 See footnote no. 214 to this chapter.

258 See, in general, R. Cornevin, *Histoire du Dahomey*, Paris, Berger-Levault, 1962; and M. Palau-Marti, *Le Roi-Dieu au Benin*, Paris, Berger-Leault, 1964.

259 Herisse, *L'ancien royaume de Dahomey*, pp. 33, 46.

260 Dalzel, *The History of Dahomey*, pp. 33, 126, 127.

261 Ibid., pp. 171–2.

262 Ibid., p. 129.

263 Ibid., pp. 135–7.

264 Ibid., p. 54.

265 Ibid., p. 47.

266 Ibid., p. 176ff.

267 *Report from the Select Committee of the House of Lords appointed to consider the best Means which Great Britain can adopt for the Final Extinction of the Slave Trade*, Session 1849, pp. 50–7.

268 William J. Argyle, *The Fon of Dahomey; a History and Ethnography of the Old Kingdom*, Oxford, Clarendon, 1966, pp. 63, 87–8; Hélène d'Almeida-Topor, *Les Amazones: Une Armée des Femmes dans l'Afrique Precoloniale*, Paris, Rochevignes, 1984, p. 43.

269 Quoted in Stanley B. Alpern, *Amazons of Black Sparta*, New York, New York University Press, 1998, p. 39.

270 Herisse, *L'ancien royaume de Dahomey*, p. 72.

271 d'Almeida-Topor, *Les Amazones*, p. 53. For the customs governing female circumcision in Dahomey, see also Melville J. Herskovits, *Dahomey, an Ancient West African Kingdom*, New York, Augustin, 1938, vol. 1, chapter 15.

272 Dalzel, *The History of Dahomey*, p. 224.

273 Robert E. Smith, *Warfare and Diplomacy in Pre-Colonial West Africa*, London, Methuen, 1976, p. 66.

274 L'Abbé Lafitte, *Le Dahomie, souvenirs de voyage et de mission*, Tours, Alfred Mame, 1876, chapter 5.

275 d'Almeida-Topor, *Les Amazones*, p. 105.

276 For the objectives of Dahomean warfare see Dov Ronen, *Dahomey between Tradition and Modernity*, Ithaca, Cornell University Press, 1975, p. 22.

277 Smith, *Warfare and Diplomacy in Pre-Colonial West Africa*, pp. 67, 151.

278 For these early campaigns see Alpern, *Amazons of Black Sparta*, chapters 16 and 17.

279 L'Abbé Lafitte, *Le Dahomie*, p. 109.

280 Richard F. Burton, *A Mission to Gelele, King of Dahomey*, London, Dent, 1864, II, p. 82; J. Alfred Skertchly, *Dahomey As It Is*, London, Murray, 1874, p. 457; see also Alpern, *Amazons of Black Sparta*, pp. 158–62.

281 Alpern, *Amazons of Black Sparta*, p. 146.

282 Dalzel, *The History of Dahomey*, p. xi.

283 Ibid., p. 48.

284 E. Chaudouin, *Trois mois de captivité au Dahomey*, Paris, Chantel, 1891, p. 91.

285 See Alpern, *Amazons of Black Sparta*, chapter 19.

286 d'Almeida-Topor, *Les Amazones*, p. 96.

287 According to Alpern, *Amazons of Black Sparta*, pp. 199–200.

288 Jean Porier, *Campagne du Dahomey, 1892–1894*, Paris, Lavauzelle, 1895, pp. 148, 199, 255.

289 d'Almeida-Topor, *Les Amazones*, pp. 13–40.

290 Margery Perham and Mary Bull, eds., *The Diaries of Lord Lugard*, London, Faber & Faber, 1963, vol. 4, p. 106.

291 Thomas Pakenham, *The Scramble for Africa, 1876–1912*, New York, Random, 1991, p. 461.

292 Henry Brackenbury, *The Ashanti War, a Narrative*, London, Cass, 1968 [1874], vol. 2, pp. 331–2.

293 See Robert Carroll, 'War in the Hebrew Bible', in Rich and Shipley, eds., *War and Society in the Greek World*, pp. 30–1.

294 d'Almeida-Topor, *Les Amazones*, p. 105.

295 See about him Keeley, *War Before Civilization*, p. 10ff.

296 Turney-High, *Primitive War*, p. 160.

297 All these songs are quoted in d'Almeida-Topor, *Les Amazones*, pp. 61–2, 65, 80.

298 Frederick E. Forbes, *Dahomey and the Dahomeans*, London, Dawsons, 1966, II, 108; Alpern, *Amazons of Black Sparta*, p. 188.

299 d'Almeida-Topor, *Les Amazones*, p. 106; Burton, *Mission*, p. 154.

300 Alpern, *Amazons of Black Sparta*, pp. 48–9.

301 Dalzel, *The History of Dahomey*, p. 205.

302 Quoted in Alpern, *Amazons of Black Sparta*, pp. 208–9.

303 For women's role in these kinds of struggles see Mary A. Tetreault, *Women and Revolution in Africa, Asia, and the New World*, Columbia, University of South Carolina Press, 1994.

304 Laura Polizzi, 'Le donne nella guerra de Liberazione', in Fabrizio Battistelli, ed., *Donne e Forze Armate*, Milan, Angeli, 1997, p. 130.

305 Information kindly provided by Prof. Fabrizio Battistelli, Archivio Disarmo, Rome, 22.9.1998.

306 Barbara Jancar, 'Yugoslavia: War of Resistance', in N. Loring Goldman, ed., *Female Soldiers, Combatants or Noncombatants?* Westport, Greenwood Press, 1982, pp. 85–105. Anton Bebler 'Women during the National Liberation War of Yugsolavia', in Johanna Hurni and others, eds., *Frauen in den Streitkraeften*, Brugg, Effingerhof, 1992, p. 109, provides slightly lower figures.

307 Djamila Amrane, 'Algeria: Anticolonial War', in Goldman, ed., *Female Soldiers*, pp. 123–35.

308 Ibid., p. 129.

309 Fieldmarshal John Dill, Chief of the General Staff, 1941, quoted in James, *Imperial Rearguard, Wars of Empire, 1919–85*, London, Brassey's, 1988, p. 96.

310 Hagana was the territorial self-defence organization associated with the Labour Party; PALMACH (short for Plugot Machats, Shock Companies), Hagana's full time striking force; ETSEL (short for Irgun Tsvai Leumi, National Military Organization) a right-wing terrorist

organization; and LECHI (short for Lochame Cherut Yisrael, Israel's Freedom Fighters) an even more right-wing one. See Martin van Creveld *The Sword and the Olive: A Critical History of the Israeli Defense Force*, New York, Public Affairs, 1998, chapter 5.

311 The most detailed figures are in PALMACH HQ., memo of 1.2.1948, PALMACH Archive, file H.109, no. 5; also D. Ben Gurion to H. Tsadok, 26.4.1948, Galili Archive, box 2, file C.

312 Laura Strumingher, 'The Vesuviennes: Images of Women Warriors in 1848', *History of European Ideas*, 8, 4–5, 1987, pp. 451–88.

313 Clemens, *Bolshevik Women*, p. 178ff.

314 Anne Eliot Griesse and Richard Stites, 'Russia: Revolution and War', in Goldman, ed., *Female Soldiers*, pp. 71.

315 James Brown and Constantina Safilios-Rothschild, 'Greece: Reluctant Presence', in Goldman, ed., *Female Soldiers*, p. 166.

316 Kyung Ae Park, 'Women and Revolution in China', in Tetreault, *Women and Revolution*, p. 142.

317 Karen Gottschang-Turner, *Even the Women Must Fight: Memoirs of the War from North Vietnam*, New York, Wiley, 1998, p. 4. Another cause behind the women's loss of their reproductive functions is said to have been Agent Orange.

318 US Admiral Elmo Zumwalt as quoted in Jean Zimmerman, *Tailspin: Women at War in the Wake of Tailhook*, New York, Doubleday, 1995, p. 118.

319 See e.g. Andres Resendes-Fuentes, 'Battleground Women: Soldaderas and Female Soldiers in the Mexican Revolution', *Americas*, 51, 4, 1995, pp. 525–33; and David T. Mason, 'Women's Participation in Central American Revolution: A Theoretical Perspective', *Comparative Political Studies*, 25, 1, 1992, pp. 63–89.

320 Gottschang-Turner, *Even the Women Must Fight*, p. 27.

321 Reed, *Insurgent Mexico*, pp. 3, 26, 45, 56, 86, 109, 141, 181, 196, 202, 258, 272.

322 The 'involuntary sex' quote is from Carolyn Nordstrom, 'Women and War: Observations from the Field', *Minerva: Quarterly Reports on Women and the Military*, ix, 1, spring 1991, p. 2, and refers to the various Tamil Liberation Movements.

323 On women in the French resistance Shelly Saywell, *Women in War*, New York, Viking, 1985, p. 42ff.

324 Salmonson, *The Encyclopedia of Amazons*, p. 170; Ellis, *Celtic Women*, p. 14.

325 Peggy R. Sanday, *Female Power and Male Dominance: On the Origin of Sexual Inequality*, Cambridge, Cambridge University Press, 1981, p. 136ff.

326 Armeebefehl des Oberbefehlabers der 6. Armee, 10.10.1941, printed in Gerd R. Ueberschaer and Wolfram Wette, eds., *Unternehmen Barbarossa*, Paderborn, Schoeningh, 1985, p. 33.

327 Anthony Mackler, *The New Mercenaries*, London, Sidgwick & Jackson, 1985, pp. 284–6, 335–6.

328 See also van Creveld, *The Transformation of War*, pp. 179–80.

329 Franz Seidler, *Frauen zu der Waffen ? Marketenderinne, Helferinnen, Soldatinnen*, Bonn, Bernhard & Graefe, 1998, p. 155.

330 For Spain see Mary Nash, 'Women in War: Milicianas and Armed Combat in Revolutionary Spain, 1936–1939', *International History Review*, 15, 2, 1993, pp. 269–82; for Yugoslavia Jancar *Female Soldiers*, pp. 85–105; for Israel van Creveld, *The Sword and the Olive*, chapter 8; for Vietnam Gottschang-Turner, *Even the Women Must Fight*, p. 9; and for Eritrea 'Eritrea: The Kitchen Calls', *Economist*, 25.6.1994.

331 Franz Weiss, 'Die Personelle Zusammensetzung der Fuehrungskraefte der Wiener Gestapoleitstelle zwischen 1938 und 1945', *Zeitgeschichte*, 20, 7–8, 1993, p. 247. To be fair, the occupants of the higher posts were all male.

332 George L. Mosse, *Fallen Soldiers: Reshaping the Memory of the World Wars*, Oxford, Oxford University Press, 1990, pp. 59–62.

333 For the Germans see Regina Schulte, 'Die Schwester des Kranken Kriegers: Krankenpflege im Ersten Weltkrieg als Forschungsproblem', *BIOS*, 7, 1,1994, pp. 87–100.

334 Jeffrey M. Tuten, 'Germany and the World Wars', in Goldman, ed., *Female Soldiers*, p. 49.

335 Nancy Loring Goldman and R. Stites, 'Great Britain and the World Wars', in Goldman, ed., *Female Soldiers*, pp. 24–6.

336 For an account of one such woman see Julie Wheelwright, 'Flora Sanders: a Military Maid', *History Today*, 39, March 1989, pp. 42–8.

337 St Williams, *Judy O'Grady*, pp. 175–6.

338 Jean Ebbert and Marie-Berth Hall, *Crossed Currents: Navy Women from WWI to Tailhook*, London, Brassey's, 1993, p. 3ff.

339 Ibid., p. 10ff.

340 Data from Jeanne Holm, *Women in the Military, an Unfinished Revolution*, Novato, Presidio, 1992, pp. 10–11.

341 Griesse and Stites, 'Russia: Revolution and War', in Goldman, ed., *Female Soldiers*, pp. 63–4.

342 According to Hirschfeld, *Sittengeschichte des Weltkrieges*, vol. 1, p. 261.

343 Denikin's memoirs are quoted in Sergei Drokov, 'The Founder of the Women's Battalion of Death' [Russian], *Voprosse Historii*, July 1993, pp. 164–9.

344 These two different locations are given by Salmonson, *The Encyclopedia of Amazons*, pp. 27–8, apparently without the author noticing she was contradicting herself.

345 Quoted in Julie Wheelwright, *Amazons and Military Maids: Women Who Dressed as Men in the Pursuit of Life, Liberty and Happiness*, Cambridge, Pandora Press, 1989, p. 129.

346 Hirschfeld, *Sittengeschichte des Weltkrieges*, vol. 1 p. 281.

347 According to Richard Stites, *The Women's Liberation Movement in Russia: Feminism, Nihilism and Bolshevism, 1860–1920*, Princeton, Princeton University Press, 1978, pp. 296–7.

348 According to William H. Chamberlain, *The Russian Revolution 1917–1921*, London, Macmillan, 1935, vol. 1, p. 318.

349 See Richard Abraham, 'Maria L. Bochkareva and the Russian Amazons of 1917', in Linda Endmondson, ed., *Women and Society in Russia and the Soviet Union*, Cambridge, Cambridge University Press, 1992, pp. 140–1.

350 Chamberlain, *The Russian Revolution*, vol. 1, p. 318; Marc Fero, *October 1917, A Social History of the Russian Revolution*, London, Routledge, 1976, p. 254. Both of these are apparently based on John Reed, *Ten Days that Shook the World*, London, Lawrence, 1926 [1920], pp. 117, 144, 155.

351 Maria Bochkareva, *Yashka: My Life as Peasant, Officer, and Exile*, New York, Stokes, 1919.

352 The Ironside memoirs as quoted by Drokov, 'The Founder of the Women's Battalion of Death'.

353 Sergei V. Drokov, 'The Interrogation Results of the Organizer of the St Petersburg Women's Death Battalion' [Russian], *Otechestrennye Arkhivy*, 1, 1994, pp. 50–66.

354 Barbara E. Clemens, *Bolshevik Women*, London, Cambridge University Press, 1997, p. 177.

355 Elizabeth A. Wood, *The Baba and the Comrade: Gender and Politics in Revolutionary Russia*, Bloomington, Indiana University Press, 1997, p. 56.

356 Abraham, 'Maria L. Bochkareva', p. 134.

357 'Memorandum for the Assistant Chief of Staff, G-1. Subject: 'Participation of Women in War', 21 September 1928, War Department, Women's Auxiliary Corps, 314.7.

358 Cf. Mario Roatta, *Otto millioni di baionette*, Milano, Mondadori, 1946.

359 The best account of the organization is given by Seidler, *Frauen zu der Waffen?*, pp. 257–61; also Sampo Ahto, 'Die finnische Lotta-Bewegung in Zweiten Weltkrieg', in Hurni and others, eds., *Frauen in den Streitkraeften*, pp. 93–9.

360 Christian Benoit, 'Des Femmes dans l'Armée de Terre, 1940–1945', *Revue Historique des Armées*, 3, 1994, pp. 39–47.

361 Saywell, *Women in War*, p. 42ff.

362 Mariano Vigano, 'Aspetti organizzativi del Servizio ausilario nella Rsi', in Battistelli, *Donne e Forze Armate*, pp. 85–115.

363 Sandra Wilson, 'Mobilizing Women in Interwar Japan: the National Defense Women's Association and the Manchurian Crisis, *Gender and History*, 7, 2, 1995, pp. 295–314.

364 Goldman and Stites, 'Great Britain and the World Wars', in Goldman, ed., *Female Soldiers*, pp. 30–1.

365 St Williams, *Judy O'Grady*, p. 191.

366 Meyer, *Creating GI Jane*, p. 13.

367 Ibid., pp. 73–5. For detailed figures see also D'Ann Campbell, 'Servicewomen in World War II', *Armed Forces and Society*, 16, 2, winter 1990, pp. 251–70.

368 *Time*, 28.9.1942, p. 60; George Quester, 'The Problem', in Goldman, ed., *Female Soldiers*, p. 225.

369 Meyer, *Creating GI Jane*, p. 108; also Holm, *Women in the Military*, chapter 8.

370 Samuel A. Stouffer and others, *The American Soldier*, Princeton, Princeton University Press, 1949, vol. 1, pp. 44–6.

371 Meyer, *Creating GI Jane*, pp. 8, 34–5, 36–9, 152–3.

372 Mitchell, *Women in the Military*, p. 4.

373 George Q. Flynn, *The Mess in Washington: Manpower Mobilization in World War II*, Westport, Greenwood, 1979, pp. 190, 209.

374 See most recently the memoirs of one of these women: Ilse Schmidt, *Die Mitlaeuferin, Errinerungen einer Wehrmachtsangehoerigen*, n.p., Aufbau, 1999, pp. 37–8, 43–5, 74–5.

375 1936 Hitler speech quoted in George Mosse, *Nazi Culture*, New York, Grosset & Dunlap, 1966, p. 39.

376 Seidler, *Frauen zu der Waffen?*, pp. 60, 74.

377 Figures from Meyer, *Creating GI Jane*, pp. 76–7.

378 See also data in Ebbert and Hall, *Crossed Currents*, pp. 89–90.

379 Meyer, *Creating GI Jane*, pp. 80–5.

380 Ibid., pp. 8, 180.

381 Holm, *Women in the Military*, chapter 8; Ebbert and Hall, *Crossed Currents*, p. 78.

382 Meyer, *Creating GI Jane*, pp. 133–4, 139.

383 Stephen J. Diensterey, 'Women Veterans' Exposure to Combat', *Armed Forces and Society*, 14, 4, summer 1988, pp. 593, 599.

384 See Holm, *Women in the Military*, chapter 6.

385 Frederick Pile, *Ack Ack*, London, Harrap, 1949, p. 186.

386 Ibid., p. 187.

387 Ibid., pp. 190–2.

388 Gerard J. DeGroot, 'Whose Finger on the Trigger? Mixed Anti-Aircraft Batteries and the Female Combat Taboo', *War in History*, 4, 4, November 1997, p. 441.

389 Griesse and Stites, 'Russia: Revolution and War', in Goldman, ed., *Female Soldiers*, pp. 68–78.

390 V.V. Pachlopkin, *The Great War and the Peace that did not Come, 1941–1945* [Russian], Moscow, Art Centre, 1997, p. 145. Pachlopkin's first name is unknown, but his surname clearly makes him male.

391 Gaby Gorodetsky, *The Myth of 'Icebreaker'*, Moscow, Progress Academia, 1995 [Russian], p. 21. For assistance with the Russian material I wish to thank Mr Alexander Epstein of the Hebrew University, Jerusalem.

392 Victor Suvorov, *M Day*, Moscow, ACT, 1994 [Russian], p. 476.

393 Campbell, 'Servicewomen in World War II', pp. 318–19.

394 Griesse and Stites, 'Russia: Revolution and War', in Goldman, ed., *Female Soldiers*, pp. 68–78.

395 Presidential Commission on the Assignment of Women in the Military, *Report to the President*, p. C–64.

396 On Soviet policies towards see Françoise Navailh, 'The Soviet Model', in Thebaud, ed., A *History of Women*, vol. 5, chapter 8; on the differential contribution of men and women to housework and the decline of the birth rate, Lynne Attwood, *The New Soviet Man and Women; Sex-Role Socialization in the USSR*, Bloomington, Indiana University Press, 1990, pp. 142–4, 170–4.

397 Pachlopkin, *The Great War*, p. 145.

398 On Israeli women see below, pp. 185-88, 207.

399 N.A. Antipenko, *In der Hauptrichtung*, Berlin, Militaerverlag der DDR, 1973, pp. 350–2.

400 Swetlana Aleksijewitch, *Der Krieg hat kein weibliches Gesicht*, Hamburg, Galgenberg, 1989, p. 170.

401 Pachlopkin, *The Great War*, p. 146.

402 Whereas the Germans always distinguished between '*Rotarmisten*' (Red Army Personnel) and '*Banditen*' (guerrillas), *all* Soviet female combatants were known either as '*Flintenweiber*' or as '*Entartete Weiber*' (degenerate women). Personal communciation from Mr Daniel Uziel, 16 November 1998, on the basis of work done in the German Archives.

403 Albert Seaton, *The Russo-German War, 1941–1945*, London, Barker, 1971, p. 89.

404 Aleksijewitsch, *Der Krieg hat kein weibliches Gesicht*, pp. 178–9.

405 Ibid., p. 165.

406 Pachlopkin, *The Great War*, p. 146.

407 A. Noggle, *A Dance with Death, Soviet Airwomen in World War II*, College Station, Texas University Press, 1994.

408 Sergeant Zoya Malkova, quoted in Noggle, *A Dance with Death*, p. 218.

409 Captain Mariya Dolina, pilot and deputy squadron commander, quoted in Noggle, *A Dance with Death*, p. 119.

410 SBS film, *The Night Witches*, 1995. I wish to thank the members of the Australian Defence Studies Centre, Canberra, for bringing this film to my attention.

411 Noggle, *A Dance with Death*, p. 105.

412 Unnamed 'Russian general officers' quoted in the Presidential Commission on the Assignment of Women in the Military, *Report to the President*, p. C–65.

413 Paul Carell, *Hitler Moves East, 1941–1943*, New York, Little Brown, 1965, p. 493.

414 Senior Lieutenant Anna Timofeyeva-Yegorova, quoted in Noggle, *A Dance with Death*, p. 225.

415 Lieutenant Olga Lisikova, quoted in Noggle, *A Dance with Death*, pp. 241, 244

416 Noggle, *A Dance with Death*, p. 84.

417 Ibid., p. 147.

418 Ibid., p. 184. Note that 'Pankration' means 'all sorts of struggle' in Greek. Is this just an accident or was Pankratova another Molly Pitcher?

419 Lieutenant Alexandra Popowa, navigator, in Aleksijewitch, *Der Krieg hat kein weibliches Gesicht*, p. 161.

420 Senior Lieutenant Alexandra Akimova, navigator, quoted in Noggle, *A Dance with Death*, p. 94.

421 Captain Maria Doma, biplane pilot, quoted in Noggle, *A Dance with Death*, p. 123.

422 Captain Alexandra Makarov, chief of staff, 125th Bomber Regiment, quoted in Noggle, *A Dance with Death*, p. 166.

423 Noggle, *A Dance with Death*, p. 202.

424 Lieutenant Olga Lisikova, quoted in Noggle, *A Dance with Death*, p. 242.

425 Senior Lieutenant Mariya Aklinia, pilot, quoted in Noggle, *A Dance with Death*, p. 98.

426 Sergeant Antonia Lepilina, mechanic, quoted in Noggle, *A Dance with Death*, p. 130.

427 Noggle, *A Dance with Death*, pp. 151, 204.

428 *The Night Witches.*

429 Noggle, *A Dance with Death*, p. 214.

430 Ibid., p. 215.

431 Ibid., p. 193.

432 See on this subject Aleksijewitsch, *Der Krieg hat kein weibliches Gesicht*, pp. 183–200.

433 Noggle, *A Dance with Death*, pp. 102–3, 126.

434 Ibid., p. 105.

435 Senior Sergeant Yekatrina Pulonina, mechanic, quoted in Noggle, *A Dance with Death*, p. 163.

436 Klaudia Pankratova, quoted in Noggle, *A Dance with Death*, p. 184.

437 On the legal status of German women working for the Wehrmacht see Rudolf Absolon, *Fraueneinsatz im Kriege*, Kornelienmunster, Personslandsarchiv des Landes Nordrhein-Westphalen, 1953, pp. 10–12.

438 Seaton, *The Russo-German War*, p. 89.

439 H. Boog, 'German Air Intelligence in the Second World War', in M.I. Handel, ed., *Intelligence and Military Operations in World War II*, London, Cass, 1990, p. 354.

440 Some women, however, flew in male regiments equipped with modern Yak-1 fighters; *The Night Witches.*

441 Alexandra Popova in Alexijewitsch, *Der Krieg hat kein weibliches Gesicht*, p. 160.

442 Noggle, *A Dance with Death*, pp. 179, 207–8.

443 *The Seven Military Classics of Ancient China*, Ralph D. Sawyer, ed., Boulder, Westview Press, 1993, p. 33. The advice is repeated on pp. 56, 57, 59, 64 and 302.

444 See Julie Wheelwright, *The Fatal Lover: Mata Hari and the Myth of Women in Espionage*, London, Collins & Brown, 1992.

445 See Michael Dewar, *The British Army in Northern Ireland*, London, Arms and Armour Press, 1985, pp. 133, 136, 144.

446 Douglas Porch, *The French Secret Services, from the Dreyfus Affair to the Gulf War*, New York, Farrar, 1995, pp. 309–10; Sandra C. Taylor, 'Long-Haired Women, Short Haired Spies: Gender, Espionage and America's War in Vietnam', *International and National Security*, 13, 2, summer 1998, pp. 61–70.

447 One example to the contrary is told by Plutarch, *Moralia*, 245c–f, about the Argive women who successfully defended their town against the Spartans.

448 Arrian, *Anabasis Alexandri*, London, Heinemann, Loeb Classical Library, 1978, VIII.9.1–13. Arrian's source for his stories concerning India was Megasthenes, a contemporary of Alexander.

449 For Greece see Xenophon, *Oeconomicus*, London, Heinemann, Loeb Classical Library, 1979, 7.5. For all these societies except Ghent, see André Burguiere and others, eds., *A History of the Family*, Oxford, Polity Press, 1996, pp. 261–3, 281, 386, 427, 447–8, 469, 500, 533, 578. For Ghent, David Nicholas, *The Domestic Life of a Medieval City: Women, Children, and the Family in Fourteenth-Century Ghent*, Lincoln, University of Nebraska Press, 1985, p. 24.

450 Information on the European marriage pattern from P.J.P. Goldberg, *Women, Work and Life Cycle in a Medieval Economy*, Oxford, Clarendon, 1992, p. 204ff.; also Peter Laslett, *Family Life and Illicit Love in Earlier Generations*, Cambridge, Cambridge University Press, 1977, p. 220.

451 Bonnie G. Smith, *Ladies of the Leisure Class: the Bourgeoises of Northern France in the Nineteenth Century*, Princeton, Princeton University Press, 1981, p. 224.

452 Laslett, *Family Life*, p. 130, table 3.3; Daniel S. Smith, 'The Dating of the American Sexual Revolution: Evidence and Interpretation', in Michael Gordon, ed., *The American Family in Socio-Historical Perspective*, New York, St Martin's, 1973, p. 323.

453 Lesley Doyal, *What Makes Women Sick, Gender and the Political Economy of Health*, London, Macmillan, 1995, p. 50; Jared Diamond, *Why Sex is Fun*, London, Weidenfeld and Nicolson, 1997, p. 38. Small, *Female Choices*, p. 78, puts the number of extra calories needed for lactation as high as 2,000.

454 Doyal, *What Makes Women Sick*, p. 110. Some researchers, incidentally, link the fact that modern women go through far more menstrual cycles with the spread of breast cancer.

455 For the life cycle of women among hunter-gathering societies see J.B. and C.S. Lancastar, 'Parental Investment: the Hominid Adaptation', in Donald J. Ortner, ed., *How Humans Adapt, a Biocultural Odyssey*, Washington DC, Smithsonian, 1983, pp. 43–51; also Ernestine Friedl, *Women and Men, an Anthropologist's View*, New York, Holt, Reinhardt & Winston, 1975, p. 17.

456 According to Jared Diamond, *Guns, Germs and Steel: A Short History of Everybody for the Last 13,000 Years*, New York, Vintage, 1998, p. 89.

457 See Alice Kessler-Harris, *Women Have Always Worked: A Historical Overview*, Westbury, The Feminist Press, 1981, pp. 28–9.

458 See Ansley J. Coale and others, *Human Fertility in Russia since the Nineteenth Century*, Princeton, Princeton University Press, 1979, p. 16, table 2.1

459 Jose Miguel Guzman and others, eds., *The Fertility Transition in Latin America*, Oxford, Clarendon, 1996, p. 5, table 1.1.

460 G.B.S. Mujahid, 'Female Labor Force Participation in Jordan', in Juanida Abu Nasr and others, eds., *Women, Employment and Development in the Arab World*, Berlin, Mouton, 1985, p. 123, table 7.

461 Iqbal H. Shah and John G. Cleland, 'High Fertility in Bangladesh, Nepal, and Pakistan: Motives Vs Means', in Richard Lefte and Iqbal Alam, eds., *The Revolution in Asian Fertility: Dimensions, Causes and Implications*, Oxford, Clarendon Press, 1993, p. 183, table 10.3.

462 Small, *Female Choices*, pp. 2, 29, 51–2.

463 See Hillary Standing, *Dependence and Autonomy: Women's Employment and the Family in Calcutta*, London, Routledge, 1991, pp. 78–90.

464 In the kibbutzim it was the women who, during the 1970s, demanded that children be taken out of communal care and back into the home. For the reminiscences of one woman who tried it see Amia Lieblich, *Kibbuts Makom*, New York, Pantheon, p. 33ff.

465 Small, *Female Choices*, pp. 189–99.

466 Wrangham and Peterson, *Demonic Males*, p. 181.

467 Data summarized in Mitchell, *Women in the Military*, pp. 141–2.

468 According to Diamond, *Guns, Germs and Steel*, p. 375.

469 Glenn Zorpette, 'The Mystery of Muscle', *Scientific American*, 10, 2, summer 1999, p. 48.

470 Jeff F. Tuten, 'The Argument against Female Combatants', in Goldman, ed., *Female Soldiers*, pp. 247–8.

471 Desmond Morris, *Manwatching; A Field Guide to Human Behavior*, New York, Abrams, 1977, pp. 239–40.

472 Presidential Commission on the Assignment of Women in the Armed Forces, *Report to the President*, p. C–74.

473 Morris, *Manwatching*, pp. 230–2.

474 Israel Radio, 20.3.1999.

475 Doreen Kimura, 'Sex Differences in the Brain', *Scientific American*, 10, 2, summer 1999, p. 27.

476 Presidential Commission on the Assignment of Women in the Armed Forces, *Report to the President*, p. C–64.

477 Sallust, *Jugurthine War*, Harmondsworth, Penguin, 1963, p. 120. In fact, for fear of them being attacked, even in the most 'progressive' modern military very few women stand guard.

478 Herodotus, *The Histories*, 9.62.3; Diodorus, *Bibliotheca Historica*, 12.70.3; 15.39.1; 87.1; Plutarch, *Moralia*, 639ff. See also John Lazenby, 'The Killing Zone', in Hanson, ed., *Hoplites*, pp. 99–100.

479 Xenophon, *Hellenica*, London, Heinemann, Loeb Classical Library, 1941, IV/3/19.

480 See the discussion in Xenophon, *Cyropaedia*, London, Heinemann, Loeb Classical Library, 1961, 2.16–18. Modern trials have shown that Roman arms and armour were best adapted to 'very strong men between 1.75 and 1.85 metres tall'; Marcus Junkelman, *Die Legionen des Augustus*, Mainz, Zabern, 1991, p. 106.

481 Anthony M. Snodgrass, *Arms and Armor of the Greeks*, Ithaca, Cornell University Press, 1967, p. 135.

482 II. Samuel, 17:8.

483 For a short list see Victor D. Hanson, *The Western Way of War: Infantry Battle in Classical Greece*, New York, Random House, 1989, pp. 55–88.

484 Victor D. Hanson, 'Hoplite Technology in Phalanx Battle', in Hanson, ed., *Hoplites*, p. 69; also *idem*, *The Wars of the Ancient Greeks*, London, Cassell, 1999, pp. 38, 58–9.

485 For experiments with Greek equipment see Walter Donlan and J. Thompson, 'The Charge at Marathon: Herodotus 6.112', *Classical Quarterly*, 71, 1976, pp. 339–43; with Roman equipment, Junkelman, *Die Legionen*, p. 196.

486 Xenophon, *Anabasis*, London, Heinemann, Loeb Classical Library, 1961, 6.1.5–13.

487 Arrian, *Anabasis*, London, Heinemann, Loeb Classical Library, 1978, VII.13.2.

488 E.g. Homer, *Iliad*, XII.445–62; Homer, *Odyssey*, XXI.405ff.

489 See R. Ewart Oakshott, *The Sword in the Age of Chivalry*, Woodbridge, Boydell Press, 1994 [1964], pp. 42–7; also Association of Vienna Museums, *Das Wiener Buergerliche Zeughaus: Ruestungen und Waffen aus Fuenf Jahrhunderten*, Vienna, Vienna Museums, 1977, p. 104ff.

490 On the Greek crossbow see Hermann Diels, *Antike Technik*, Leipzig, Teubner, 1924, p. 23; on the force needed to draw bows, David Edge and John M. Poddoch, *Arms and Armor of the Medieval Knight*, New York, Brompton, 1990, pp. 89–90.

491 See Ralph Payne-Gallway, *The Crossbow, Medieval and Modern*, New York, Bramhall, 1958, p. 309.

492 See Martin van Creveld, *Technology and War, from 2000 BC to the Present*, New York, Free Press, 1988, p. 54.

493 See William L. Rodgers, *Greek and Roman Naval Warfare*, Annapolis, Naval Academy Press, 1938 [1934], pp. 230–1.

494 For what could happen if strength did not suffice see Plato, *Laches*, London, Heinemann, Loeb Classical Library, 1952, 183D.

495 See H.T. Wallinga, The Boarding Bridge of the Romans, Gronigen, Wolters, 1956.

496 For boarding John Guilmartin, *Gunpowder and Galleys*, Cambridge, Cambridge University Press, 1974, pp. 92–3; also Richard Harding, 'Naval Warfare, 1453–1815', in Jeremy Black, ed., *European Warfare 1453–1815*, New York, St Martin's, 1999, pp. 103–7.

497 Guilmartin, *Gunpowder and Galleys*, p. 207.

498 Elting, *Swords around a Throne*, pp. 490–1.

499 Maximilian von Poseck, *Die deutsche Kavallerie in Belgien und Frankreich*, Berlin, Mittler, 1921, *passim*.

500 Elting, *Swords around a Throne*, p. 259.

501 F. Gies, *The Knight in History*, New York, Harper and Row, 1984, p. 201.

502 For a detailed inventory see Christopher Duffy, *The Military Experience in the Age of Reason*, London, Routledge, 1988, p. 188.

503 Ulrich Braeker, *Der Arme Mann in Trockenburg*, Osnabrueck, Biblio, 1980 [1852], p. 138.

504 Martin van Creveld, *Supplying War*, London, Cambridge University Press, 1977, chapter 3.

505 For the 'insane' physical effort that German infantry training involved see Guy Sayer, *The Forgotten Soldier*, London, Brassey's, 1967, p. 142

506 All these figures from Junkelman, *Die Legionen*, p. 199.

507 William Greider, *Fortress America*, New York, Public Affairs, 1998, p. 125.

508 For Freud's views see Elisabeth Young-Bruehl, *Freud on Women*, New York, Norton, 1990, pp. 272–82 346–62.

509 Karen Horney, 'The Flight from Womanhood', *International Journal for Psycho-Analysis*, 7, 1926, p. 330; *idem*, 'The Dread of Women', ibid., 13, 1932, p. 359; H.L. and R.R. Ansbacher, eds., *The Individual Psychology of Alfred Adler*, New York, Harper & Row, 1956, pp. 50, 452; Peggy R. Sanday, *Female Power and Male Dominance; on the Origins of Sexual Inequality*, Cambridge, Cambridge University Press, 1987, p. 78; Jill K. Conway and others, eds., *Learning about Women*, Ann Arbor, University of Michigan Press, 1989, p. xxvi; and J. Rutherford, *Men's Silences*, London, Routledge, 1990, pp. 180–1.

510 Nancy C. Chodorow, *Feminism and Psychoanalytic Theory*, New Haven, Yale University Press, 1989, pp. 32–41; Walter Ong, *Fighting for Life*, Ithaca, Cornell University Press, 1973, p. 71.

511 Andrea Dworkin, *Pornography: Men Possess Women*, New York, Perigee, 1981, pp. 49–51.

512 Philip L. Newman and David J. Boyd, 'The Making of Men: Ritual and Meaning in Awa Male Initiation', in Gilbert H. Herdt, ed., *Rituals of Manhood: Male Initiation in Papua New Guinea*, London, Transaction Publishers, 1998, p. 278.

513 See Elisabeth Badinter, *XY: On Masculine Identity*, New York, Columbia University Press, 1995, chapter 3.

514 See most recently David G. Gilmore, *Manhood in the Making: Cultural Concepts of Masculinity*, New Haven, Yale University Press, 1990.

515 Fitz John Porter Pole, 'The Ritual Forging of Identity', in Herdt, ed., *Rituals of Manhood*, p. 123.

516 Gilbert H. Herdt, 'Fetish and Fantasy in Sambia Initiation', in Herdt, ed., *Rituals of Manhood*, p. 79.

517 Pole, 'The Ritual Forging of Identity', p. 123.

518 Deborah B. Gewertz, 'The Father Who Bore Me: The Role of *Tsambunwuro* during Chambri Initiation Ceremonies', in Herdt, ed., *Rituals of Manhood*, p. 298.

519 Nancy C. Lutkehaus, 'Feminist Anthropology and Female Initiation in Melanesia', in Nancy C. Lutkehaus and Paul B. Roscoe, eds., *Gender Rituals; Female Initiation in Melanesia*, London, Routledge, 1995, p. 29.

520 Mead, *Blackberry Winter,* p. 204.

521 See Arnold M. Cooper, 'What Men Fear: the Facade of Castration Anxiety', in Gerald I. Fogel and others, eds., *The Psychology of Men: New Psycholoanalytic Perspectives*, New York, Basic Books, 1987, p. 113.

522 Plato, *Republic*, 455 D.

523 For the view of war as sport see above all Friedrich Nietzsche, *Thus Spake Zarathustra*, Harmondsworth, Penguin, 1961, pp. 73–5; van Creveld, *The Transformation of War*, chapter 6; and Barbara Erhrenreich, *Blood Rites: Origins and History of the Passions of War*, New York, Holt, 1997, chapter 7; and Cora Stephen, *Das Handwerk des Krieges*, Berlin, Rohwolt, 1998, pp. 158–63.

524 Exodus, 12: 36–7.

525 Tacitus, *Germania*, London, Heinemann, Loeb Classical Library, 1965, 18.

526 Joachim Bumke, *The Concept of Knighthood in the Middle Ages*, New York, AMS, 1982, pp. 79–81. The terms used were '*zu man werden*' and '*swert leisten*', respectively.

527 Thomas Spears, *Kenya's Past*, London, Longman, 1981, pp. 63–7; Ifi Amadiume, *Male Daughters, Female Husbands: Gender and Sex in an African Society*, London, Zed, 1987, pp. 94–6; Turney-High, *Primitive War*, pp. 162–3.

528 M.B. Davie, *The Evolution of War: A Study of Its Role in Early Societies*, New Haven, Yale University Press, 1929, p. 33; Gilmore, *Manhood in the Making*, p. 67.

529 Homer, *Iliad*, VI.124; VII.114. For an in-depth discussion of the Greek link between war and manhood see above all Blok, *The Early Amazons,* pp. 181, 251–5.

530 For a discussion of the Greek terminology see E. Vermeule, *Aspects of Death in Early Greek Art and Poetry*, Berkeley, University of California Press, 1979, p. 101; of the Hebrew one, Sion, *Images of Manhood*, pp. 90–2. For a general discussion of the terminology that war and sex have in common see Denis de Rougemont, *Passion and Society*, London, Faber & Faber, n.d., pp. 248–50.

531 See D.H.J. Morgan, 'Theater of War: Combat, the Military and Masculinities', in H. Brod and M. Kaufman, eds., *Theorizing Masculinities*, Los Angeles, Sage Publications, 1994.

532 Margaret Mead, *Male and Female*, London, Gollancz, 1949, pp. 159–60.

533 See Robert Wenke, *Patterns in Prehistory: Humankind's First Three Million Years*, New York, Oxford University Press, 1990, pp. 120–1.

534 Chawwa Wijnberg, 'If Men were to Bleed', in Elly de Waard, ed., *Die niewe wilden in the poezie* 2. Amsterdam, van Gennep, 1988, trans P. Niewint.

535 For some attempts at an explanation see Freud's 1932 lecture, 'Femininity', in Young-Bruehl, ed., *Freud on Women*, pp. 346–62; Horney, 'The Flight from Womanhood'; also Dworkin, *Pornography*, pp. 17–18.

536 Lynne Segal, *Is the Future Female?* New York, Peter Bedrick, 1987, p. 14; Elizabeth Reardon, *Sexism and the War System*, New York, Teachers' College, 1985, p. 47; Violet Klein, *The Feminine Character*, London, Kegan Paul, 1946, p. 72.

537 Kate Millett, *Sexual Politics*, New York, Avon Books, 1971, p. 119.

538 Francke, *Ground Zero*, p. 41.

539 L.R. Goldberg, 'Simple Models of Simple Processes?' *American Psychologist*, 23, 1968, pp. 483–95; G.I. Peterson and others, 'An Evaluation of the Performance of Women as a Function of their Sex, Achievement and Personal History', *Journal of Personality and Social Psychology*, 19, 1971, pp. 114–18.

540 For the evidence see Katherine Hakim, *Key Issues in Women's Work: Female Heterogeneity and the Polarisation of Women's Employment*, London, Athlone, 1996, pp. 108, 115, 117.

541 Christine E. Bose, *Jobs and Gender, a Study of Occupational Prestige*, New York, Praeger, 1985, p. 53; see also Elizabeth Fox-Genovese, *Feminism is not the Story of My Life*, New York, Anchor Books, 1996, p. 122.

542 Friedrich Nietzsche, *Beyond Good and Evil*, Harmondsworth, Penguin, 1969, p. 145.

543 Bose, *Jobs and Gender*, pp. 36, 98; Bernard E. Whitely, Jr., 'Sex Roles and Psychotherapy: A Current Appraisal', *Psychological Bulletin*, 86, 6, 1979, pp. 1309–21.

544 For the situation as it exists in the US see Barbara F. Reskin and Patricia A. Roos, *Job Queues, Gender Queues: Explaining Women's Inroads into Male Occupations*, Philadelphia, Temple University Press, 1997, pp. 122–5, 133–41, 157–63, 175–81, 193–202; for Western Europe, Rose-Marie Lagrave, 'A Supervised Emancipation', in Thebaud, ed., *A History of Women* vol. 5, p. 470ff.

545 Carol Tavris and Carole Wade, *The Longest War*, New York, Harcourt Brace Jovanovich, 1984, p. 24; Rose-Marie Lagrave, 'A Supervised Emancipation', in Thebaud, ed., *A History of Women*, vol. 5, p. 486; Betty Friedan, *Beyond Gender*, Washington DC, Woodrow Wilson Press, 1997, p. 34.

546 Reskin and Roos, *Job Queues, Gender Queues*, p. 15.

547 *Economist*, 26.9.1998, p. 108.

548 See most recently van Creveld, *The Rise and Decline of the State*.

549 Aristophanes, *Lysistrate*, London, Heinemann, Loeb Classical Library, 1979, 672–83 (my adaptation).

550 Queen of Halicarnasus. According to the anonymous *Tractatus de Mulieribus*, 13, she joined Xerxes in his invasion of Greece in 480 BC.

551 Micon was the painter who decorated the Parthenon. He did a painting of Amazons on horseback, which became famous.

PART III

1 The best work about the breaking of the link between victory and survival and indeed nuclear strategy in general, remains Thomas Schelling, *Arms and Influence,* New Haven, Yale University Press, 1966.

2 Bernhard Brodie and others, *The Absolute Weapon*, New York, Columbia University Press, 1946, chapter 1; also *idem*, 'The Atom Bomb as Policy Maker', *Foreign Affairs*, 27, 1, October 1948, pp. 1–16.

3 The best history of nuclear 'strategy' remains Lawrence Freedman, *The Evolution of Nuclear Strategy*, New York, St Martin's Press, 1981.

4 See e.g. John F.C. Fuller, *The Conduct of War*, London, Eyre & Spottiswoode, 1961, p. 321ff.

5 P.M.S. Blackett, *The Military and Political Consequences of Atomic Energy*, London, Turnstile Press, 1948, chapter 10.

6 For the Soviet road to the bomb see most recently David Holloway, *Stalin and the Bomb*, New Haven, Yale University Press, 1994.

7 See Aalan Enthoven, *How Much is Enough? Shaping the Defense Budget, 1961–69,* New York, Harper & Row, 1971, for the kind of calculation involved.

8 See most recently Tariq Rauf, 'Disarmament and Non-Proliferation Treaties', in G.A. Wood and Lewis S. Leland, Jr., eds., *State and Sovereignty, Is the State in Retreat?*, Dunedin, University of Otago Press, 1997, pp. 142–88.

9 See e.g. *Public Opinion Quarterly*, 14, spring 1950, p. 182 (the Soviet bomb); Roberto Ducci, 'The World Order in the Sixties', *Foreign Affairs*, 43, 3, April 1964, pp. 379–90 (the Chinese bomb); and A. Myrdal, 'The High Price of Nuclear Arms Monopoly', *Foreign Policy*, 18, spring 1975, pp. 30–43 (the Indian bomb).

10 For a more detailed discussion of the decline of inter-state war since 1945 see Martin van Creveld, *Nuclear Proliferation and the Future of Conflict,* New York, Free Press, 1993, chapter 1; also Edward Luard, *The Blunted Sword: The Erosion of Military Power in Modern World Politics,* London, Tauris, 1988.

11 The International Institute of Military Studies, *The Military Balance, 2000–1,* (London, IISS, 2000, gives a country by country overview of the armed forces currently in existence.

12 Richard Overy, *The Air War 1939–1945,* London, Europa, 1980, pp. 308–9.

13 Dr Daniel Goure (CSIS), lecture, Bonn, 22.9.1999.

14 The best analysis of cost trends remains Franklin Spinney, *Defense Facts of Life*, Boulder, Westview, 1986.

15 BBC, 25.2.1998.

16 For some calculations pertaining to his subject see Neville Brown, *The Future of Air Power*, New York, Holmes & Meier, 1986, p. 88; John A. Warden, III, 'Air Theory for the Twenty-First Century', in Karl P. Magyar, ed., *Challenge and Response: Anticipating US Military Security Concerns*, Maxwell, Air Force University Press, 1994, pp. 313 and 328; also Daniel T. Kuehl, 'Airpower vs. Electricity: Electric Power as a Target for Strategic Air Operations', *Journal of Strategic Studies*, 18, 1, March 1995, pp. 250–60.

17 Cf. van Creveld, *Technology and War*, chapters 9 and 11.

18 For the effect of nuclear weapons on the Arab-Israeli conflict see Shlomo Aronson, *The Politics and Strategy of Nuclear Weapons in the Middle East*, Albany, State University of New York Press, 1992.

19 See Mary Kaldor, *New Wars for Old*, London, Pergamon, 1998.

20 Quoted in Francke, *Ground Zero*, p. 24.

21 Dwight David Eisenhower, *Crusade in Europe*, New York, Doubleday, 1948, pp. 132–3.

22 See Holm, *Women in the Military*, chapter 10; Ebbert and Hall, *Crossed Currents*, p. 97ff.

23 Meyer, *Creating GI Jane*, pp. 177–8.

24 Holm, *Women in the Military*, p. 148.

25 Martin Binkin and Shirley J. Bach, *Women in the Military*, Washington DC, Brookings, 1977, p. 12.

26 Holm, *Women in the Military*, pp. 163–4; Judith H. Stiehm, *Arms and the Enlisted Woman*, Philadelphia, Temple University Press, 1989 pp. 32–3.

27 Holm, *Women in the Military*, p. 181; Ebbert and Hall, *Crossed Currents*, p. 122; Breuer, *War and American Women*, pp. 70–1.

28 Holm, *Women in the Military*, p. 184.

29 Ebbert and Hall, *Crossed Currents*, pp. 120–1.

30 For an overview see Jean E. Klick, 'Utilization of Women in the NATO Alliance', *Armed Forces and Society*, 4, 4, August 1978, pp. 673–94; also Seidler, *Frauen zu der Waffen?* part 2.

31 For a short account see Melva Crouch, 'The Role of Women in the Army', *United Service*, 45, 1, July 1991, pp. 19–21.

32 Michel L. Martin, 'From Periphery to Center: Women in the French Military', *Armed Forces and Society*, 8, 2, winter 1982, pp. 303–33.

33 Figures on women from Binkin and Bach, *Women in the Military*, Washington D.C. Brookings, 1977, p. 123; figure on total strength from International Institute of Strategic Studies, *The Military Balance, 1976*, London, IISS, 1977, p. 9.

34 Attwood, *The New Soviet Man and Woman*, p. 131ff.

35 Details and quotation from Griesse and Stites, 'Russia's Revolution and War', in Goldman, ed., *Female Soldiers*, p. 78ff.

36 A useful survey of female members of Eastern Bloc armies is provided by Seidler, *Frauen zu der Waffen?* pp. 197–204.

37 See above, pp. 121.

38 Xiaon Li, 'Chi Women in the People's Liberation Army', *Armed Forces and Society*, 20, 1, fall 1993, pp. 69–83.

39 Netiva Ben Yehuda, *When the State Broke Out* [Hebrew], Jerusalem, Keter, 1991, p. 1; Alon Kadish, *To Arms and To Farms* [Hebrew], Tel Aviv, Tag, 1995, p. 234.

40 Hedva Avigdori-Avidav, *The Road We Took: From the Diary of a Convoy-Escort* [Hebrew], Tel Aviv, Ministry of Defence, 1988.

41 Based on the casualty list in Aryeh Yitschaki, *Latrun: The Battle for the Road to Jerusalem* [Hebrew], Jerusalem, Kanah, 1982, pp. 564–71.

42 Uri Ben Ari, *Follow Me* [Hebrew], Tel Aviv, Maariv, 1994, p. 169ff.

43 Zehava Ostfeld, *An Army is Born: Main Stages in the Buildup of the Army Under the Leadership of Ben Gurion* [Hebrew], Tel Aviv, Ministry of Defence, 1993, vol. 2, p. 819.

44 See the statistics in van Creveld, *The Sword and the Olive*, pp. 99, 119.

45 Avigdori-Avidav, *The Road We Took*, p. 154ff.

46 For all this see van Creveld, *The Sword and the Olive*, p. 119ff.

47 The figures given in Presidential Commission on the Assignment of Women in the Armed Forces, *Report to the President*, Washington DC, 1992, 11.9.1992, p. C–31 confuse the conscript force with the standing one and are therefore highly misleading.

48 See Reuven Gal, *A Portrait of the Israeli Soldier*, Westport, Greenwood Press, 1986, p. 49.

49 Israel's Women's Lobby, 'Women's Service in the IDF: Reality, Will, Vision' [Hebrew], mimeographed, Tel Aviv, Tel Aviv University, 1995, p. 13.

50 For current figures on Israeli military manpower see IISS, ed., *The Military Balance, 1997–98*, pp. 128–9.

51 *Yediot Acharonot*, 1.12.1998, p. 16.

52 Term used by CHEN Commander Colonel Stella Levy, quoted in J. Larteguy, *The Walls of Israel*, New York, Evans, 1969, p. 195.

53 See the collection of articles on this subject in Giuseppe Caforio, ed., *The Sociology of the Military*, Cheltenham, Elgar, 1988, part D.

54 See, for the US, Susan Householder van Horn, *Women, Work, and Fertility, 1900–1986*, New York, New York University Press, 1988, chapter 10; for Canada, Yolande Cohen, 'From Feminine to Feminism in Quebec', in Thebaud, ed., *A History of Women*, vol. 5, p. 550; for Western Europe and Australia, Gisela Bock, 'Poverty and Mothers' Rights in the Emerging Welfare States', *ibid*, vol. 5, p. 434.

55 See on these subjects Betty Friedan, *The Feminine Mystique*, New York, Dell, 1963, *passim*.

56 Binkin and Bach, *Women in the Military*, p. 12.

57 See Eric V. Larsen, 'Ends and Means in Democratic Conversation: Understanding the Role of Casualties in Support for US Military Operations', RAND Corporation, 1995, p. 205, figure 2.3.1.

58 Holm, *Women in the Military*, chapter 15; Breuer, *War and American Women*, p. 79; Rogan, *Mixed Company*, p. 16; Ebbert and Hall, *Crossed Currents*, pp. 160–1, 168, 222–3; Jean J. Mansbridge, *Why We Lost the ERA*, Chicago, University of Chicago Press, 1986, p. 72; Mitchell, *Women in the Military*, pp. 24–5.

59 Breuer, *War and American Women*, p. 82.

60 Ibid., pp. 72–3, 76.

61 Ebbert and Hall, *Crossed Currents*, pp. 156–568; Holm, *Women in the Military*, chapters 16 and 17. For some of the women's own stories see Kathryn Marshall, *In the Combat Zone: An Oral History of American Women in Vietnam, 1966–1975*, Boston, Little Brown, 1987.

62 Lawrence J. Korb, *The Fall and Rise of the Pentagon*, Westport, Greenwood, 1979.

63 See Colin L. Powell, *My American Journey*, New York, Random House, 1995, p. 157. Since then, incidentally, the army has gone down to 497,000.

64 See the testimonies quoted in Binkin and Bach, *Women in the Military*, p. 49ff.

65 Quoted in Stiehm, *Arms and the Enlisted Woman*, p. 55.

66 Binkin and Bach, *Women in the Military*, pp. 62–3; Holm, *Women in the Military*, p. 381.

67 See Mansbridge, *Why We Lost the ERA*.

68 Binkin and Bach, *Women in the Military*, pp. 2, 12–13.

69 Ebbert and Hall, *Crossed Currents*, pp. 163–4.

70 See Holm, *Women in the Military*, chapter 18.

71 See Breuer, *War and American Women*, p. 116ff.

72 Holm, *Women in the Military*, p. 205.

73 Japan: K.M. Wiegand, 'Japan: Cautious Utilization', in Goldman, ed., *Female Soldiers*, pp. 184, 187. Australia: V.H. Billington, 'Broadening the Recruiting Base for ARA Soldiers', Fort Queenscliff Papers, 1991, pp. 56–7. Sweden: Kurt Tornqvist, 'Sweden, the Neutral Nation', in *ibid*, p. 208. Greece: J. Brown and C. Safilios-Rothschild, 'Greece: Reluctant Presence', *ibid*, p. 168. Britain: Christopher Dandeker, 'New Times for the Military', *British Journal of Sociology*, 45, 4, December 1994, p. 649. The Netherlands: Loes van Tuyl, 'Vrouwen tegen Vergrjizing', *ARMEX*, December 1997, p. 16. Belgium: Seidler, *Frauen zu der Waffen?*, p. 243. FGR: *ibid*, p. 223.

74 Yael Jerby, *The Double Price: the Status of Women in Israel Society and Military Service for Women* [Hebrew], Tel Aviv, Ramot, p. 149.

75 Rogan, *Mixed Company*, p. 62; see also Gutman, *The Kinder, Gentler Military*, pp. 31–43, 72–3.

76 Rogan, *Mixed Company*, p. 65.

77 US Army Research Institute for Environmental Medicine, *Incidence of Risk Factors for Injury and Illness among Male and Female Army Basic Trainees*, 1988.

78 Figures from Lis B. de Fleur, David Gilman, and William Marshal, 'Sex Integration at the US Air Force Academy: Changing Roles for Women', *Armed Forces and Society*, August 1978, p. 615.

79 Gutman, *The Kinder, Gentler Military*, p. 266.

80 See Karen J. Colson, Stephanie A. Eisenstadt, Terra Ziporyn, *The Harvard Guide to Women's Health*, Cambridge, Harvard University Press, 1996, pp. 238, 241, 322, 379, 388.

81 Mary J. Festle, *Playing Nice: Politics and Apologies in Women's Sports*, New York, Columbia University Press, 1996, p. 270ff.

82 Gutman, *The Kinder, Gentler Military*, p. 248; *Wall Street Journal*, 3.12.1999.

83 See Gregory K. Stanley, *The Rise and Fall of the Sportswoman: Women's Health, Fitness, and Athletics, 1860–1940*, New York, Lang, 1996, chapter 6.

84 On these problems see also GAO, *Improved Guidance and Oversight are Needed to Ensure Validity and Equity of Fitness Standards*, Washington DC, Government Printing Office, 1998, pp. 3, 4, 5, 9, 12, 16, 26 and 28.

85 Rogan, *Mixed Company*, p. 36.

86 Radio Israel, 21 July 1998, announced the opening of a mixed anti-aircraft defence course for men and women in which the latter would have to meet different (i.e. lesser) physical standards.

87 For a plethora of such complaints see Mitchell, *Women in the Military*, *passim*; Francke, *Ground Zero*, p. 200; Gutman, *The Kinder, Gentler Military*, pp. 260–1.

88 See on these cases Stiehm, *Arms and the Enlisted Woman*, p. 113ff.

89 Ibid., pp. 23–4.

90 Ibid., p. 55.

91 van Horn, *Women, Work, and Fertility*, p. 202ff.

92 See below, pp. 210–11.

93 Holm, *Women in the Military*, p. 388.

94 For details see Klick, 'Utilization of Women in the NATO Alliance'.

95 *Die Welt*, 10.4.1997, quoted in Seidler, *Frauen zu der Waffen?*, p. 330.

96 US, Canadian, British, Norwegian and Dutch figures (1980) from Cynthia. Enloe, 'Women in NATO Militaries – a Confence Report', *Women's Studies International Forum*, 5, 3/4, 1982, pp. 330–1. French figure (1988) calculated by me on the basis of J. Boulegue, '"Feminization" and the French Military: Anthropological Approach', *Armed Forces and Society*, 17, 3, 1991, pp. 343–62. Britt Dohile, 'Women in the Military of Foreign Countries', *Minerva: Quarterly Reports on Women and the Military*, vi, 4, winter 1988, pp. 76–7 has a somewhat different set of figures, but the conclusion is the same.

97 For the details of this curious story see Mitchell, *Women in the Military*, pp. 195–8; also Francke, *Ground Zero*, pp. 48–71.

98 Figures from Holm, *Women in the Military*, p. 397.

99 Ibid., p. 429.

100 See figures in Stefan Busch, 'Frauen in der US Army – Standpunkt zum Combatverbot und Grenzen der Integration', *Mars, Jahrbuch fuer Wehrpolitik und Militaerwesen*, 3/4, 1997–8, p. 383, table D.

101 Lillian A. Pfluke, 'Every Day is a Fight', *Newsweek*, 48/1996, p. 22.

102 The army alone was to lose 5 out of 18 divisions; Benjamin F. Schemmer, 'Pentagon's 5 Year Defense Plan', *Armed Forces Journal International*, March 1990, p. 16.

103 For Iraqi military strength at the time see IISS, ed., *The Military Balance, 1990–91*, pp. 104–6.

104 General Accounting Office, *Report to Sec/Def*, US GAO,Washington DC, 1993, p. 2.

105 Mitchell, *Women in the Military*, p. 211.

106 *News Weekly*, 23.8.1997, p. 10. Mike Lynch Testimony to the Presidential Commission on the Assignment of Women in the Armed Forces, *Report to the President*, p. 59.

107 According to P.J. Edwards and J.E. Edwards, *Incidence of Pregnancy and Single Parenthood among Enlisted Personnel in the Navy*, San Diego, Navy Personnel Research and Development Center, Report TN–92–8, February 1992. Other sources give slightly higher figures.

108 Office of the Assistant Secretary of Defense for Manpower, Reserve Affairs and Logistics, Background Review: *Women in the Military*, Washington DC, Department of Defense, October 1981, p. 7.

109 A. Clymer, 'At Home with No Parents at Home', *New York Times*, 16.2.1991, p. 10.

110 Francke, *Ground Zero*, pp. 134, 136.

111 Mitchell, *Women in the Military*, p. 210.

112 Proceedings of the Presidential Commission, *Report to the President*, 13–15.7.1992.

113 Holm, *Women in the Military*, p. 470.

114 Mitchell, *Women in the Military*, p. 209.

115 Ibid., p. 211.

116 E. Smith, 'Head of Army Sees Chance of Female Fliers in Combat', *New York Times*, 2 June 1991, p. 20.

117 See Breuer, *War and American Women*, pp. 68–70.

118 Ibid., pp. 77–9.

119 Martin van Creveld, 'Why Israel Doesn't Send Women into Combat', *Parameters*, 23, 1, spring 1993, pp. 5–9.

120 Presidential Commission on the Assignment of Women in the Services, *Report to the President*, p. C–86.

121 Mitchell, *Women in the Military*, p. 231.

122 Ibid., p. 127.

123 See Breuer, *War and American Women*, pp. 198–9.

124 See Mitchell, *Women in the Military*, p. 289.

125 John Chapman, 'No Bayonets Please, We're Women Soldiers', *Express*, 23.10.1997, p. 31.

126 Glenn W. Goodman, 'Ruling the Skies', *Armed Forces International*, June 1999, p. 30.

127 Presidential Report on the Assignment of Women in the Military, *Report to the President*, p. C–91.

128 Data provided by Dr Sergei Rogov, head of the US-Canada Institute, Moscow, Bonn, 22–3.9.1999.

129 *Bundeswehr Aktuell*, 6.3.2000, p. 6; ZDF 3, 21.3.2000.

131 Pierre Montagnon, *Histoire de la Légion*, Paris, Pygmalion, 1999, p. 400. Present plans call for its size to go down by only 8.4 per cent.

132 Martin van Creveld, *The Sword and the Olive*, chapters 17 and 20.

133 For the resistance to the Lebanese adventure see Ruth Linn, 'Conscientious Objection', *Iyunim-Bechinuch* [Hebrew], 49/50, 1989, pp. 51–2.

134 Jerby, *The Double Price*, p. 149.

135 Orri Schwartz, 'Women in Combat – Legal Aspects of the Alice Miller Case' [Hebrew], unpublished paper, the Hebrew University, Jerusalem, 1998.

136 Israel TV, 29.10.1996.

137 *Yediot Acharonot* [Hebrew], 8.5.1997, p. 17; 9.5.1997, p. 6; 21.9.1997, pp. 8–12.

138 Ibid., 8.5.1997, p. 7.

139 Ibid., 15.1.1999, pp. 20–1.

140 Ibid., 16.12.1998, p. 13.

141 Israel TV, 8.7.1999.

142 *Le Point*, 24.2.1996, p. 50.

143 Paul Vennesson, 'De L'esprit de Défense au Sentiment Patriotique', in Bernhard Boenne and Christopher Dandeker, eds., *Les armées en Europe*, Paris, La Découverte, 1998, pp. 287–304.

144 See Geoffrey Best, *War and Society in Revolutionary Europe*, London, Fontana, 1982.

145 On the link between the two phenomena see also Karl W. Haltener, 'Le Déclin final des armées de masse', in Boenne and Dandeker, eds., *Les armées en Europe*, pp. 150–2.

146 *Newsweek*, 18.1.1980.

147 Mansbridge, *Why We Lost the ERA*, chapter 8.

148 Presidential Commission, p. 40.

149 For the relevant calculations see Kommission fuer die Langzeitplannung der Bundeswehr, *Bericht*, Bonn, Ministerie fuer Verteitigung, 6.5.1982, particularly articles 402–3.

150 Lieselotte Funcke, 'First Lady' of the Free Democratic Party, as quoted in *Emma*, no. 6, 1978; also Astrid Albrecht-Heide and Utemaria Bujewski-Crawford, *Frauen-Krieg-Militaer, Images und Phantasien*, Tuebingen, Verein fuer Friedenspaedagogik, 1991, pp. 90–1.

151 Press declaration of various feminist groups, 6.12.1980, printed in: Friederich Naumann Stiftung, *Frauen und Bundeswehr*, Bonn, Friedrich Naumann Stiftung, 1983, p. 228; also Renate Janssen, *Frauen ans Gewehr?*, Cologne, Ruegenstein, 1983.

152 Harald Wust, 'Frauen zu den Waffen?' *Mars*, 3–4, 1997–8, p. 59.

153 Meyer, *Creating GI Jane*, pp. 76–7.

154 Pile, *Ack Ack*, pp. 187–8.

155 See above, p. 147.

156 Interview with Brigadier General Chedva Almog, CO, CHEN, in A.R. Bloom, 'Women in the Defense Forces', in Barbara Swirski and Marylin P. Safir, eds., *Calling the Equality Bluff: Women in Israel*, New York, Pergamon Press, 1991, p. 15; interview with Brigadier General Yisraela Oren, CO, CHEN, *Yediot Acharonot* weekend magazine, 15.8.1997.

157 See, for the US, Stiehm, *Arms and the Enlisted Woman*, p. 1; Rogan, *Mixed Company*, pp. 125–6; Sarah Wood and others, 'Migration of Women to and from Nontraditional Military Occupations', General Research Corp., Final Report Prepared for Commander, Office of the Assistant Secretary of Defense, 15.7.1979, pp. 33–5. For the situation in Canada see Cheryl D. Lamerson, 'Integration of Women in the Canadian Forces', in Hurni, *Frauen in Streitkraeften*, pp. 219, 225; also Gutman, *The Kinder, Gentler Military*, pp. 268–71. For Australia, see Pam Wood, 'The Airwoman of the 1990s', *United Service*, 45, 1, July 1991; for Norway, Seidler, *Frauen zu der Waffen?* p. 334; for Sweden, *ibid*, pp. 369–70.

158 Lionel Tiger, *Women in the Kibbuts*, New York, Harcourt Brace Jovanovich, 1975, pp. 254–5; Henry Near, *The Kibbutz Movement: A History*, London, Littman, 1997, vol. 2, pp. 300, 324.

159 See Lance Morrow, 'Men: Are They Really that Bad?' *Time*, 14.1.1994, pp. 56–7.

160 Stiehm, *Arms and the Enlisted Woman*, p. 100.

161 *Newsweek*, 5.8.1991.

162 Laura Miller, *Feminism and the Exclusion of Army Women from Combat*, Harvard University, John M. Olin Institute for Strategic Studies, n.d., p. 19. I wish to thank Prof. Charles C. Moskos for putting this study at my disposal.

163 David Anderson, 'The Challenge of Military Service: Defence Personnel Conditions in a Changing Social Context', Canberra, ACT, Parliamentary Information and Research Services, 1997, p. 145.

164 Miller, *Feminism*, pp. 1–2.

165 Kathleen Jones, 'Dividing the Ranks: Women and the Draft', in Jean B. Ehlstain and Sheila Tobias, eds., *Women, Militarism and War*, Savage, Rowman & Littlefield, 1990, p. 133.

166 Miller, *Feminism*, pp. 2, 35.

167 Ebbert and Hall, *Crossed Currents*, p. 14.

168 Ibid., p. 78.

169 Alexijewitsch, *Der Krieg hat kein weibliches Gesicht*, p. 138.

170 Cf. DeGroot, 'Whose Finger on the Trigger?', p. 437; Pile, *Ack Ack,* pp. 190–1.

171 Goldman and Stites, 'Great Britain and the World Wars', in Goldman, ed., *Female Soldiers,* p. 32.

172 Stiehm, *Arms and the Enlisted Woman*, p. 145.

173 Francke, *Ground Zero*, p. 149.

174 Griesse and Stites, 'Russia: Revolution and War', in Goldman, ed., *Female Soldiers,* p. 80; also Seidler, *Frauen zu der Waffen?,* p. 361.

175 Brown and Safilios-Rothschild, 'Greece: Reluctant Presence', p. 173.

176 Klick, 'Utilization of Women in the NATO Military', p. 675; *Moniteur belge,* 7.5.1977, p. 6236.

177 Seidler, *Frauen zu der Waffen?,* p. 381.

178 According to Seidler, *Frauen zu der Waffen?,* p. 324.

179 *Yediot Acharonot*, 16.12.1998, p. 13.

180 Enloe, 'Women in NATO Militaries – a Conference Report', p. 330.

181 Cf. Boulegue, 'Feminization' and the French Military', p. 343 for figures on the French military as of 1985. The situation in the old USSR was similar.

182 For the US see testimony of Lt. John Calgett, USN, 6.8.1992, Presidential Commission, 15.11.1992; also David Hackworth, 'War and the Second Sex', *Newsweek*, 5.8.1991, p. 26. For Israel see *Yediot Acharonot*, 8.5.1996, p. 17, and *ibid.*, 9.5.1996, p. 6.

183 DeGroot, 'Whose Finger on the Trigger?', pp. 437–8.

184 M. C. Devilbis, 'Gender Integration and Unit Deployment: a Study of GI Jo', *Armed Forces and Society*, 11, 4, summer 1985, p. 538. While I was unable to establish Devilbis's first name, she is clearly female.

185 Mitchell, *Women in the Military*, pp. 107–9.

186 Cf. GAO Report to Sec/Def, US GAO, Washington DC, 1993, pp. 2–5.

187 Gutman, *The Kinder, Gentler Military*, pp. 15, 258.

188 Personal communication from Lt. Col. Ian Wing, Australian Army.

189 The text is quoted in Nancy G.Wilds, 'Sexual Harassment in the Military', *Minerva: Quarterly Report on Women and the Military*, viii, 4, winter 1990, p. 3.

190 See the definition in Lois M. Beck, 'Sexual Harassment in the Army: Roots Examined', *Minerva: Quarterly Reports on Women and the Military*, ix, 1, spring 1991, p. 29. For a discussion of the way in which the definition of 'sexual harassment' has expanded, see Larry May, *Masculinity and Morality*, Ithaca, Cornell University Press, 1998, chapter 6.

191 *Washington Times*, 25.11.1998.

192 All these quotes from Timothy Beneke, *Proving Manhood: Reflections on Men and Sexism*, Berkeley, University of California Press, 1997, pp. 180–8.

193 Wilds, 'Sexual Harassment', p. 12.

194 For the US armed forces see Juanita A. Firestone and Richard J. Harris, 'Sexual Harassment in the US Military', *Armed Forces and Society*, 21, 1, fall 1994, pp. 24–43; for the Australian ones Kathryn Quinn, *Sexual Harassment in the Australian Defence Force*, Canberra, ACT, Defence Centre, 1996, p. 15.

195 *Los Angeles Times*, 11.10.1998.

196 See, for example, the controversy that followed after the publication of a letter by Warrant Officer 2 M. Thorp of the Australian Infantry School in *Army*, 23.7.1998, p. 15.

197 'Follow Military Lead', *USA Today*, 5.2.1998.

198 The latest masterpiece to emerge from this situation is the Australian Defence Force Academy, *Report of the Review into Policies and Practices to Deal with Sexual Harassment and Sexual Offences*, Canberra, ACT, ADFA, June 1998.

199 See Rogan, *Mixed Company*, p. 248, for the men's reactions.

200 *USA Today*, 21.10.1998, p. 35.

201 Between 1980 and 1991 the percentage of West Europeans who felt proud of their nations' military declined by 8 per cent on average: Joseph L. Seoters, 'Valeurs militaires, valeurs civiles; vers le "soldat communicateur"', in Boenne and Dandeker, eds., *Les armées en Europe*, p. 271.

202 See *Washington Times*, 19.11.1999, on the attempts of recruiters to meet targets by cheating on standards.

203 *USA Today*, 23.10.1999.

204 *Financial Times*, 12.8.1998.

205 See van Creveld, *The Sword and the Olive*, *passim*.

206 *Yediot Acharonot* [Hebrew], 15.1.1999, pp. 20–1; *ibid*, weekend magazine, 2.7.1999, pp. 80–5.

207 Till Schroeder, 'Der Soldaten-Job hat an Attraktivitaet eingebuesst', *Berliner Zeitung*, 27/8.5.2000, p. 97.

208 Presidential Commission to the Assignment of Women in the Armed Forces, *Report to the President*, p. C–22.

209 van Tuyl, 'Vrouwen tegen Vergrijzing'; also Seidler, *Frauen zu der Waffen?*, pp. 329–30.

210 Nigel South, *Policing for Profit: the Private Security Sector*, London, Sage, 1989.

211 *Der Spiegel*, 1996, no. 46, p. 37; also Bernard Jean d'Heur, 'Von der Gefahrenabwehr als staatlicher Angelegenheit zum Einsatz privater Sicherheitskraefte', *Archiv des Oeffentlichen Rechts*, 119, 1, March 1994, pp. 107–36.

212 *Der Spiegel*, 27/2000, p. 75.

213 All American figures based on Brian Jenkins, 'Thoroughly Modern Sabotage', *World Link*, March–April 1995, p. 16.

214 In Israel, as of summer 1998, private security personnel are even used to guard police officers who need protection.

215 For example, in New Zealand as of 1997 there was a serious debate as to whether they should be allowed to join the police on roadblocks to collect debts; Auckland *Herald*, 27.6.1997, p. 1.

216 For some relevant figures (US) see Reskin and Roos, *Job Queues, Gender Queues*, p. 61. Remarkably enough, the figure for a traditional society such as India is exactly the same: Hilary Standing, *Dependence and Autonomy: Women's Employment and the Family in Calcutta*, London, Routledge, 1991, p. 53.

217 For a general explanation of the working of the industry see Dennis Phipps, *The Management of Aviation Security*, London, Pitman, 1991.

218 For example, in one group of about forty medium-level aviation security specialists that this author once addressed there was exactly one woman.

219 A picture of Indonesian policewomen parading with specially made shields was carried by the Israeli newspaper *Yediot Acharonot*, 3.9.1998, p. 7.

220 Even in the US, the country that has made the greatest 'advances' in including women in the police, only 9 per cent of all police departments had women in policy-making positions; whereas fewer than 1 per cent (123 out of 17,000) had women chiefs. *USA Today*, 24.11.998.

221 See the short discussion in Adam Roberts, 'The United Nations: a System for Collective of International Security?' in G.A.S.C. Wilson, ed., *British Security 2010*, Camberley Staff College, Strategic and Combat Studies Institute, 1996, pp. 59–60.

222 For a list of these companies and the services that each of them provides see David Shearer, 'Private Armies and Military Intervention', *Adelphi Paper* 316, London, IISS, 1998, p. 25.

223 Ibid., pp. 55–7.

224 Kaldor, *New Wars for Old*, p. 49.

225 A. J. Venter, 'Today's Dogs of War', *Soldier of Fortune*, August 1998, pp. 55–6.

226 Nordstrom, 'Woman and War', p. 2.

227 The percentage of victims who are civilians – and thus often female – has increased dramatically since 1945. See Amnesty International, *Donne in prima linea. Contro I violazioni dei diritti ummani*, V. Piattelli, ed., Fiesole, Cultura della Pace, 1995, p. 58. Also Kaldor, *New Wars for Old*, p. 8.

CONCLUSION

1 See e.g. Dorothy Goodman, ed., *Women and World War 1: The Written Response*, New York, St Martin's Press, 1993.

2 *Report to the President*, pp. C–65–6.

3 Barbara Ehrenreich, *Blood Rites: Origins and History of the Passions of War*, New York, Metropolitan, 1997, p. 230.

4 Aileen S. Kraditor, *The Ideas of the Woman Suffrage Movement, 1890–1920*, Garden City, Anchor Books, 1965, pp. 54, 56, 157.

5 This is the central argument of Jerby, *The Double Price*.

6 According to Sigmund Freud, *Civilization and its Discontents*, London, Hogarth Press, 1930, pp. 50–1, 73.

7 Sandra Witleson, 'Exchange on Gender', *New York Review*, 24.10.1985, p. 53.

8 Reskin and Roos, *Job Queues, Gender Queues*, p. 302.

9 Mady Wechsler Segal, 'Women in the Armed Forces', in Howes and Stevenson, eds., *Women and the Use of Armed Force*, p. 92. A good illustration of this process is provided by the US Navy. From 1948 on it allowed women to serve aboard transports and hospital ships; at the same time it got rid of both categories. See Binkin and Bach, *Women in the Military*, p. 24.

10 Bose, *Jobs and Gender*, p. 68.

11 *Herald International Tribune*, 12.3.1998, p. 3.

12 *Life Special Issue*, spring–summer 1985.

13 For the continued domination of men in other fields see Rose-Marie Lagrave, 'A Supervised Emancipation', in Françoise Thebaud, ed., *A History of Women in the West*, vol. 5, pp. 453–89.

14 Figures and job descriptions from US General Accounting Office, Report to the Ranking Minority Member, Subcommittee on Readiness, Committee on Armed Services, US Senate, *Gender Issues: Information on DOD's Assignment Policy and Direct Ground Combat Definition*, Washington DC, GAO, 1998.

15 Anonymous twelfth-century French poem, quoted in Maurice de Freville, ed., *Les Quatres Ages de l'Homme*, Paris, Société des Anciens Textes Français, 1888, pp. 38–9.

16 Figures calculated from IISS, *The Military Balance, 1970–71*, p. 22; and IISS, *The Military Balance, 1999–2000*, pp. 20, 24.

17 See most recently *USA Today*, 23.10.1999; also David A. Anderson, 'Should the [Marine] Corps be Concerned about Retention?', *US Naval Institute Proceedings*, 125/7, July 1999, p. 40.

18 For this line of reasoning see Brit As, 'A Materialistic View of Men's and Women's Attitudes towards War', *Women's Studies Forum*, 5, 3/4, 1982, pp. 355–64; Ruth Greber, 'Unser Kampf gegen Frauenwehrdienst ist Gleichzeitig ein Kampf fuer Abruestung in Ost und West', in Friedrich Nauman Stiftung, *Frauen und Bundeswehr*, pp. 201–2.

19 Genesis 3:16.

20 Mary J. Salter, 'Annie, Don't Get Your Gun', *The Atlantic Monthly*, June 1980, p. 83.

21 Gina Lombroso, *La femme dans la société actuelle*, Paris, Payot, 1929, p. 12.

22 See above, p. 57.

23 Letter to Martha Bernays, 5 November 1883, quoted in Ernst Jones, *The Life and Work of Sigmund Freud*, New York, Basic Books, 1953, vol. I, p. 176.

INDEX

Aal the Dragoon 101
Abeokuta, Battle of (1851) 111,
  113
Achilles 51, 55, 86, 88
Acrotatus 18
Adahoonzou, King of Dahomey
  108, 109
Adelita 122
Aeneas 29
Aethelflaed 72
Afghanistan 122
AFZ see Anti Fascist Women's
  Organization
Agnes of Saarbruecken 73
Ago-li-Agbo, King of Dahomey
  114
aircraft
  see also pilots
  declining numbers 175, 176
Aischylos 55
Albert, Archduke 83
Alexander, Clifford 192
Alexander the Great 31, 73, 86–7,
  89, 155
Alexander I, Tsar 103
Algeria 119
Amazon 59–60
Amazons 36–7, 54–60, 66, 69,
  228
Amazons of Dahomey 107–16
American Civil War
  camp followers 97
  rape myths 35
  women disguised as soldiers
    104, 105
American Revolution see War of
  the American Revolution
Anath 49–50
Anderson, Pamela 65
Andromache 34
Angola 225
animals 45–7
Anna, Empress of Russia 76–7
Anne, Queen of England 76–7,
  78, 83

Anne of Austria 76–7
Anti Fascist Women's
  Organization (AFZ) 118
anti-aircraft batteries 215
anti-aircraft units, Second World
  War 139–40
anti-war movements 26
Antigone 89
Antiochus III, King of Syria 89
ants 45–6
Antwerp, Maria van 100
Arab-Israeli War (1948–1949) 17,
  35, 185–6
Arab-Israeli War (1973) 26, 35,
  177, 178, 186
Arctinus 55
Ares 50, 55
Ariosto 58–9
Aristophanes 167
armed forces
  see also combat, women in
  camp followers 88–98
  declining size 174–6, 232
  loads carried 158–9
  women in disguise 60–1,
    99–106
  women in 126–31, 133–48,
    180–8, 200, 201–9
armour 154–5, 157, 158
Aronson, Sarah 149
Arrian 86, 150
Artaxes II 88
Artemis 51–2
Artemisia of Caria 68, 69, 79
artillery 155–6, 157–8, 207
Asmat 28
Aspasia 88
Aspin, Les 205
Atalante 81–2
Athene 50–1
Athens 164
athletes 81
Atossa 69, 70
ATS see Auxiliary Territorial
  Service

Aud the Deep-Minded 72
Augustus, Emperor 89, 90
Aurelian, Emperor 58, 71
Australia
  recruitment 221
  sexual harassment 219
  women in the armed forces
    194, 216
Austrian Army, women in disguise
  100
Auxiliary Territorial Service (ATS)
  139

Baker, Louisa 104
Bangladesh 151
Barbarella 63
Barbed Wire 65
Bataan 32, 138
Bayard, Pierre de 31–2
Beauvoir, Simone de 34
Behanzin, King of Dahomey
  111–12, 113–14
Belgium, women in the armed
  forces 214
Ben Yehuda, Netiva 185
Berlin Blockade (1948) 180
Bickerdyke, Mary 97
Bochkareva, Maria Leontief
  129–32
Bolsheviks 131–2
Bonet, Honoré 31
Borodino, Battle of (1812) 103
Bosh, Evgenia 121
Bosnia-Herzegovina 29, 225
Bossa Ahadee, King of Dahomey
  109
Boudicca, Queen 71, 73–4
bows 155
boxing 85, 86
Braeker, Ulrich 159
Bray, Captain Linda 199
Brewer, Lucy 104
Briseis 34
Brittain, Vera 22

Brown, Harold 197
Bry, Theodor 107
Burdina, Galina 148
Burton, Richard 110
Bush, George 199, 201
Byron, Beverly 204

Caesar, Julius 30, 70–1
Calpurnius Piso, Gnaeus 89
Camilla 58
camp followers 88–98, 122, 231
Canaanites 49–50
Canada, women in the armed
　forces 194, 198, 200, 206,
　214, 218
Carter, Jimmy 192, 210
Carvajal, Friar Gaspar de 59–60
Casius Longinus 71
Cassandra 17
Catherine I, Empress of Russia
　76–7
Catherine II (the Great), Empress
　of Russia 76–7, 78, 80
causes of war, women as 27, 38
cavalry 157
celebrations, warriors return 17
Celts
　camp followers 90
　treatment of prisoners 32
　warrior goddesses 52
　warrior women 61–2
　women rulers 71
Charles I, King of England 21
Charles VI, King of France 74
Charles VII, King of France 19–20
Charles XII, King of Sweden 76
Charlie's Angels 63–4
'chaste Suzanne' 106
Chastillon, Agnes de 63
CHEN 186–8, 212
Cheney, Richard 203
Cherokee, prisoners 17
children 150–2, 189, 203
chimpanzees 46–7
China 62, 175, 184
Christina, Queen of Sweden 76–7,
　80
Christine de Pizan 41, 58
Churchill, Winston 139
Claudius, Emperor 90
Clausewitz, Karl von 81, 161
Cleopatra VII, Queen of Egypt
　70–1
Clinton, Bill 220

Clotilde 58–9
Clytemnestra, Queen 17, 55, 88
codes of behaviour 30–2
Cohen, Geula 120–1
Cold War 173, 174–5, 180,
　198–9, 201
collaboration 33–4, 37
collateral damage 29
combat, women in 138–9, 188,
　199–209, 212–13, 230
combatants 31
commanders, women as 67–80,
　230
conscription 210–11, 229
　First World War 126, 128
　French Revolution 42–3
　Israel 186–8
　Revolutionary France 94
　Second World War 134
cowboy activities 223
Crimean War 97
crowd control 224
Crusades, camp followers 91–2
Cuchulainn 62
Culloden, Battle of (1746) 95
Cumberland, Duke of 95
Cunaxa, Battle of 88
Cushman v. Crawford 196
Cynane 73
Cyrus, Emperor of Persia 18, 69
Cyrus the Younger 88

DACOWITS see Defence Advisory
　Committee on Women in the
　Services
Dahomey, women warriors
　107–16
Dakota Indians 17
Damatria 18
dancing 16–17
Daniels, Josephus 213
Darius, Emperor of Persia 29, 88
de Gaulle, Charles 134
Dees, Staff Sergeant Tatiana
　Khaghani 202
Defence Advisory Committee on
　Women in the Services
　(DACOWITS) 204–5
Degrelle, Leon 32
Dennen, Jan van der 27
Deutsch, Helene 24–5, 41
developing wars 12
Diana see Artemis
Dido 68

Dio Cassius 83
Diomedes 50
discipline 213–14
disguise, women in 99–106
duals 81
Dugm Dani 30
Durova, Nadezha 102–4, 106

East Timor 10, 29, 226
Easter Rising (1916) 123
Edward III, King of England 67
Egypt, warrior goddesses 52–3
Eisenhower 205–6
Eisenhower, General Dwight D.
　180–1
Elazar Ben Yair 34–5
Eleanor of Aquitaine 74
Elizabeth, Empress of Russia 76–7
Elizabeth, Queen of England
　75–6, 79–80, 84
employment 165–7, 189–90
enfranchisement 77–8
English Civil War 21, 73
enlistment, First World War
　126–30
Equal Rights Amendment (ERA)
　210–11, 229
equality 42–3
ERA see Equal Rights Amendment
Erik's Saga 72
Eritrea 125
espionage 149
Ethiopia, Italian invasion 25
ethnic cleansing 29
ETSEL 120
Euripides 88
Everett, Major 204
Eyeo 109

Falkland War (1982) 80, 159, 177
Farmborough, Florence 130
Fascism 25, 134
femininity 231
feminism 9
　commanders 80
　equality 42–3, 210–11
　First World War 22–3
　women in armed forces 210–11,
　228–9, 232–3, 236
　women rulers 79–80
　world without war 38
feminization 166–7, 233–4
film 63–5

Finland 133–4
firearms, weight 156–7, 158–9
First World War 213, 228
  camp followers 96
  cavalry 157
  loads carried 159
  rape 35–6
  treatment of prisoners 32
  war hysteria 21–5
  women in the armed forces
    126–30
  women disguised as soldiers
    104–5
FLN see Front de Liberation
    Nationale
Fonda, Jane 63
France
  Algeria 119
  camp followers 94–5
  collaboration 37
  Dahomey 113–14
  First World War 21, 22–3, 126
  Jeanne d'Arc 18–21
  Paris revolutions 1848 121
  Second World War 34, 134
  size of armed forces 176
  women in the armed forces
    183, 198, 207
  women disguised as soldiers 100
Frederick II, Duke of Swabia 73
Frederick II (the Great), King of
    Prussia 76, 77
Frederick William I, King of
    Prussia 77
Frederick William III, King of
    Prussia 21
Free French Forces 134
French Revolution 42–3
French Revolutionary Wars 21
Freud, S. 161, 228
Freya 52
Freydis 17
Friedland, Battle of (1807) 103
Frisia 74–5
Froissart, Jean 74
Front de Liberation Nationale
    (FLN) 119
Frontiero v. Richardson 196

Gandhi, Indira 78–9, 80
Gebusi 30
Geneva Convention (Second)
    1949 32
Genghis Khan 33

German tribes 16, 90, 164
Germany
  camp followers 92–3
  First World War 21, 23, 24–5,
    126
  Nazi Party 25–6
  private security firms 222
  Second World War 34, 134,
    137
  women in the armed forces 206,
    207
Ghezo, King 110–11, 112
GI Jane 64–5
GI Joe 65
gladiators 81, 82–3
Glele, King of Dahomey 111–12
goddesses 48–53
Godolphin, Sydney 78
Gorbachev, Mikhail 173, 201
Gorgo 17–18
Great Armada 75–6
Great Britain
  camp followers 93–4, 96
  English Civil War 21, 73
  First World War 22, 23–4,
    126–9
  loads carried 159
  marriage and pregnancy 150–1
  Palestine 120, 123, 185
  private security firms 222
  recruitment 221
  Second World War 134–6,
    139–40, 215
  women in the armed forces
    195–6, 198, 206–7, 213, 215
  women disguised as soldiers 100
Greece
  Second World War 121
  women in the armed forces
    214
Greeks, ancient
  Amazons 54–8, 66, 228
  arms and armour 154
  camp followers 88–9
  masculinity 164
  sport 81–2
  warrior goddesses 50–2
  weapons 155
  women as objects of war 27–8
Groenlendinga Saga 17
Guidinild of Catalonia 72
Gulf War (1991) 16
  propaganda 36
  size of armed forces 175
  weapons 177

women in the armed forces
    200, 201–4, 205, 216
Gyrtias 18

Hackworth, Colonel David
    212–13
Hagana 120, 125, 185
Hart, Nancy 105
Haslett, Caroline 139
Hays, Anna Mae 190
Hector 34, 51
Helgi, King of Norway 28
herfang 28
Herodotus 66, 69, 88
heroism 234–5
Hesiod 50
Hessel, Phoebe 101
Hirschfeld, Sanitaetsrat Magnus
    105
Hitler, Adolf 26, 124, 133, 137
Hobby, Colonel Oveta 138, 139
Hodges, Jennie 104
Hoisington, Elisabeth 190
Homer
  Amazons 54–5, 55
  camp followers 88–9
  masculinity 164
  prisoners 34
  rape 34
  women as objects of war 27–8
Horace 38
Howard, Robert E. 63
Hughes, Major Everett S. 132
Huli 30
Hundred Years' War 74–5
hunting 83, 85
Hussein, Saddam 201

Iceni 71
IDF see Israel Defence Force
Illyria 70
Imad a Din 91
Inanna 48–9
India 175, 178, 208–9
Ingle, Sue 124
initiation rites 162–3
instigating war 16–26
instigators of war, women as 38
insurgencies 117–25
intelligence agents 149
Iphigenia 52
Iraq 201–4
Ireland, Easter Rising (1916) 123

Iron Cross 21
Iroquois, prisoners 17
Isabella of Castile 76
Isabella Clara Eugenia,
    Archduchess of Austria 83
Israel 212
    Arab-Israeli War (1948–1949)
        17, 35, 185–6
    Arab-Israeli War (1973) 26, 35,
        177, 178, 186
    PLO 124
    recruitment 221
    women in the armed forces
        185–8, 193, 195, 207–8,
        214–15, 228, 229
Israel Defence Force (IDF) 141,
    186–8, 207–8
Israelites
    protection of women 30–1
    women as causes of war 27
Issus, Battle of 88, 89
Italy
    Fascism 25
    Second World War partisans 117
    women in the armed forces 207

Japan
    Second World War 32, 134
    sports 84–5
    warrior women 62
Jeanne d'Arc 18–21, 106
Jivaro 30
Johnson, President Lyndon 190
Jordan, women in the armed
    forces 209
Juvenal 82–3

Kali 50
Kerensky, Alexander 129
khaki fever see war hysteria
Khaled, Leila 122
Kipling, Rudyard 17
knights, tournaments 81, 84
Kollentai, Alexandra 132
Kollwitz, Kaethe 21
Korb, Lawrence 191, 197
Korean War 181–2, 184, 204
Kosovo 226
Kurdish Liberation Movement
    (PKK) 122
Kuwait 36, 201–2

Lactantius 90
Lapiths 34
Lassik 28
Lavinia 29
LECHI 120–1
Leningrad 149
Leonidas 17–18
Levin, Don 131
Levy, Colonel Stella 188
Little Bighorn, Battle of (1876) 17
Lottas 133–4
Louis VII, King of France 74
Louisa, Queen of Prussia 21
Lugard, Frederick 114
Luo Maodeng 62
Luukonen, Fanni 133
Lysias, Amazons 56–7

Mabille of Belleme 72
Macaulay, Rose 24, 26
Machiavelli, Niccolò 74–5
Mae Enga 30
Manhatten Project 177
Mao Zedong 121
Maori 27
marching, loads carried 158–9
Marfisa 58–9
Maria Theresa, Archduchess of
    Austria 76–7, 78
Mark Antony 71
Markievicz, Constance 123
Markov, Major Valentin 144,
    146–7
marriage 150–1
Marshal, General 204
Marx, Karl 16
Masada 34–5
masculinity 126, 161–7, 229–30,
    232, 237
Massegetae 69
Mata Hari 149
Matilda, Countess of Tuscany 67,
    72–3
Matilda, Queen of England 73
Mattole 28
Mead, Margaret 164–5, 229
Medb 61–2
Medusa 50
Meir, Golda 78–9, 80
mental illness, women disguised as
    soldiers 104–5
mercenaries 224–6, 235
Mermerus, King of Parthia 68–9
Mexican Revolution 122

Mexican War 104
Mill, John Stuart 43
Miller, Laura 212–13
Mojave 28
Monfort, Jeanne de 74
Moore, Demi 64–5
Mujahedin 122
Munatia Plancina 89
Mussolini, Benito 25, 134
myths
    Amazons 54–8
    warrior goddesses 48–53, 231

Nanking 32
Napoleon 21, 77, 94–5
Napoleon, Louis (Napoleon III)
    77
Napoleonic Wars
    weapons 157
    women disguised as soldiers
        102–4, 106
    women as instigators of war 21
National Liberation Army (NOV)
    117–19
Native Americans
    prisoners 17
    rape 35
    women as causes of war 27
    women as instigators of war
        16–17
    women as objects of war 28
navies
    ancient 156
    camp followers 95–6
    declining numbers of vessels
        175–6
    USA 182–3, 205–6
    women in disguise 99
    women in 192, 196
Nazi Party 25–6
Nemea, Battle of (394 BC) 154
Nero, Emperor 82
Netherlands
    recruitment 221
    women in the armed forces
        198, 206
    women disguised as soldiers
        99–100
Nicetas 74
Nichola de la Hay 73
Nicotris, Queen of Babylonia 68
Nicotris, Queen of Egypt 68
Nietzsche, Friedrich 162, 165–6
Nigeria 123

Nightingale, Florence 97
Nisenan, women as objects of war 28
Nixon, Richard 191
non-combatants 31
Nongatl 28
Norway, women in the armed forces 198, 206
NOV *see* National Liberation Army
nuclear weapons 169, 170–9, 231–2
nurses
American Civil War 97
Britain 215
First World War 126, 127
Second World War 135
Vietnam War 190–1

objects of war, women as 27–9, 38
occupied territories, sex with forces of occupation 33–4
Ojibway 17
Omaha Indians 17
Onomaris 69
Orellana, Francesco 59–60
Oviedo 59–60
Owens v. Brown 196

pacifism, First World War 22
Pakistan 178
Palataea, Battle of 88
Palestine 120, 123
Arab-Israeli War (1948–1949) 17, 35, 185–6
terrorism 122, 124
Palestinian Liberation Organization (PLO) 124
PALMACH 120, 185, 186
Palmyra 71
Pamphile of Epidaurus 69
Panama 199
Pankhurst, Christabel 23
Pankhurst, Emmeline 22, 130, 131
Pankratova, Klaudia 145
Papua New Guinea 162
partisans, Second World War 117–19, 121, 124, 147
passivity 41
patriarchy 9
patriotism, First World War 21–5
peacekeeping 232

Penthesilea, Queen 36–7, 55
Persians 18, 88
Petronius 82
Philip II, King of Spain 75, 76
Philotas 89
physical strength 151–60, 193–5, 205, 236
Pile, General Frederick 139
pilots
China 184
Israel 187, 208
Second World War 135, 137, 143–8, 228, 231
USA 192, 205–6, 207
pitched battle, women as objects of war 28
Pitcher, Molly 95
PKK *see* Kurdish Liberation Movement
Plato 163
PLO *see* Palestinian Liberation Organization
Plutarch 17–18, 162
Pomo, women as objects of war 28
Pople, Jessie 23–4
Popova, Senior Lieutenant Nadezha 144
pregnancy 150–1, 189
First World War war hysteria 25
women in the armed forces 134, 196, 203, 206, 216
primates 46–7
prisoners
collaboration 33–4
killing of 17
treatment of 31–2
women as 30
women as objects of war 27–9
private security firms 12, 222–4, 235
propaganda, fear of rape 35–6
protection of women 33–7, 38
Prussia
camp followers 92–3
load carried 158–9
Napoleonic Wars 21
psychology 41
Ptolemy, camp followers 89

Quenchan 28
Quintus Smyrnaeus 36–7

raiding parties, women as objects of war 28
railways, camp followers 96–7
rape 32, 33
causes of war 27
myths 35–6
protection of women 34–6
women as victims of war 29, 31–2
Raskova, Marina 143–4
Reagan, Ronald 173, 197–8, 201
Reed, John 122
Reichenau, General Walter von 123
religion, warrior goddesses 48–53
Renatus Vegetius, Flavius 43
resistance, Second World War 117–19, 121, 124, 147
revolutions 117–25
Rhodogyne 69
rodeos 86
Romans
armour 154–5
Boudicca 71
camp followers 89–90
gladiators 81, 82–3
masculinity 164
naval warfare 156
rape and defeat 35
women as instigators of war 16
Roosevelt, Eleanor 23
Rousseau, Henri 53
Rousseau, Jean Jacques 42
Rowlandson, Mary 105
rulers 67–80, 230
Russia
see also Soviet Union
Civil War 121, 131–2, 141, 228
First World War 22, 126, 129–31
marriage and pregnancy 151
private security firms 222
Revolution 131, 141
women in the armed forces 129–32
women disguised as soldiers 104
Russian Civil War 121, 131–2, 141, 228
Russian Revolution 131, 141

Sabine women 26
Sampson, Debora 101
Sanbao 62
Sancherib, King of Assyria 30

Sauromatians 57, 66
Scanagatta, Francesca 100
Schellink, Maria 100
Schroeder, Patricia 199
Scipio Aemilianus 89
Scipio Africanus 31
Second Crusade 74
Second World War 213
  air attack 172
  intelligence agents 149
  Leningrad 149
  partisans 117–19, 121, 124,
    147
  propaganda 36
  rape 36
  sex with forces of occupation 34
  size of armed forces 174–5
  treatment of prisoners 32
  women in armed forces 133–48,
    180, 215, 231, 234
  women collaborators 37
Sekhmet 52–3
Semiramis 68, 70
Septimus Severus, Emperor 82, 90
Serbs, rape 29
Seven Years War (1756–63) 78
sex
  see also rape
  occupied territories 33–4
  war hysteria 21–2, 25, 26
sexual harassment, women in the
  armed forces 10, 208, 217–20,
  234, 235
Seychelles 123–4
Sforza, Caterina 73
Shakespeare, William 66
Shaw, Anna Howard 23
Sheena, Queen of the Jungle 63
shields 154–5
sieges 149–50
Sierra Leone 225, 226–7
Sin 65
Sinkyone 28
slavery 107–8
Slovokhtova, Nina 148
Smith, Elizabeth C. 104
Smmuramat, Queen of Assyria 68
Snell, Hanna 101–2, 105
soldiers see armed forces
Sophia of Bavaria 73
Soviet Union
  see also Russia
  nuclear weapons 171, 172
  Second World War 121, 134,
    140–8, 147, 228, 231

size of armed forces 175–6
  women in the armed forces
    183–4, 207, 213, 214, 228,
    231
Spanish Civil War 124
Sparta 17–18, 162, 164
sports 81–7, 194
Sri Lanka 226
Statius, Publius Papinius 82
Strabo 57
Stryangaeus, King of Persia 68–9
suffragettes 22, 229
Sumer 48–9
sumo wrestling 84–5
Sun Tzu 43
Swanwick, Helene 25, 41–2
Switzerland, women in the armed
  forces 214

Tacitus 16, 82, 164
Talbot, Mary Anne 102
Tamara, Queen of Georgia 76, 83
Tasso, Torquato 58–9
terrorism 122–3
Teuta 70
Thais 89
Thalestris, Queen 57–8
Thatcher, Margaret 78–9, 80, 165
Theiso, Queen 68
Theristes 55
Thompson Indians 16
Tiberius, Emperor 89
Tito 118
Titus, Emperor 83
Tojan War, Artemis 52
Tomoe 62, 65
Tomyris 69
torture, of prisoners 17
total war 126–48, 169, 170
tournaments 81, 84
training, women in the armed
  forces 186, 187–8, 192,
  193–6, 198
transvestism 60–1
tribal warfare
  camp followers 88, 90
  Dahomey 107–16
  masculinity 164–5
  prisoners 33–4
  victims of war 29–30
  women as causes of 27
  women as objects of 27–9
Trieu 122
Trojan War 50–1

Troy, camp followers 89
Turney-High, Harry Holbert 115
Turnus, King 29
Tyrtaeus 154

United States of America
  First World War 23, 36, 126,
    128–9
  Gulf War 201–4
  loads carried 159
  nuclear weapons 171–2
  private security firms 222–3
  recruitment 220–1
  Second World War 134, 135–9
  sexual harassment 218, 219–20
  size of armed forces 175, 176
  women in the armed forces
    180–3, 190–206, 207,
    213–14, 216
  women disguised as soldiers
    100, 104
US Marine Corps 182, 199–200,
  235

Valkyries 52, 53
Vattel, Emmerich 31
Vesuviennes 121
victims, women as 29–32, 38
victory dances 17
Vietnam, female revolutionaries
  121, 125
Vietnam War 190–1, 204–5
Vikings
  prisoners 17
  women commanders 72
  women as objects of war 28
Virgilius 29, 58
virginity
  Amazons 58, 59
  goddesses 49, 51, 52
Volkova-Tikonova, Captain
  Valentina 146
voting 210, 229
Vraede, Lotta 133

WAAC see Women's Auxiliary
  Army Corps
Wackenhut Ltd 223
Wailaki 28
Walker, Dr Mary 97
War of the American Revolution
  21

camp followers 93, 94
Molly Pitcher 95
women disguised as soldiers 105
War of the Austrian Succession
(1740–48) 78
War of the Bretonnic Succession
74–5
war hysteria, First World War 21–5
war nymphomania 21
War of the Spanish Succession 78
warrior goddesses 48–53, 231
warrior queens 68–74
warrior women of Dahomey
107–16
Warwick, Countess of 23
Washington, George 94
Washington, Martha 93
weapons 155–9, 175–7
see also nuclear weapons
WEC *see* Women's Emergency
Corps
Weinberg, Chawwa 165
Weinberger, Caspar 197–8
Welch, Christian 100, 101
Wellington, Duke of, camp
followers 93–4

West Germany
conscription 211
women in the armed forces
198, 229
Winniet, Captain William 110
Winnington, Rev. A.E. 32
Winter War 133
Wollstonecraft, Mary 42–3, 85
Wolseley, General Sir Garnet 114
*Women Intelligent and
Courageous in Warfare*
(anonymous) 68–70
Women of the Royal Navy (WRN)
127
Women's Auxiliary Army Corps
(WAAC) 127–8
Women's Emergency Corps
(WEC) 126–7
Women's Royal Air Force (WRAF)
127
Wonderwoman 64
Woolf, Virginia 38
WRAF *see* Women's Royal Air
Force
WRN *see* Women of the Royal
Navy

Xena the Warrior Queen 64
Xenophon 154, 155
Xerxes 69

Yanomamo-Nanowei, victims of
war 30
Yanomamo-Shamatari, victims of
war 30
Yossi Beylin, M.K. 26
Yrsa, Queen of Sweden 28
Yugoslavia, Second World War
117–19, 124
Yuki 16
Yurok 28

Zabdas 71
Zaire 225
Zarathustra 49
Zarya 52
Zemliachka, Rozalia 121
Zenobia, Queen of Palmyra 58, 71
Zerinea, Queen of Parthia 68-9
Zulus 18
Zumwalt, Admiral Elmo 192